The Transformational Power of DREAMING

Discovering the Wishes of the Soul

Stephen Larsen and Tom Verner

Inner Traditions

Rochester, Vermont • Toronto, Canada

154.63
LAR

Inner Traditions
One Park Street
Rochester, Vermont 05767
www.InnerTraditions.com

Text stock is SFI certified

Library of Congress Cataloging-in-Publication Data

Names: Larsen, Stephen, author. | Verner, Tom, author.
Title: The transformational power of dreaming : discovering the wishes of
 the soul / Stephen Larsen and Tom Verner.
Description: Rochester, VT : Inner Traditions, 2017. | Includes bibliographical
 references and index.
Identifiers: LCCN 2016056372 (print) | LCCN 2017006710 (e-book) |
 ISBN 9781620555149 (pbk.) | ISBN 9781620555156 (e-book)
Subjects: LCSH: Dreams.
Classification: LCC BF1078 .L36 2017 (print) | LCC BF1078 (e-book) |
 DDC 154.6/3—dc23
LC record available at https://lccn.loc.gov/2016056372

Printed and bound in the United States by Lake Book Manufacturing, Inc.
The text stock is SFI certified. The Sustainable Forestry Initiative® program
promotes sustainable forest management.

10 9 8 7 6 5 4 3 2 1

Text design by Priscilla Baker and layout by Debbie Glogover
This book was typeset in Garamond Premier Pro with ITC Leawood Std, Gill
Sans MT Pro, Cronos Pro, and ITC Legacy Sans used as display fonts

Plate 6 appears courtesy of its creator through https://creativecommons.org
/licenses/by-sa/2.5.

To send correspondence to the authors of this book, mail a first-class letter to the
authors c/o Inner Traditions • Bear & Company, One Park Street, Rochester, VT
05767, and we will forward the communication, or e-mail Tom Verner at **verner@
gmavt.net** and Stephen Larsen at **Stephen@stonemountaincenter.com**.

The
Transformational
Power *of*
DREAMING

"More than a thousand books have been written about dreams. If you had to choose just one, you could not do better than this beautiful integration of the biological, psychological, cultural, mythological, and spiritual dimensions of these mysteries of the night. The best, most practical techniques for remembering and understanding your dreams are placed in the rich context of humanity's best dream interpreters, from ancient shamans through Freud, Jung, and contemporary authorities with whom the authors have studied, up to the authors themselves. Just reading this book has enriched our dream lives, and it is bound to stimulate your psyche as well!"

DONNA EDEN AND DAVID FEINSTEIN, PH.D.,
COAUTHORS OF *THE ENERGIES OF LOVE*

"A deep well of knowledge from two of the world's most respected dream cartographers. This book is mythically oriented, historically detailed, and everyday practical. It also serves as a fascinating personal memoir about the crucial role of dream practices in contemporary mythopoetics. A fine feat! Highly recommended for all dream enthusiasts looking to remember who we really are."

RYAN HURD, AUTHOR OF *SLEEP PARALYSIS*, COEDITOR OF
LUCID DREAMING, AND EDITOR OF THE *DREAM STUDIES PORTAL*

"*The Transformational Power of Dreaming* is a beautiful synthesis of scholarship, science, mythology, and the many fascinating but little-known facts about the lives of those dreamers who have had an outsized influence on humanity—scientists and inventors, philosophers, and even some of the great spiritual heroes of our kind. For me this book is a delightful balance of insight and human touch with generous openings into clinical practice and growth. A great bedside read to usher you into the night's journey."

EDWARD BRUCE BYNUM, PH.D., A.B.P.P., AUTHOR OF
THE DREAMLIFE OF FAMILIES AND *DARK LIGHT CONSCIOUSNESS*

"I have read numerous books about dreams and dreaming, but Stephen Larsen and Tom Verner have revealed insights that are both new and old, both practical and entertaining. *The Transformational Power of Dreaming* takes the reader on a wild trip that spans centuries and continents. Its description of contemporary brain neuroscience is solid but the book also delves into Greek dream incubation, Tibetan lucid dreaming, Jungian dreamwork, and an innovative procedure by which readers can enter the portals of their own dreams. Actual dream reports from the authors' clients and students illuminate novel ideas, conveying personal touches that will touch the heart and move the soul."

STANLEY KRIPPNER, PH.D.,
ALAN WATTS PROFESSOR OF PSYCHOLOGY
AT SAYBROOK UNIVERSITY AND COEDITOR OF
WORKING WITH DREAMS AND PTSD NIGHTMARES

"The power of *The Transformational Power of Dreaming* as told by Stephen and Tom is the story of the dreams of history—of how they were incubated, used, and valued by our ancestors—dreams that gave them directions to find health and harmony in the ways they lived. By listening to the dream spirits of our ancestors and of the Earth, these spirits can carry us into a world that heals both us and the Earth and can bring us peace. This book needs to be read and practiced by all."

NICHOLAS E. BRINK, PH.D.,
AUTHOR OF *ECSTATIC SOUL RETRIEVAL*
AND *TRANCE JOURNEYS OF THE HUNTER-GATHERERS*
AND PAST BOARD MEMBER OF THE INTERNATIONAL
ASSOCIATION FOR THE STUDY OF DREAMS

"The authors lucidly map how consciousness and unconsciousness 'look' at each other and can be brought into deeper, more intimate conversation. This insightful, entertaining book is also an immensely practical guide to working with dreams. Verner and Larsen's fascinating stories, meticulous explications, and poetic intelligence inspire our dreaming selves and lead us toward more concentrated, richer lives. They make a wise and convincing case for how, as our roots deepen, our branches blossom."

TONY HOAGLAND, POET AND TEACHER

*Both Stephen and Tom have been mentored by
a Wise Old Man who has also helped several
generations of psychologists climb out of the box
(the one that can never really contain our discipline)!
To the immortal Alan Watts Professor of Psychology
at Saybrook Institute: Dr. Stanley Krippner*

*To my beloved partner and lifetime companion, who
always shares my dream pillow: Robin Searson Larsen*
STEPHEN LARSEN

*Anne
Janet
Mirabai and Orion
Sangeeta and Amaya
Four generations of love and inspiration*
TOM VERNER

Contents

Foreword by Edward Tick, Ph.D.   ix

Introduction   1
Big Dreams, Little Dreams

Part One

Dreams, Past and Present, Open Us to Meaning and Healing

1   **Ancient Dreaming**   6
The Many Faces of Morpheus

2   **The Dreaming Brain**   39

3   **Remembering Our Dreams**   67
(And a Few Tips for Beginning to Work with Them)

4   **What Makes for a Big Dream?**   86

5   **Standing Naked Before the Dream**   109

6   **Archaeologist of Morning, a Digger of First Things**   137

Part Two

Dreams Unite and Inspire Us

7   Precognition, Telepathy, and Synchronicity
in Dreams   158

8   Dream Incubation   196
Seeding the Unconscious

9   The Cauldron of Inexhaustible Gifts   222

10   Dreaming While Awake, Waking in the Dream   251

11   Dreams and the Poetic Imagination   272

Epilogue   295
What Dreams May Come . . .

Appendix   307
The Dream Portal Method

Notes   309

Bibliography   316

Index   329

Foreword

Edward Tick, Ph.D.

His eyes are wild, his mind swirling, his sleep torn by nightmares. As an air force lieutenant in his late twenties, John had been in command of a first-strike team of our country's nuclear weapons forces. If orders were given, he would have to push the proverbial button to help destroy the world. John posted images of mushroom clouds on his desktop. Time went on, and as it did, John could not evolve his identity beyond that of an immoral and evil agent of annihilation.

Fortunately he found his way to Tom Verner, who, through his dream incubation workshop, led this tormented veteran from personal hell into healing. John had once been an actor. With Tom's guidance he reembraced that calling and was able to use the catharsis offered by theater as a means by which to share his torment and purge some of his demons. (See the story of Tom's work with Kevin, another traumatized veteran, in chapter 8.)

I was John's graduate school faculty mentor. As our studies advanced, he was able to reframe his military history in archetypal terms. He saw that he had embodied the warrior archetype but was possessed by its shadow—its denied, destructive side. At this point I gave him Stephen Larsen's book *The Mythic Imagination*. He found himself inspired by Stephen's work, because it offered him a road map for tracing his own hero's journey through his service career. For his graduate school thesis, John was able to write the myth of his own life. With a deeper understanding of his own personal mythology, he finally returned to us as an elder warrior devoted to witnessing truth and healing others trapped in the hell he knew too well.

In this story, as in many instances over the decades, Stephen, Tom, and I have become a kind of mythopoeic healing team, laboring in the fields of imagination and spirit. Our work together embraces dreams, healing rituals, psychodrama, and art. Stephen's work also includes neurofeedback for the rebalancing and restoration of brain functioning. Tom's work entails his own special brand of healing magic, which you will read about later in this book.

In Robert Frost's poem "The Tuft of Flowers" the poet wrote, "'Men work together,' I told him from my heart, / 'Whether they work together or apart.'" In their long careers as teachers, healers, and creative spirits, Stephen and Tom have worked synergistically, "whether together or apart." This new book that they have written, *The Transformational Power of Dreaming,* is the latest effort of their lifelong friendship and professional collaboration. Herein, Stephen and Tom bring great love and respect, fresh insights and syntheses, and new reports on dreamers and dreams and their creative and healing potentials to our contemporary world—a world that is seriously and tragically deprived of an imagination that is meant to be fostered and nourished by dreamwork. Tom and Stephen tell dream stories, report dream practices, and consult dream visionaries down through the ages. In so doing, we the readers are initiated into millennia of dream practices and guided through numerous creative exercises to make these practices our own.

At the onset, the authors beautifully state that the dream is "a magic crystal ball that lets us gaze into the mystery of ourselves." Their book stands like an oracular volume of old—a compendium of dreams, dream practices, and forms of dreamwork and interpretation from all times and peoples that serve as testimony, record, and guidebook. Our wonderful guides, Stephen and Tom, guide us and help us learn how to gaze in to this crystal ball of the dream.

I will always remember a dream incubation retreat that I co-facilitated at the Center for Symbolic Studies in the Hudson River valley of New York, which Stephen and his wife, Robin, run. In the Asclepian practices of ancient Greece, as the sleepers lay in a dormitory called an *Abaton,* sacred serpents—believed to be the animal form of the god—came out and visited them as they slept. To this modern enactment, Serpentessa, a snake priestess and dancer, brought her pythons and boa constrictors. It was a deep, freezing winter, and participants were offered a choice—to sleep in the big room with the fireplace, but with the snakes present, or to put their sleeping bags elsewhere, where they wouldn't be disturbed. With some trepidation from certain members, the whole group chose to sleep in the room with the snakes.

The sleepers were warm in their bags and under their quilts, and the snakes made a beeline for the warm places. They crawled, wrapped, hissed, or kissed their way among the sleepers in such unique ways that we had little doubt the snakes had "read" the sleepers' unconscious. What could have been a phobia turned into a blessing—as we discovered when we shared our amazing stories the next day.

These are but a few of the precious moments and efforts revealed as we strive to bring the practice of true soul work into our suffering world. We seek to bring that which awakens, activates, resuscitates, and deepens our essence and reconnects us to the cosmos. In all of this, Stephen and Tom bring us countless "meetings with remarkable people." As well, we are privy to the many dreams of literary, scientific, and religious figures down through the ages. Interwoven are contemporary dreams from the coauthors' patients and workshop participants, who have been kind enough to share them here. And, inspiringly transparent, the authors share their *own* dreams and the work they have done in trying to understand them.

Communal dream-sharing is a fundamental component of the traditional dream practices that the authors report on in this book. They tell us of dream-revering peoples who gather over morning meals or around the lodge fire in winter snows to share their dreams for all to witness and be part of reenacting. This tribal sharing transforms dreams into community property, stimulates more dreaming in others, and allows everyone to seek and share mystical guidance together.

As in varied traditions from indigenous peoples to the Asclepian Greeks, to Carl Jung and his patients, we declare that dreams are not "just dreams" but also portents, oracles, revelations, exposures, and awakenings. As Stephen's mentor Edward Whitmont put it in a book title (see chapter 5) they are a "portal to the Source."

Drenched in images, ideas, visitations to other cultures and their dream practices, teachings from masters, immersions in patients' and other explorers' dream and inner worlds, and memoirs, reflections, and autobiographical revelations by our guides, in this book we find ourselves in a world of *dream immersion*. This book enlists you, the reader, to be an active member of a timeless dream-witnessing tribe.

Herein, Stephen and Tom teach that our layers of consciousness are readily accessible, rather than discrete and walled off, and we are invited in to the journey that embraces and reveals them all: the subconscious, the personal unconscious, the creative unconscious, and the collective unconscious. Tom and Stephen show how dreams can be revelatory of *any* of these levels or *all of them simultaneously*. Dreams are the imaginal vehicles by which we travel through and access these layers. And in dreaming big enough, going deep enough, peeling off enough, we pass through the portal to the universal Source. There we connect to the wisdom of the cosmos.

Our dream guides also present compelling examples of the practice of dream incubation. Dream incubation occurs when we prepare to enter into the sacred space and practice known as "temple sleep." During this time and practice we seek a big dream—a dream from transpersonal sources. Tom and Stephen both use dream incubation in retreat or therapeutic settings and present stories that evidence the healing power of this practice. I attest to it as well, for I have led dream incubation retreats to Greece since 1995, where the practice of dream incubation originated under the healing god Asclepius more than thirty-five hundred years ago. As detailed in my book *The Practice of Dream Healing*, this practice was at the forefront of the fields of medicine and psychotherapy in the Western world. We know of the holistic philosophical/medical theory combined with the profound spiritual devotion that informed it. We know of thousands of miraculous cures through big dreams that the practice facilitated—and does so even today. By taking guidance from this ancient path, all three of us, Stephen, Tom, and I, have brought forth the same healing from within—not only to wounded warriors as in the story we began with but also to many on the precarious battleground of life itself.

As Stephen and Tom demonstrate, we can use these principles and practices today to restore holistic healing and attain life-shaping, life-changing big dreams that foster profound transformation. In this new introduction to a very old science, the coauthors relay something like this: Dreams are not only Freud's "royal road" to the (personal) unconscious, but they also truly reveal who we are and help us to see how psyche and cosmos are structured—and related. They reveal truths about our personal past and directions for growth in the present. However, they also reveal future needs, events, and intentions. They awaken our creativity and lead to discoveries in every field of human endeavor (see chapter 9, "The Cauldron of Inexhaustible Gifts"). They see deeply behind, into, and ahead of us. They connect us to the Earth, the Ages, and the Divine. They connect us to all of humanity and the cosmos itself. In the dream we participate in self and cosmic unfolding, revelation, and re-creation.

Stephen and Tom tell us to love our dreams; play with them; embrace them; tell their stories; act them out; write poems from them; draw them; record them; journal them; dance them; share them; value them as essential messages and actions of the soul. They connect them to the dreams of others in our community, all over the planet, and to the dreams of the ages. *In the dreamworld we are always connected, never alone, and never without guidance.* Learn again what Erich Fromm once called "the forgotten language" as Stephen and Tom have done in a lifetime of wise and loving study.

With Stephen Larsen and Thomas Verner's guidance, and with the wisdom and dreams of the ages inspiring you, the dreams you dream

xiv ☺ Foreword

will never be *"only* a dream." Do as *The Transformational Power of Dreaming* teaches us to do—believe in your dreams and allow them to bring you closer to the ultimate realities we all share.

EDWARD TICK, PH.D., cofounder and executive director of the humanitarian organization Soldier's Heart in Troy, New York, is an internationally recognized transformational healer, psychotherapist, writer, and educator. He specializes in using psychospiritual, cross-cultural, and international reconciliation practices to bring hope and healing to veterans, communities, and nations recovering from the trauma of war and violence. He is the author of five books, including the groundbreaking *War and the Soul: Healing Our Nation's Veterans from Post-Traumatic Stress Disorder.* His newest book is *Warrior's Return: Restoring the Soul After War.*

Big Dreams, Little Dreams

This book is the outcome of years of dreamwork and research by the authors, who have also been friends for more than forty years. Stephen Larsen and Thomas Verner have both served as university psychology professors as well as practicing psychotherapists. But more important than any academic standing, they feel, is their mutual love of dreams. Each has recorded more than fifty years' worth of dream journals and thousands of personal dreams, as well as the analytic dreamwork they have done on these dreams.

Both Stephen and Tom have used dreams as a source of creative inspiration for books, festivals, music, and yes—magic! Tom is a practicing and stage magician who founded the philanthropic organization Magicians without Borders, which works with children in refugee camps all over the world. Stephen, with his wife, Robin, began the not-for-profit Center for Symbolic Studies in the Hudson River valley of New York. Focusing on the study of myth, dream, and creativity, the center works with budding young cultural creatives—sometimes also called "youth at risk."

Stephen and Tom have apprenticed to some of the great dream-teachers and mythological scholars of our time. Both have studied with Stanley Krippner and Ira Progoff. Tom has also studied with Robert Bly, Renee Nell, and James Hillman; Stephen with Joseph Campbell, Stanislav Grof, and Jungian training analyst Edward Christopher Whitmont. In this book they recount what it was like to learn from these influential twentieth-century thinkers and writers. Is there such a thing as a lineage of myth and dream? If so, this book offers to bring this living tradition out of the twentieth century and into the new millennium.

We begin the book with the ancient dreamers of prehistory, moving into the oldest records that we have (chapter 1, "Ancient Dreaming"). This chapter discusses shamanism and then moves on to the topic of Greek dream incubation and a discussion of the first modern dream interpreters (who lived more than a thousand years ago). Chapter 2, "The Dreaming Brain," shows how inseparable the lore of yoga is from modern dream research. This chapter details how dreams both depend upon and yet reach far beyond the brain and its states. Chapter 3, "Remembering Our Dreams," moves to the practical concerns of a reader who might wish to become a dream apprentice: How do we remember, and begin, in a systematic way, to work with our dreams? Chapter 4, "What Makes for a Big Dream?" takes up the intriguing notion of the big dream and moves into a discussion of how dream and myth are related in the timeless world of the archetypal imagination. In chapter 5, "Standing Naked Before the Dream," Stephen tells of his early encounters with Jungian psychology and those formidable pioneers Joseph Campbell and Edward C. Whitmont. (The appendix, "The Dream Portal Method," outlines the elegant dreamwork method Stephen learned from Whitmont.) The first half of the book concludes with Tom's equally magical story found in the book's sixth chapter, "Archaeologist of the Morning, a Digger of First Things."

The last six chapters of the book help remind us how dreams unite us with each other as well as with the past and future dreamers of all time.

Although the science of materialism has dismissed prophecy and extrasensory perception as quaint and outdated, in chapter 7, "Precognition, Telepathy, and Synchronicity in Dreams," the authors take exception to this reductionist thinking. We feel we have help; the timeless magic of dreaming itself shows us a world far larger than our own historically bound notions. Chapter 8, "Dream Incubation," shows that this time-honored practice (of dream incubation) lives on in the present time and articulates how it can bring healing and inspiration to the wounded warriors of our current world, as traumatic in its own way as that of the ancient Greeks. Chapter 9, "The Cauldron of Inexhaustible Gifts," recites the inspiring history of how dreaming, time and again, has gifted our world. Great contributions in literature, music, and art, as well as scientific discovery, have been birthed by the alchemical cauldron of dreaming. Chapter 10, "Dreaming While Awake, Waking in the Dream," explores the intriguing notion first introduced in chapter 2: how dreams and waking life interpenetrate each other. What is a waking dream? While awake, can we use the mythic imagination to fathom the mysteries of the night? And how can the will and clarity of our waking mind make the hero's journey into the mythic realm of the dream?

Chapter 11, "Dreams and the Poetic Imagination," reveals how the timeless beauty and metaphor of poetry is woven deep into the fabric of our dreams and may help us to understand that dream interpretation is an art perhaps more than a science. This is Tom's chapter—with excursions into poetry from Stephen and Robin's dream groups. What is the mythopoetic imagination, and how does it help our lives become more profound, meaningful, and beautiful? With the epilogue, "What Dreams May Come," we close our study, as we glimpse that sleep, dreams, and death have always been the brothers Greek mythology has held them to be. Is there an immortality waiting hidden behind our inescapable mortality, and how do dreams themselves regard this transition called dying?

Our Collaborative Process
In the Words of Coauthor Stephen Larsen

As Tom and I worked on this book together, more than three hundred miles apart, time and space dissolved, and something amazing began to happen: We who thought we were, perhaps, "old hands" in the business, found ourselves beginners contemplating a process at least as old as humanity and yet as fresh as the dawning of each new day. Again and again, we found ourselves apprentices to an age-old wisdom that surprised us with its novelty and creativity. Not a little humor accompanied the process. I (Stephen), woke up one day with what seemed like an inner reprimand: "You're asleep on the job!" Immediately following came: "Get it?" I laughed out loud as I "got" that my current, most important job was to keep moving seamlessly through sleep, dreams, and waking!

I called Tom in Vermont, in the predawn light as has been our custom, and after sharing this incident with him we laughed together. "We cannot predict the next mythology," said Joseph Campbell, "any more than you can predict tonight's dream."[1] Dreams always catch us by surprise, and if we are awake to their meanings, they carry us to brand-new questions to live out—and dream about again!

Here at the start of our collaborative endeavor that we now wish to share with you, the reader, we would like to expunge one phrase from the common vocabulary: the dismissive "just a dream" that makes this timeless gift that has graced the lives of our ancestors, ourselves, and our children seem a distraction from the very real business of living. We hope to show that it is anything but, for the fine art of dreaming may be compared to a magic crystal ball that lets us peer in to the mystery of our own becoming and of who we really are. We hope, in the pages that follow, to show you how very true this is!

Part One

Dreams, Past and Present, Open Us to Meaning and Healing

1

Ancient Dreaming

The Many Faces of Morpheus

We don't know what Lucy dreamed. That is to say, our ancestress, who lived probably three million years ago, walked upright during the day, like we do, and probably lay down at night, as we do. And no doubt she dreamed, as do all mammalian organisms. What we do know is that her children and grandchildren survived, and her great-great-grandchildren, to the extent of thousands of generations, survived. We ourselves are the manifest outcome of this process (and thanks to the Human Genome Project* we all know from whence we came and how very long this walk has been going on!). So although we don't know *what* Lucy dreamed, according to neurobiology, we know *that our species has likely been dreaming* for at least three million years!

From the archaeological records we have and the examination of contemporary shamanic societies, we are led to believe that most preliterate people valued their dreams and visions far more than we do, as most precious gifts—gifts from the universe. We know that they dreamed, but we have no idea when they began to share their dreams or deliberately use them to solve problems. As best we understand,

---

*The Human Genome Project is an international effort to map the entire human genetic sequence—about 20,500 genes—conducted over about fifteen years and likened to an inner version of the Apollo Space Mission; it was completed in 2004 (www.genome .gov/10001772).

they didn't really have much else in the way of resources. Something allowed those many generations to survive: larger brains, opposable thumbs, the use of tools, social bonding, an astonishing creativity? None of these attributes may be discounted, but neither can we, in our dream-impoverished and dream-denigrating society, omit that their rich dream life and appreciation of same may have tipped the balance in helping the naked, relatively helpless creatures survive. By the end of this book, if we the authors have done our job well, you will have little doubt that dreams are one of humankind's most valuable allies.

Preliterate societies, as we know, left imagery behind. Some of it, probably thirty thousand years old, is depicted in *Cave of Forgotten Dreams* (Werner Herzog's award-winning documentary film featuring the Chauvet Cave in France).[1] Similar imagery may also be found at other sites such as Lascaux and Les Troix Freres in the Dordogne region in France and Altamira in Spain (they are twenty thousand years and older). Uluru, also called Ayers Rock, a treasure trove of pictographs in central Australia, is unquestionably ancient. Aboriginal scholar Robert Lawlor, in his comprehensive book *Voices of the First Day,* says Aboriginal lore of the dreamtime (*alcheringa*) is much older than that associated with the aforementioned European sites—perhaps as old as 60,000 BCE.[2] All of these vestiges are prehistoric, and no language, of course, was written down; but the pictorial evidence is breathtakingly clear: these artist-magicians were as intelligent as modern *Homo sapiens sapiens*—or at least their right hemispheres were!

Some of the earliest representations of human figures from the European sites seem to suggest shamans in trance, or feature them dancing or impersonating animals. Furthermore, all the evidence comes from deep and relatively inaccessible caves, which is not only why they are preserved but also, as Joseph Campbell says, why these were locations for magic and visionary activity, not dwellings, by any stretch of the imagination.[3]

In addition to the relatively scarce pictograms and paintings from the ancient past, we have a few statues and ritual objects. (That we have so few is in large part attributable to the fact that most shamanic

*Fig. 1.1. Lascaux cave imagery of aurochs, horses, and deer
(photo credit: Prof. Saxx)*

artifacts were made of perishable and fragile materials such as feathers, fur, wood, and bark.) More enduring are the Neolithic remnants studied and interpreted by meticulous scholar Marija Gimbutas in her books *Goddesses and Gods of Ancient Europe* and *The Language of the Goddess*. At the end of his long and distinguished career, Joseph Campbell would say that if he had studied Gimbutas's work before he wrote *The Hero with a Thousand Faces* and the monumental four-volume *The Masks of God* (Gimbutas's work wasn't yet available) he would have written quite differently about the mythological beginnings of civilization. "Caves and tombs," says Gimbutas, "are interchangeable with womb, egg and uterus symbolism." As we will see, in the ancient tradition of dream incubation (chapter 8) this is a symbolic reminder of how humans have always sought dreams and regeneration in caves—the womb of the Earth.[4]

Thus is our early history shamanic as well as iconic.

To learn more about the practices of ancient shamanism and how dreaming may have played a role in them, many scholars of shamanism, beginning with the great Mircea Eliade, are comfortable with extrapolations from contemporary shamanic societies, which include remote Siberian or Inuit tribes, peoples from the jungles of South America, African tribals, and Australian Aboriginals.[5] We think that ancient shamans must have performed similar techniques to these "remnant" traditions: drumming or trance-dancing to induce altered states; visionary journeys to the underworld, including soul retrieval; bargaining with the spiritual realm; and/or invoking magical spells and incantations to change the weather or even the future outcome of events. The modern shamanic peoples also told their interlocutors—from the Jesuit priests of New York state who interviewed the Iroquois in the sixteenth to eighteenth centuries, to the countless anthropologists interviewing indigenous people all over the globe—that their dreaming was important to their shamanic practice. However, even with these modern instances we have no direct knowledge of precisely *how* our ancestors used their dreams. What we *do* have is an undeniable understanding that dream lore and mythology emerge from a common source in the human mythic imagination. To paraphrase Joseph Campbell, "A dream is a private myth, a myth, a public dream."[6]

Mesopotamian, Egyptian, and Greek Dreaming

Literate history is only, perhaps, five thousand years old. From the ancient Near East we have cuneiform, hieroglyphics, Chinese ideograms, and more recently, Proto-Indo-European, Sanskrit, Hebrew, and the Greco-Roman alphabets. As we enter the era of recorded history, with its written records of Mesopotamia (and/or those records figured in hieroglyphs), we find that dream lore is inextricably woven with magic, the lore of gods and goddesses, and with demonology. As cultural historians have long pointed out, the more tenuous our knowledge of "how things work," the more the mythic imagination fills the landscape with the wondrous and the strange—and definitely the fearful. In Sumerian and Babylonian myth and magic, for example, dreams may not only foretell the future, but they also may give specific knowledge of what demons might be involved in a particular situation. Babylonian demonology and the spells needed to avert disaster or countervail demonic action are elaborate, and sordidly and vividly spelled out.

Perhaps the earliest recorded dream is from Mesopotamia. It is called "the dream of Dumuzi" (Tammuz) and involves Dumuzi's sister Geshtin-anna (Inanna). The dream is interwoven with the story of the descent of Inanna to the underworld (1900–1600 BCE).[7] With it we see an early intimation of the connection of dreams with death, the underworld, and rebirth. (Interestingly enough, Inanna herself was also reputed to be a skilled dream interpretress.)

Egyptian dream lore involves the soul-journeying of the Ka and the Ba (integral spiritual parts of the soul) and the encounters with mythological entities associated with the underworld, such as Anubis, Isis, and Osiris.

One of the earliest examples of dream lore in the world is a papyrus from the Egyptian Dream Book dating from the reign of Rameses II from 1279–1213 BCE (see color insert, plate 1). It states the following: "Example: 'If a man sees himself in a dream looking out of a window, good; it means the hearing of his cry.'"[8] On the papyrus the good dreams are listed first, followed by the bad ones written in red (believed to be the color of bad omens).

Approximately 108 dreams, which describe 78 activities and emotions, are recorded in the Egyptian Dream Book. These activities may be said to be things commonly undertaken by the average person. Most of these activities deal with some form of sight or seeing. The second largest category deals with eating and drinking, and a few more deal with receiving and copulating.

The cult of Serapis, a syncretic deity combining Osiris and Apis, began under Ptolemy II in the third century BCE. Sleeping in the temple of Serapis was said to bestow important or big dreams. The cult lasted almost seven centuries, until the great Serapeum in Alexandria was destroyed by a Christian mob led by the patriarch Theophilus (389 CE), who wished to destroy all remnants of the pagan gods.[9]

A Greek named Zoilos dreamed several times of Serapis and peti-

Fig. 1.2. Serapis, the god of big dreams, was imported by Ptolemy to Alexandria in the third century BCE. (photo credit: Marie-Lan Nguyen, 2006)

tioned the royal treasurer under Ptolemy that he must bring a statue of him to Alexandria. Misfortune bedeviled the ruler until he obeyed the dream (and the god who apparently wished to be worshipped).

Dream Incubation:
Laying Down in a Lair Like an Animal

The tradition of cave occupation for the pursuit of shamanic practices, dreaming, and mythology enters Western history through the same area of Anatolia (present-day Turkey) that Marija Gimbutas believed was so important to the (Neolithic) goddess cult. From the ancient cities of Phocaea and Miletus the cult spread throughout the Panhellenic world, as far west as Velia in modern Italy, and even to Marseilles in France. We are talking about a truly Western mystical tradition with ancient roots; it is the equivalent of the better-known Eastern wisdom traditions from India or China.

Fig. 1.3. Pediment of dedication to the iatromantis, a place sacred to the iatromantis tradition (shamanic healing with dreams), in Velia, Italy, which was founded circa 538–535 BCE.

In his fascinating study *In the Dark Places of Wisdom,* scholar of ancient philosophy Peter Kingsley shows how, with just a few written clues engraved on marble blocks or the pediments of statuary, elements from the preliterate shamanic world of dreaming gave birth to over-looked, archaic features of Greek civilization, including the Eleusinian Mysteries and dream incubation.[10] It is one thing to go to sleep every night, willy-nilly, as we all do. It is something entirely different, as Kingsley suggests, to sleep in a cave or a sacred place that is dedicated to a goddess or a hero, ritualistically, *consciously* going into the *unconscious* with a purpose. This is the incubation principle—or the vision quest, as it has clearly been practiced since the dawn of time.

The modern world of depth psychology, especially after Carl Jung and Karl Kerényi, associates dream incubation mainly with the fifteen-hundred-year-old cult of Asclepius (roughly 1000 BCE–500 CE). There are references to Asclepius throughout Greek history but famously in the Trojan War of 1200 BCE, wherein the two sons of Asclepius—Machaon (the first battlefield surgeon) and Podalirius (the first mental health worker to treat PTSD)—are mentioned. Asclepius also appears in Socrates' death scene, where he asks Crito to dedicate a cock to Asclepius.[11]

Fig. 1.4. Statue of Asclepius exhibited in the Museum of Epidaurus Theatre (photo credit: Michael F. Mehnert)

Kingsley postulates even more ancient roots to the incubation tradition, showing how shamanic elements widely permeate less well-understood aspects of Greek mythology through the cult of Apollo. Often perceived to be merely a solar deity, Apollo's roots are much more chthonic. In Anatolia, Apollo Oulious was known as "deadly, destructive, and cruel," but also, paradoxically, "he who makes whole." "That, in a word," says Kingsley, "is Apollo—the destroyer who heals, the healer who destroys."[12] Thus we have the archaic shamanic idea of death and dismemberment as the other side of healing.

Kingsley traces the words related to Apollo and his initiates through ancient inscriptions, from Asia Minor to southern Italy (also the later extended geography of the Asclepius shrines). When people faced enormous problems that were related to their very survival, they went and lay down in the darkness, in a cave, in the manner of hibernating animals in their lair, to await a transformative dream. One of the words Kingsley traces from Anatolia to Velia in Italy is *Pholarkos,* which means "Lord of the Lair." This chthonic mythology is also connected, as Gimbutas would have predicted from the Neolithic evidence, with the Goddess and the idea of the cave as a second womb in which the initiate may be spiritually reborn, achieving the "stillness" associated with the Pythagorean initiates, also called *hesychia.*

Not surprisingly, the goddess named in the incubation lore is Persephone, goddess of the underworld and consort of Hades, its ruling deity. In her role as Kore, Persephone presided over the Eleusinian Mysteries and the spiritual rebirth vouchsafed to the initiates.

The later association of Apollo primarily to the sun forgets the mythology of where the Sun goes on his nightly journey when he is down. Thus we are connected back to the pre-Olympian mythology of Morpheus and his brothers and their cave on the Western Sea, facing the sunset, darkness, and shadow. The myth is inescapably anthropomorphic: When the bright sun of our conscious awareness dims and sinks, we are in the realm where sleep and death, dream, nightmare, and illusion prevail. We ourselves rise and fall with the sun. Thus the association of the death and rebirth of the hero and his night-sea journey, so fascinatingly explored by Leo Frobenius (the German culture morphologist and ethnographer who had such a powerful influence on Joseph Campbell).

The archaeological findings revealed two words in ancient Greek: *Pholarkos,* which again, means "Lord of the Lair," and *Iatromantis,* which means "Diviner, who heals by dreams." However, these were not just ordinary dreams; they were *big* dreams. We will encounter a number of these big dreams in the ensuing chapters of this book and glimpse how they may set the tone of a lifetime, heal us from a wound or crisis, or introduce an unexpected *metanoia* (a change of mind or heart). The pivotal question, really, is whether we live in an indifferent or a "friendly" universe; one that cares for us as a mother cares for her children.

Peter Kingsley writes:

> To most people nowadays a dream is nothing, it's just a dream and that's that. And yet for people in the ancient world, there were dreams and there were dreams. Some were meaningful, others weren't; and some could take you into another kind of reality altogether.
>
> If you look at the old accounts of incubation you can still read the amazement as people discovered that the state that they entered continued regardless of whether they were asleep or awake, whether they opened their eyes or shut them. Often you find the mention of a state that's like being awake but different from being awake, that's like sleep but not sleep; that's neither sleep nor waking. It's not the waking state, it's not an ordinary dream, it's not dreamless sleep. It's something else, something in-between.[13]

Soon we will explore the yogic *turiya* state that threads *AUM* and represents a "fourth" state. In this realm, past, present, and future commingle, and the "doors of perception" are opened, so that we may glimpse creative insights beyond anything we can imagine in more ordinary states.

Kingsley writes of the healing dreams of the iatromantis that "the God of this other state of consciousness was Apollo. In his consciousness, space and time mean nothing. He can see or be anywhere; past and future are as present as the present for us . . . there was a single word in Greek to express this; it meant taken by Apollo . . . the name given to those priests [Iatromantis] of Apollo was 'skywalker' . . . a term used as far east as Tibet and Mongolia in just the same way."[14]

In another book by Kingsley, titled *A Story Waiting to Pierce You,* he explores this magical realm (the same one that Alexandra David-Neel explored in *Magic and Mystery in Tibet*). Its synthesis is otherwise either unknown or ignored in Western scholarship for the most part. This realm is the spiritual "fertile crescent" stretching from Siberia and Mongolia to Greece and Anatolia—even up to Finland and Scandinavia. In those places we find the following residues of shamanism: the soul journey, visits to the underworld or sky world, dismemberment in the service of initiation, and profound states of trance and altered consciousness—particularly Tibetan yoga. The West seems largely ignorant of its own legacy regarding the mysteries of consciousness and its alterations. But we submit that it persists in the Western (specifically Anatolian and Greek) traditions of dream incubation and hesychia (stillness).[15]

If you will, this world opened by Peter Kingsley is the "missing link" between prehistoric shamanism and the early historical world of the Greek mystery tradition and dream incubation. It is a profound one, especially when we live in a world that "has lost its soul"—at least the soul of dreaming, that is. Carl Jung has pointed out how "modern man in search of a soul" dives rather recklessly into Eastern traditions to find that soul. This is not going to work, he says, because cultures have their own weltanschauung, and their own zeitgeist. We cannot become yogis by wearing robes and chanting, nor can we acquire Zen by being enigmatic and paradoxical. We need to find our own roots.

We believe these are in the tradition of dream incubation and the mysteries. They are the missing link between the archaic worldwide tradition of shamanism and both Eastern and Western traditions. We do better to go back to the roots that are older than either, rather than adopt the latter-day Eastern versions that are derivative themselves—and hence reveal ourselves as pitiful cultural imitators. More will be told about Asclepius and his tradition in chapter 8 on dream incubation (ancient and modern) and how to "seed the unconscious mind."

Morpheus and His Brothers

In a cave on the Western Sea, facing the region where the sun dives down on its long night journey, are said to dwell the Oneiroi, "the dreaming ones." Morpheus, the "shape-changer" (and the root of whose name is embedded in the word *metamorphosis*) is the official god of dreams.

Hesiod's *Theogony*, one of the most ancient narratives of the gods and their origins, details the chthonic background of Greek mythology and the tales of the ancient Titans and Demiurges, who long preceded the colorful Olympians whose more familiar doings are woven into all of Western literature. Not so much is memorialized of these deities (or really, principles), because their origin (appropriately) is shrouded in the darkness from which all bright and daylit manifestations emerge.

From primordial Chaos comes Nyx, "night," and Erebus, "deep shadow." Nyx is thought to be female and Erebus male, and so from them come children: Somnia and Hypnos (both of which mean "sleep") and their darker brother, Thanatos (death). Their three sons, in turn, are the Oneiroi, who look out on that Western Sea.[16] The darker brothers of Morpheus are Phoebetor, god of nightmares, and Phantastos, god of false and fantastic dreams.

The earliest account of the idea of true versus false dreams in Greek mythology is preserved in the *Odyssey,* in the musings of Penelope on whether she has dreamed truly or wishfully of the return of her husband, Odysseus (also called Ulysses). Penelope, who has had a dream that seems to signify that Odysseus is about to return, expresses, by a play on words, her conviction that the dream is false. She says:

> Stranger, dreams verily are baffling and unclear of meaning, and in no wise do they find fulfillment in all things for men. For two are the gates of shadowy dreams, and one is fashioned of *horn* and one of *ivory*. Those dreams that pass through the gate of sawn *ivory deceive* men, bringing words that find no *fulfillment*. But those that come forth through the gate of polished *horn bring* true issues *to pass,* when any mortal sees them. But in my case it was not from thence, methinks, that my strange dream came.[17]

The theme of the gates of horn and of ivory, true dreaming versus the illusory kind, is fascinating enough to have been repeated throughout Western literature, from the *Aeneid* to T. S. Eliot, and even fantasy writer Ursula LeGuin. In his enigmatic and mythic treatise, *A Vision,* Yeats reports that the informing spirits that come through his wife's automatic writing say, "We will fool you if we can!"[18] (But later in this chapter we meet an early and profound scholar of dreams who takes issue, saying, "There are no false dreams!")

We have here some basic underlying mythologems that will be found throughout this book, among them the idea that chaos, night, and deep shadow give birth to dreams, nightmares, and illusions. Death (Thanatos) is in the same fraternity. Sleep resembles death, and death, sleep. The body is immobilized, paralyzed, in fact, while dreams are occurring (more on this in the next chapter). Certainly to "fall" into sleep is to relinquish conscious control; in fact, we cannot sleep until we do. Then, as we see in chapter 2, "The Dreaming Brain," every ninety or so minutes during the night the morphology of brain waves changes and resembles the waking state ("paradoxical sleep," as it has been called). These periods subside again and the brain drops back into a more "deathlike" sleep state (one that is vital, however, for physiological recuperation).[19]

In the Words of Coauthor Stephen Larsen

Morpheus Still Alive and Well . . . Well!

My dream student and friend Yiskah, who has a lifelong fascination with dreams, finally met the patron deity himself, in a totally unexpected dream. In fact, "Morpheus" was what the dream itself called the mysterious electrical man who appeared in her dream, but Yiskah had no conscious knowledge of the Greek mythological figure. Despite that, the dream was clearly a big dream, and one that shook her profoundly!

Yiskah called me in excitement and consternation, and we met a couple of nights later to discuss the disturbing dream. Here it is, as she told it.

I am at a beach hotel. A dark-haired guy who is named Morpheus wants to kill a young woman who is there with her dad. At one point, I take her by the hand and we run. We take the open stairway and run upstairs. We open the first door, a bathroom, and she hides in there. The second door on the right is like a laundry room, with a chair, and an afghan [blanket] slung over the side. I go to a corner of the room and pull the afghan blanket over me to hide my body. Morpheus first looks in the bathroom door, but somehow the girl got away. He opens my door twice but doesn't see me. I wait awhile until I don't hear anything, then I open the door and follow other vacationers down the hall.

I see a stairway leading to the beach, run down it, and hide in sand under the boardwalk. Further under I go. At the left side, there is Plexiglas. I am planning my escape if I need to run. Then I notice: Morpheus is hunched down beside me! He grabs me! I yell for the people on the beach to help me. They cannot and do not. Morpheus is shocking them with electricity from his fingertips; Morpheus drags me out and pulls me down the beach. He has decided that he likes me.

I say, "No! I'm scared of you!"

Then he starts shocking me (this is why others didn't help).

I ask him to stop.

He says, "We will make love! We will not touch (at first)—then only touch." Foreplay; then we have sex. It is ecstatic. Then he wants sex again right by the water on the beach. Now he is talking about throwing me into the waves.

I say, "But I might be carrying your baby."

He says, "You are! It's a son! I will figure out when the baby will be born."

I guess he decides to let me live. He leaves me in a heap at the top of the beach and walks away.

Yiskah, who has always had (as I tell her) a somewhat romanticized relationship with dreaming (emphasizing the light, inspirational, and creative side and trying to avoid the darker, numinous, even dismembering possibilities present in dreaming), here meets the "god" in charge of dreaming himself. Like Dionysus, he presents as the Lord of Sex and Death. He can kill people—even nice, innocent ones, and shock them (he is filled with a numinous energy that has destructive as well as erotic dimensions).

Yiskah acknowledged that since a breakup with her husband several months previously there had been no sex; it was indeed shocking for her that this dark, frightening figure could not only turn her on but actually impregnate her; his powers include fertility (and presumably creativity). He appears in character (as one of the Oneiroi) by the sea (the dark, unfathomable unconscious that contains all kinds of things that could surprise and frighten us—primordial things).

After she'd had the dream, she couldn't get it out of her mind—the dream was under her skin. Yiskah already has two beautiful sons by two different fathers. One is a charismatic rabbi, the other a music teacher and cultural creative. A wonderful poet as well as educator and dreamer, Yiskah's own creative life had become stagnant with household and mothering duties. But her demon lover will not allow her to languish; instead he electrifies her and impregnates her. I told her I suspected the child she was carrying was not any kind of earthly child but rather one with "bright fiery wings" as the great artist William Blake and his wife, Catherine, called their books of dreams, drawings, and poems. The dream promises her, in the fullness of time, a renewal of her creativity.

The only reason Yiskah didn't call this a "nightmare" (Phoebetor), is because we have encouraged members of our dream groups not to use the automatic negative label—which could negate the energy of the dream. Instead we may say, "I had a really amazing, upsetting, and electrifying dream!" The goal is to take the energy out of fear (phobia) and put it into excitement and creativity.

THE MYTHIC FAMILY OF NIGHT, SLEEP, DEATH, AND DREAMS

From Erebus (darkness) and Nyx (night) come Somnia and Hypnos (sleep). Hypnos's three sons are called the Oneiroi (dreams).

THE ONEIROI
MORPHEUS: God of Dreams

PHOEBETOR: Ruler of Nightmares

PHANTASTES: False and confusing dreams

The genealogy of Erebus below details (with both Greek and Latin terms), the mysterious relatives who rule both dreams and mental distortions.

PARENTS OF EREBUS

[1.1] KHAOS (no father) (Hesiod, *Theogony, 123;* Hyginus, preface)

[2.1] KHRONOS and ANANKE (Orphic Fragment, 54)

OFFSPRING PROTOGENOI (PRIMORDIAL GODS AND GODDESSES)

[1.1] AITHER, HEMERA (by Nyx) (Hesiod, *Theogony,* 124; Cicero,
De Natura Deum, 3.17)

[1.2] AITHER (Aristophanes, *Birds,* 1189)

[1.3] EROS (by Nyx) (Hyginus, preface)

[1.4] AITHER, HEMERA, EROS (by Nyx) (Cicero, *De Natura Deorum,* 3.17)

OFFSPRING DAIMONES (DIVINE SPIRITS)

[1.1] MOROS (FATUM), GERAS (SENECTUS), THANATOS (MORS),
KER (LETUM), SOPHROSYNE (CONTINENTIA), HYPNOS
(SOMNUS), ONEIROI (SOMNIA), EROS (AMOR), EPIPHRON,
PORPHYRION, EPAPHOS, ERIS (DISCORDIA), OIZYS
(MISERIA), HYBRIS (PETULANTIA), NEMESIS, EUPHROSYNE,
PHILOTES (AMICITIA), ELEOS (MISERICORDIA), STYX,
MOIRAI (PARCAE), HESPERIDES (by Nyx) (Hyginus, preface)

[1.2] EROS (AMOR), DOLOS (DOLUS), DEIMOS (METUS), PONOS
(LABOR), NEMESIS (INVIDENTIA), MOROS (FATUM), GERAS
(SENECTUS), THANATOS (MORS), KERES (TENEBRAE),
OIZYS (MISERIA), MOMOS (QUERELLA), PHILOTES (GRATIA),
APATE (FRAUS), ? (OBSTINACIA), THE MOIRAI (PARCAE),
THE HESPERIDES, THE ONEIROI (SOMNAI) (by Nyx) (Cicero,
De Natura Deorum, 3.17)

I Will Not Let You Go Unless You Bless Me

In the biblical story of Jacob and the angel (Genesis 32:22–31), the antagonist with whom Jacob wrestles through the course of the night is alternatively rendered a man, an angel, or God himself. Jacob is alone on one side of the River Jabbok while his family and entourage are on the other side. The wrestling goes on all night—until the dawn, we are told—and neither one prevails. The numinous being touches Jacob in the socket of his hip, puts it out of joint, and thereafter Jacob has a limp.

But Jacob refuses to let go until the being either tells him his name or blesses him. The mysterious being withholds his name, but not the blessing. This becomes a decisive event in Jacob's journey, because through this legendary event, Jacob, whose other name is Israel, becomes a great patriarch. He, along with Abraham and Isaac, gives his name to his entire people (called thenceforth Israel).

Likewise, in an earlier part of the Greek story, Telemachus, son of Odysseus, must encounter the mysterious semidivine sea being Proteus. Telemachus must wrestle but hold on to this old man of the sea to get him to reveal his oracular secrets—in this case, the fate of the other Greek warriors who are returning (or failing to return) home from the Trojan War. The point is that to receive the gift of the oracle (the blessing), one must hold on to the primal energy while it metamorphoses into a serpent, a panther, a waterfall, or one of many other forms.

Morpheus is in essence *the dream itself in its essential being of shape-changer.* He is the primordial energy of the living psyche—the *cittavritti* (as we discuss in the next section). He (she) is by nature dangerous, numinous, the brother of the primordial powers of death (Thanatos), dangerous illusion (Phantastos), nightmare or psychosis (Phoebetor). The accounts of holding on to the energy of the dream and wrestling with the angel until the dawn breaks have several things in common. One is a special mission, a destiny, an anointing, that allows and empowers one to be in this dangerous, sacred encounter. (Jacob is the progenitor, the patriarch of his people who wrestles the primal power to bring a great destiny into being.) Telemachus is destined to inherit his father's kingdom, blessed by the goddess Athena (who accompanies him in the form of Mentor). He is given the secret to Proteus's oracular wisdom by the old man's beautiful daughter Eidothea (literally, "the form of the goddess"). It is she who reveals the secret of how to extract Proteus's power and his prophecy without being torn apart in the process. From her name, of course, comes the root of *eidolon* and *eidetic imagery* that, like Jungian *active imagination,* can also be used to contact and work with the energy of the dream (more on this in chapter 11).

The other secret seems to be in the holding on (wrestling, holding, keeping mindful of the prize even as one passes through the changing waves of consciousness, and passing from sleep to wakefulness, as we will discuss in the next chapter on the dreaming brain). This is why wisdom traditions, from the incubation practice of the Asclepiae to the dream yoga of Indian and Tibetan Buddhism, identify work with dreams as a true yoga. It is no less demanding and no less rewarding than any other form of sacred mindfulness practice.

My colleague Yiskah's dream shows the extremely dangerous, possibly even lethal, power of this encounter with Morpheus. Electricity crackles around him and off his fingers. He can kill people. He even seems to fall in love with and can impregnate women (he evidently carries inside him the genetic code required to mate with a human woman). In her dream, as in the ancient Greek myth, his element is the vast and mysterious sea, or the border between the land and the sea; he is under the boardwalk or in the sea cave with his changeable and perilous brethren: death, nightmare, illusion.

As I write these words (at the time of All Hallows' Eve and Dia de los Muertos, 2015), I realize how they resonate, both in their power and in their peril, with the culture of our time. Teenagers in our community flirt with or are captured by powerful hallucinogenic drugs. The urge to dream while awake or waken in the dream seems irresistible to our (secular, materialistic) culture. As authors and dream guides, our daily business seems to be to help them find their way back—or back and forth—from the shadowlands. One beautiful and talented young woman of fifteen, beclouded with an experimental cocktail of mind-shifting drugs, just took her own life, to the horror not only of her family but also of the entire community. Others demonstrate their addiction to the liminal realm by sneaking into an abandoned mental hospital, ingesting LSD, reading the records of the patients who lived (and perhaps died) there, and then sleeping in its bleak, cluttered hallways in the arms of Phantastos or Phoebetor—to see what dreams may come. It is a curious, dark inversion of classical incubation and a perilous courting of the deity in charge of nightmare. With one particular young patient, the nightmares were not slow to come, for his life fell apart, his college expelled him, and his parents thought, indeed, of placing him in a mental hospital. The same patient courted and received numerous nightly visits from Phoebetor by smoking dope and watching a horror movie every night, with his girlfriend, before going to sleep. (One of his presenting symptoms was frequent nightmares.)

Fortunately he was truthful about confiding these actualities of his life to me (Stephen), his therapist. Through thoughtful, empathic work, we were able to ease and break the spell that the dark brothers of Morpheus had thrown over his sorcerer's apprentice–like activities. In mutual moments of insight into his family and social life, we were able to recognize that his journey into the heart of darkness began with a flight from meaninglessness, *and the fear of a meaningless life,* in a shallow, narcissistic culture (our own). A culminating moment came when we discovered a crack between the worlds, literally, and a numinous— and frightening—black dog who passed back and forth through the portal showed himself to the dreamer. I (the therapist) was able to help him identify the dog, big and scary as he was—but with a knowing look in his eye, a possible ally. After he had been befriended, the dog revealed himself as a psychopomp, a helpful guide of souls, and the complexion of the nightmares changed. A more positive attitude dawned, as did a willingness to see the creativity latent in his own flirtation with darkness.

In another dream, a big dream to be sure, the same young man found himself in a Mediterranean landscape, throwing himself off a high precipice above the sea, and somehow turning in to Odysseus as a mythic hero and saving his community. He was not slow to recognize that the dream guides were introducing him to the same timeless journey that Joseph Campbell wrote about in *The Hero with a Thousand Faces.*

Which world would you rather live in: dream or nightmare? The myths—and the media—tell us that both are present, interpenetrating our schools, our theaters, our airplanes, and the poor, benighted minds of those whose raison d'être seems to be to inflict terror! Both are powerful indeed. They are, after all, the myths tell us, brothers, children of night and deep shadow.

In what ways have Morpheus or his brothers "shocked" you? Have you had nightmares as well as dreams? Have you courted realms where ordinary reality trembles, shimmers, and lets in Phantastos (fantasy)? Do you daydream a lot? Do you have desires for mind-altering drugs so reality doesn't seem so concrete and literal? And what are the upsides (not just downsides) of these activities? Do they open to creativity or alternative ways of visioning your life? Try to find positive as well as negative aspects of them, and think of how you can limit—or draw boundaries around—them.

Keep a dream journal or journal of daydreams that offers to relate to, if not tame, Morpheus and his brothers.

The Origins of Yoga and Understanding the Shape-Changer Patanjali

In terms of tracing the origins of spiritual traditions, all of them go back to shamanism: It is the urgrund, the progenitor, whose origins stretch back into prehistory. From it come both the great traditions of the East—Indian yoga and Chinese Taoism (and all their descendants)—and the traditions of the West, which we are now identifying with Greek dream incubation, the cult of the hero (and his descent to the underworld), the hesychia of Eastern Orthodoxy, and the contemplative exercises of St. Ignatius of Loyola.

Because we are following a time line from the ancient past forward, we move now to a not-so-well-understood aspect of yoga tradition, close to its origins, but one that flavors and offers to enrich the Western traditions, answering some vital questions. Included in those questions are these: What is human consciousness? What are its modifications? Why are they important to us?

(Forgive us for saying what this aspect yoga is not: It is not about simple flexibility, nor weight loss, nor a chic lifestyle! It is something quite different!)

The great progenitor Patanjali (who was writing around 400 CE) put it in a deceptively simple phrase: "Yoga is the intentional stopping of the involuntary movements of the mind substance."[20] There are so many assumptions in this phrase that elude classical Western philosophy that it's astounding! What? There is something called "a mind substance" (a classical translation of the Sanskrit word *cittavritti*)? And it moves involuntarily? (Why the very idea! Humph!) But all you have to do is sit down for twenty minutes and try to meditate, or for that matter engage in any serious mindfulness practice, to find how very true it is! *The mind moves ceaselessly by itself.*

We will penetrate this last idea more specifically in the next chapter, on dreaming and the brain, but the idea we want to bring forward here is that, simply, *the human mind is a living thing.* Yoga, and all its descendants in the sometimes bewildering variety of Hindu and Buddhist disciplines, all aim at this core truth. The corollary is that the mind in its involuntary movements is an amazing generator of illusions and illusory thinking. Only when it is held still for many minutes, hours, days, months, and years do we begin to glimpse the truth, that *even when awake, we are dreaming.* The undisciplined mind searching for the clarity of enlightenment is portrayed in the image of trying to see the moon in a surface of turbulent waters.

A simple map of this model of consciousness is given in the Sanskrit syllable *AUM* (see the box on page 28) in the venerable Mandukya Upanishad.* *A* stands for the realm of waking consciousness, wherein the (illusion-prone) mind seeks to grapple with the exigencies of time and space (the outer world). *U* stands for the realm of self-luminous forms, really the world of dreams. It is called "self-luminous" because we don't need a flashlight to see our dreams (they glow in the dark and move by themselves through shifting scenes and with unexpected casts of characters that are human, animal—even angels and aliens). The denizens of the dreamworld walk and talk, swim and fly, and morph unexpectedly. This is, of course, what our mythic imagination

---

*The Vedic treatise the Mandukya Upanishad is a relatively late work from about 300–100 BCE. It is based on the much earlier Chandogya Upanishad, which introduces the same concept—dated variously from the ninth to sixth century BCE.

does when not otherwise employed in grappling with the outer world. (Imagination and perception are not so far apart, after all.) The dream yogas in all the Eastern spiritual disciplines ascend toward the heights (literally) in the form of Tibetan Buddhist dream practices, which are highly developed and nuanced, probably emerging from the exquisitely trained imaginations of practitioners who meditate on tankas—with their depictions of the multiple realms among which humans live.

Tankas, with their special enclosure in a mandalic circle, are symbolic representations of the intentional stopping of the involuntary movements of the mind-substance. There they are, frozen in place, the earthly mountains and temples and people, the demons (*yakshas* and *rakshasas*) and the sublime *dakinis,* meditating arahats and avatars, exquisitely affixed in place for our contemplation. Of course they may seem dreamlike—they are based, if you will, on congealed dreams. Coauthor Stephen can vouch for the vividness and luminosity of dreaming at high altitudes—say, above twelve thousand feet. These dreams, especially if you meditate during the day, are of a luminous quality seldom experienced in the lowlands. Dream yoga is an intimate and potent part of all the Vajrayana (Tibetan Buddhist) traditions.

The last letter of *AUM* is *M,* which the Upanishad says corresponds to deep sleep, in which it is cheerfully affirmed that we all are one with the universe, in "cosmic consciousness"—*only unfortunately we are deeply unconscious!* So in a circadian cycle, we visit all of the possible permutations of consciousness, from waking through dreaming into deep immersion in the sleep state and then back to waking again—in a twenty-four-hour period. A healthy human being may not omit any of these stages. If we lack deep sleep, we get increasingly exhausted and ill—even to the point of death. If we lack dreams, we become anxious, restless, and highly anxious (as psychologist William Dement showed in controlled experiments in dream deprivation during the 1950s). And if we lack a dynamic and engaged outer life we grow stir-crazy, or share the fate of those in solitary confinement. We seem to

---

THE STAGES OF *AUM*

A = Waking (Aristotelian) consciousness

U = Dream, or self-luminous forms

M = Deep sleep (an unconscious "cosmic consciousness")

The *turiya,* the thread that sutures them all together!

---

need all the states of consciousness, cycling regularly in a twenty-four-hour (circadian) period.

Last but definitely not least is the *turiya,* the thread that sutures them all together. This thread is only as strong as the practice of the yogi who does it, maintaining a thread of conscious awareness and intention through each of the three daily realms we visit. In our Western journeying, lacking the ability to meditate twenty-four hours a day as people may do in ashrams or Zendos, several aids exist to help the seeker on their spiritual path. They are spelled out in subsequent chapters of this book and include the gift of biofeedback/neurofeedback, where we are trained to keep attention present through the metamorphoses (brain waves) of the mind (chapter 2). Also explored are lucid dreaming—not so different from the Tibetan practices—in which we wake up a little in the dream and exert waking prerogatives (chapter 9); active imagination or guided affective imagery, where we let the spontaneity of the cittavritti take over for a little while and "mind" the results (chapter 10). Also the use of dreaming for creativity is explored (chapters 9 and 11). Here we see that to utilize this perennial technique we must formulate or work on a problem, see what dreams may come, and then apply the symbolic or metaphoric information that the unconscious produces—back and forth in a cycle of perspiration, inspiration, and perspiration again.

In chapter 7 we also explore why dreams are truly magical and revelatory and how they have a secret connection with our waking world that never crosses our consciousness—and often bypasses our intention, as when we dream of a disaster or the death of a loved one, which we would rather not think about! In this section, we revisit some stories deliberately left out of this chapter to see how the ancients were in many ways more advanced than we who think of ourselves as, well, advanced. In this chapter we also explore the literalistic myth or fundamentalism that keeps us trapped and prevents us from opening our minds to the incredible possibilities present in dreamwork.

🌙 Exercise: The Three Minute Meditator[21]

Try holding your mind still for just three minutes at a time. Be honest and see if it wanders—make jottings in a meditator's notebook. Gradually expand the three minutes to five, to ten, to twenty—if you can! Believe that the more you practice, the quieter your mind can become—then let it take a little excursion, fantasy, do whatever it wants. See if you can detect a commonality between dream, daydream, and deep fantasy. When do you crave to let your fantasy loose? When might you prefer an empty mind?

See how your mental climate changes between dream or deep sleep, and waking. When in the evening might you prefer fantasy? When an empty mind?

Write about altered states of consciousness in your journal.

The First Modern Dream Interpreter (405 CE)

Then let us deliver ourselves to the interpretation of dreams, men and women, young and old, rich and poor, private citizens and magistrates, inhabitants of the town and the country artisans and orators. . . . Sleep offers itself to all, it is an oracle always ready, and an infallible and silent counsellor; in these mysteries of a new species each is at the same time priest and initiate.

SYNESIUS OF CYRENE, *ON DREAMS*

The authors would like to acknowledge dream scholar Robert Moss who, in his book *A Secret History of Dreaming,* initially called our attention to Synesius of Cyrene (circa 373–414 CE). Synesius, in referring to "the mysteries," was not just being mystical in our modern sense. Since ancient times the rulers of Greece had consulted the Oracle of Delphi; the Roman leaders, the Cumaean Sibyl. Such counsel was *not* available to everyone, but could be accessed by kings, senators, the nobility, and generals entering war. And mysteries, such as those practiced at Eleusis (the Eleusinian Mysteries) were the most solemn and life-transforming events in which one could participate. Consulting the oracle required elaborate ritual and propitiation. Synesius was announcing a new *democracy of the mysteries,* by saying, essentially, "You don't have to be royalty or a military commander; you have the oracle within you!"

Synesius was born circa 373 CE, descended from wealthy parents who traced their origins to ancient Sparta and had estates in what is now Libya in North Africa. He had access to the best classical education of his time. His great enlightenment, in which the eye of his soul was opened and he saw into the deep inner workings of the universe, happened in Alexandria sometime between 400 and 405 CE and while he was under the tutelage of the famed woman philosopher and mathematician Hypatia. (Only after this fertile period was he elevated to the status of bishop of Cyrene and consecrated by the controversial pope Theophilus in 410.) Thus Synesius's thinking contains three wisdom traditions—Classical Greek literature and mythology, Neoplatonism, and Christianity (which he accepted fairly late in his life)—but goes beyond them all, it seems, in depth and scope of insight.

He begins his treatise *On Dreams* by noting that Archimedes thought he could move the world with a lever and fulcrum if he *were outside of it.* But this is the wrong idea, Synesius says. *If you wish to know the world, and move it—you must be in it!* Why? Because the world is really an indivisible whole in which all the parts are interconnected. Second, all divination is obscure, dreams no less than the pronouncements of the oracle at Delphi. Therefore we should not judge dreams as impenetrable, but it takes a special attention and art to decipher them.

Third, the soul contains in itself the images of "becoming"; thus it can be used to read the future or obtain knowledge at a distance. The "animal" he says, presumably our physiological selves, has to learn to read, through the agency of the imagination, knowledge present in the soul, and so it is, by definition, he says "most marvellous and obscure."[22]

It is the imagination that leads human beings to understanding. "While awake, he learns from men, while asleep from God . . . to know God by means of the imagination is a higher intuition. . . . Imagination is the sense of senses." (Put in modern psychological terms, imagination is impossible to dissociate from perception.) And again, "Imagination is the vehicle of the soul."[23] In the following, we see Patanjali's *cittavritti* in Synesius's *imagination:* "To wholly transcend the imagination is a thing not less beautiful than difficult," and "This breathing animal, which the wise have called a soul endowed with breath, takes all species of forms and becomes a god, a demon, a phantom, in whom the soul receives the punishment for its faults."[24] (In yoga, the root of mastering the cittavritti lies in the control of breath—*pranayama*.)

When the soul is "warm and dry," he says, "it rises toward the heaven realms." When it is "thick and humid" it is "drawn by its weight toward the lower regions, into the subterranean depths, the abode of the bad spirits."[25] Synesius mentions that life offers us two roads: good dreams come to the person who practices virtue and restraint, whereas bad dreams (Phoebetor) come to those who indulge themselves in greed, or crime, or mischief. He anticipates Freud's "day residues" but casts the problem in a deeper spiritual context: Daytime concerns give texture and quality to our dreams, and the dreams give the same to waking life (or, as a man is, so he dreams). When the soul loses track of its original nature, in the realm of spirit it is drawn into a romance with matter, which pulls it on a descending spiral of desire and self-forgetfulness as the following words from the Sibyllene oracles indicate.

> *Do not drag it down into this muddy world,*
> *Into its deep gulfs, its sad and black kingdoms,*
> *Sombre hideous hells, entirely peopled with phantoms.*[26]

(It is hard to tell, at times, whether Synesius sounds more gnostic, or more Buddhist.) With matter comes preoccupation, even obsession with physical things. "It is not a small affair," he says, "to have to break, sometimes even violently, contracted habits."[27]

A professional associate of coauthor Stephen, once addicted to heroin before he found a spiritual path that liberated him, had a dream (a nightmare) that Synesius would have understood.

> *I go to the house of my friend I used to party with. There are people taking drugs on every floor of the three-story house. There is paraphernalia lying around everywhere: bongs, pipes, needles, crack equipment. You can't get away from it. I look outside, and the entire house is sitting in a field of poppies. I get really, really scared.*

This dream came at a pivotal time in this man's life. It urged him, in no uncertain terms, to clean up his act. It is hard to say whether it was desperation, inner resolve, or the inescapable in-your-face quality of the dream that brought about his successful metanoia (profound change of mind and heart). Synesius comments, bringing in myth to dream lore: "Without doubt, it is this [freeing oneself from addictions] that is meant by the labours of Herakles, which we read of in the sacred legends, and those combats which other heroes so valiantly sustain. . . ."[28]

But the heroic soul may bring back the essence of its flirtation with matter and carry it up to the heights. As the Sibylline verses have it:

> *The flower of matter into the terrestrial abysses*
> *The phantom has its place upon the brilliant summits.*[29]

In a comparable insight, some sixteen hundred years later the fourteenth Dalai Lama wrote to Peter Goullart (quoted by James Hillman): "I call the high and light aspects of my being, 'spirit' and the dark and heavy aspects, 'soul.' Soul is at home in the deep shaded valleys. Heavy torpid flowers grow there. The rivers flow like warm syrup. They empty into huge oceans of soul. Spirit is a land of high white peaks and glittering, jewel-like lakes and flowers. Life is sparse and sounds travel great distances."[30]

And here is the counter for the dissolute or self-indulgent life: "It is necessary to, as much as possible, prevent the blind and disordered movements of our imagination."[31] When the imagination is "thickened, contracted, and dwarfed, to the point of not being able any more to fill the place destined for it by Providence when it formed man (I intend by that, *the habitation of the brain*), as nature abhors a vacuum, it introduces into us an evil spirit. And what sufferings does this detestable guest bring to us!" (emphasis added)[32] Here Synesius captures the next place we will visit in this book: the relationship between dreaming and the brain. Notice that he doesn't dismiss the brain as irrelevant to the soul or the imagination. Nor does he confuse the two (as does modern science, seeing all mental activity as an epiphenomenon of the physiological brain). But he hints that enslavement to "lower order thinking" brings a condition to the brain in which demons (not daemons in Socrates' sense) really, *evil spirits,* occupy us—nature abhorring a vacuum.

It is not hard, as a practicing psychotherapist, to catch glimpses of such demons: We call them "complexes," or "dissociated instincts." In dreams, they masquerade as robbers, thugs of all kinds, even vampires or zombies. (Why are we so preoccupied with these mythologems in our "socially enlightened" times?)

For years, kind and talented Yiskah—whom you met earlier through her dream of Morpheus—a dedicated primary schoolteacher, would dream recurrently of violent terrorists taking over the school and killing or torturing the children. (Was this the child nature in her? I wondered, as she brought the dreams to me.) This was an early example of the power of dreams (Morpheus) to shock her. (And he does, as in the dream, also shock lots of other people.) Indeed, all we have to do is open a paper or watch the media to be shocked in this manner. Here we see the ghastly truth that some people may not distinguish between nightmare and ordinary reality and allow their bad dreams to go on rampage in schools, theaters, shopping malls, dragging us all into their nightmare and thus causing very bad things to happen to very good people. (Given that would-be terrorists often nurture their violent fantasies in isolation, do we have some hints for how to listen to and help them cope with their nightmares before they become the nightmares of a whole generation, a whole world? Could dream interpreters in the mental health profession help us head off some terrible things in waking life?)

Synesius waxes very Gnostic, in that he depicts the world as filled with dark forces who will try to drag us down if we reach for the light. And yet the light is whence we come, he insists, woven into our essential natures, and accessible through the daily oracle of dreaming. "It is religious exercise which renders us adept at divination."[33] "Are you in the right condition? God, who holds himself afar comes to you. You have no need to give yourself trouble: He presents himself always during your sleep." And "External divination demands costly preparations . . . divination by dreams is placed within the reach of all. . . . To practice it there is no need of neglecting any of our occupations, or to rob our business for a single moment . . . no one is advised to quit his work and go to sleep, especially to have dreams."[34]

I know of no single expositor of dreams in the past century who has spoken so plainly and clearly to our sadly dream-deprived culture. Very much the classical scholar, Synesius uses Penelope's dream in the *Odyssey,* and her doubts about it, to tell us that dreams always speak the truth, only our conscious minds distort its message. "If the Penelope of Homer tells us that two different gates allow the passage of dreams, and that one permits the escape of deceiving dreams, it is because she lacks a correct knowledge of the nature of dreams: better instructed she would have made them all go out of the door of horn . . . *If we do not deceive ourselves in our dreams,* [italics added] the dream itself is not deceptive."[35]

Here Synesius declares against the elaborate cover-ups and deceptions that Freud will postulate as the essential dynamics of dreaming fourteen centuries later. Synesius is closer to Jung or Fromm, who say that the dream is not a cover-up but instead speaks in a language that we have forgotten or don't take the time to understand. (In this he is very close to the essential message of Edward C. Whitmont, Stephen's mentor, whom you will meet in a few chapters.)

Remember that while Ulysses (Odysseus) is at the Trojan War for ten years and spends ten years getting home, dissolute suitors from among the local nobility have decided he is long dead and have come to see Penelope and Ulysses' house and kingdom of Ithaca as a great prize. They are abusing the laws of hospitality by lingering at the house as guests and squandering its substance. They are also plotting to kill Telemachus, Odysseus's son and the heir apparent, who stands in their way. Penelope is terrified that the dream of her returning husband is mere wish-fulfillment (she is an early Freudian, perhaps). But actually, having survived wars, whirlpools, cannibals, temptresses, Odysseus is finally at her doorstep, but she dares not to allow herself to believe what she hopes for beyond all other hopes.

Penelope dreams of "a majestic eagle, and geese who are scattered. . . ." Synesius interprets (retrospectively) that the suitors are the geese and Ulysses the eagle who will descend upon them. (Indeed, the now centuries-old story has Ulysses pouncing upon the usurping geese and annihilating them!)

Dreams speak the truth, but only the righteous and disciplined mind can receive it. Synesius goes on to talk about the incredible gifts the dream has brought to him. As they had seemed to with the Aboriginals and Zulu hunters, dreams instructed him how to find and catch game animals. When he was sent to a hostile and dangerous court situation in Byzantium dream divination "preserved me from ambushes that certain magicians laid for me, revealed their sorceries, and saved me from all danger."[36] Through his dreaming he was led to favorable audiences with people of power, including the emperor himself, and was able to prevail upon the emperor in obtaining tax relief for his country.

Nearing the end of *On Dreams*, Synesius then gives a disquisition that should be dear to any writer (including the authors of this book). "As for me, how often dreams have come to my assistance in the composition of my writings! Often they have aided me to put my ideas in order and my style in harmony with my ideas. . . . When I allowed myself to use images and pompous expressions in imitation of the new Attic style, so far removed from the old, a god warned me in my sleep . . . and brought me back to a natural style."[37]

Synesius says there is no universal formula for understanding dreams, "on account of the diversity of minds" therefore obviating the need for such things as a valid dream dictionary, or universal interpretive manual, "for there is nothing so variable as the spirit." He encourages readers (as do the writers of this book) to avoid wasting their time with stock interpretations of images or events in dreams and instead consult one's own memory and affective associations.

In a visionary conclusion of his wonderful little book, Synesius waxes eloquent. We will let him speak for himself and then lead you into the rest of *our* book, where we think you will also find many wonders "marvellous to tell!"

> In dreams one is a conqueror. We walk, we fly. Imagination lends itself to all. . . . Sometimes we dream that we sleep, that we are dreaming, that we arise, that we shake off sleep, and yet we are asleep. We reflect on the dream we have just had; even that is still a dream, a double dream. We think no more of recent chimeras; we imagine ourselves now awake and we regard the present visions as if they are realities. Thus is produced in our mind a veritable combat; we think that we make an effort for ourselves, that we have driven away the dream, that we are no longer asleep, that we have taken the full possession of our being, and that we have ceased to be the dupe of an illusion.[38]

This calls to mind the film *Inception,* where the protagonist, played by Leonardo DiCaprio, works his way through dreams inside dreams inside dreams—as do the other characters—or as Joseph Campbell says of Vishnu's dream: "The cosmic god dreams a dream *in which all the characters dream too*!" (emphasis added)[39] In whose dream do we live, in whose dream do we dream?

"We perceive the earth from afar, we discover a world which even the moon does not see," Synesius incants in his conclusion to his immortal book, which should be read by every contemporary schoolchild or college student. "We can talk with the stars, mingle with the invisible company of the gods who rule the universe."[40]

Synesius exemplifies the possible human, of his—or any century. There is a democracy of the imagination implicit in everything this fourth-century original thinker writes. Every night you dip into wisdom; you need not be emperor, senator, or philosopher.

Synesius's identity as a Christian cleric was relatively new to him after his years of Alexandrian studies with the brilliant and charismatic Hypatia, a Neoplatonist and Pythagorean mathematician. But the endorsement of Pope Theophilus, a passionate and opinionated early church father, precipitated him into his prominence in the early church, despite his spiritual universalism. Fortunately he died a couple of years before an aroused Christian mob (not unlike the one that destroyed the Serapeum), inflamed by the fundamentalist Theophilus, ripped Hypatia from her coach and brutally dismembered her. It would have pained him immensely to see the religion of Jesus, the gentle teacher, come to such a pass.

☺ Gates of Horn and Ivory Exercise:
True Dreams and False Ones

Have your dreams portrayed something you didn't expect? A friend suddenly seems inimical; an enemy (or so you thought) appears in a friendly light. Your hoped-for love shows up but behaves antagonistically. Someone you overlooked or dismissed suddenly appears as helpful—even miraculous. A daydream reflecting a reality in which you were inadequate—or behaved badly—turns out better than you thought (and then real life confirms the change). Think of the differences between how you originally daydreamed a situation and how it turned out! Are your dreams (daydreams) true or illusory?

Carl Jung made much of the compensatory nature of dreaming. What we thought was a certainty from our ego perspective now appears in a different light. The gates of horn and ivory mythologem seems instructive.

Ivory would seem fair, valuable, decorative—but what appears initially attractive may hide its opposite. Horn is plainer, common, undistinguished—but may contain truth or a hidden value. Try to identify how this principle may have worked for you in the past. (Jung tells a story of a woman he had dismissed appearing in a high place in a dream, so he had to look up—and even get a crick in his neck—to see her. He used this as a way of reexamining the value of this person and found his initial impression had been superficial.) See if you can find similar instances in your own biography, or perception. Make a little dream shrine using horn or bone and invite your dreams to arrive through that portal!

Western Dreaming

The reader may have learned from this chapter that there is human wisdom related to dreaming to be drawn from both the Eastern and Western traditions. We have introduced the lore of *AUM,* and the involuntary movements of the mind-substance, that underlies most of the Eastern meditative traditions. We can learn about the dreamlike qualities of waking consciousness from a study of dreams and about the dreaming state from attempting to still the waking mind in the solitude of incubation or the quietness of the hesychia.

In this next chapter on the dreaming brain, we find an even more advanced understanding of the states of consciousness from Western science and its knowledge derived from neurobiology. If Eastern disciplines have gained their profound knowledge of consciousness from meditation and concentration, then the West has contributed the discipline of careful scientific observation and studies such as biofeedback (also called the yoga of the West) and neurofeedback, which uses electronic measurements to track consciousness through its changes. In this, Western science *confirms* the lore of Patanjali and the Mandukya Upanishad, leading us to ever deeper and more textured knowledge of both dreaming and waking.

2

The Dreaming Brain

In the Words of Coauthor Stephen Larsen

Dreams occur in the brains of all living mammalian organisms (including you and me). They are not discernible in an identical form in reptiles, fish, or insects as far as we know at this point.

Fortunately, we now have reliable physiological evidence that warm-blooded animals, including birds, dream. Birds rehearse their songs, or seem responsive to hearing them played on recording devices. Dogs growl in their sleep or make little motions with their legs. (When dreaming, they are paralyzed, as we are, so that they don't act out their dreams.) Of course we are guessing, from external observation, what the dog might be dreaming about. The dreams of nonverbal human babies are mysteries too. *Only after children become verbal are they able to talk about their dreams.*

We know from studies that involve tracking the movements of intrauterine babies and their mothers that communication is going on all the time between them, and this communication may be more than simply hormonal or biochemical. Of course, we understand the hormonal or even proprioceptive (movement or body language) communication, but some provocative studies suggest that there is more going on in this most proximate nexus in which we all begin. Specifically, there is intriguing physiological evidence indicating that when mothers dream, the fetus is activated. Whether it dreams the mother's dreams cannot ever be ascertained or proved, but what is known is that when a sleeping pregnant mother dreams (usually in the REM state, which we will discuss in greater detail later in this chapter), there are activation patterns in the perinatal child. Some psychologists have suggested that the root of what is described as extrasensory perception (ESP) may lie in this state in which the mother and child are so intimately connected. (There will be more on this intriguing topic later as well!)

The work of distinguished perinatal specialist Dr. Thomas Verny suggests that the mother-child relationship is far more intimate than has been articulated in the existent literature. Anxiety and depression are certainly biophysical and hormonal states that could be communicated. But can unborn children feel a mother's terror at a dangerous situation or a violent act? Verny's work suggests that this, unfortunately, may be true![1] Can the unborn child feel the interminable existential angst of the mother as she confronts a life crisis? (Some dreams and clinical material suggest that this is so.)[2]

Later on in this section we will talk about the relation between neurofeedback (biofeedback for the brain) and psychotherapy, but two of the most poignant and seemingly unresolvable cases of anxiety I have worked with in my clinical practice have been of a grown woman whose pregnant mother was held in a detention camp in World War II, while the child (my patient) was in the womb—later to be born in the camp. In therapy, my client gave voice to why being in the presence of her mother, now long dead, always made her anxious! They would fight like cats and dogs.

In another even more dramatic case, I treated a woman (now in her seventies) whose mother, to avoid the invading Nazis, had had to ski over a dangerous pass in the Italian Alps while pregnant with my patient. She came to neurofeedback treatment for intractable lifelong anxiety, which no amount of talk therapy seemed to have mitigated (because the catalyzing experience was visceral and preverbal).

In both of these clinical cases, neurofeedback, because it works on the primordial, nonconscious nervous system, proved quite helpful. With these two clients, when the abysmal, nonverbal terror they had lived with all their lives was reduced, we could talk about what it must have been like to live through those times—and lots of tears and compassion for their mothers ensued.

Psychiatrist Stanislav Grof posits that our birth impacts us in ways that are very real, even though they may not be all that tangible to us. To best articulate these impacts he devised a model of them and named them the Basic Perinatal Matrices (BPM).[3] Not only dreams, but almost every subsequent experience in waking life, activate the dynamics of one of these underlying matrices.

If Grof is right, and his deep LSD work supports his theory, many waking events as well as dreams symbolize these core mythic or existential dilemmas.

The matrices are as follows:

- BPM I (Basic Perinatal Matrix): Undisturbed intrauterine experience. All intimations of total peace and harmony or paradise before the Fall are located here.
- BPM II: The beginnings, or the premonition, of the birth process, marked by anxiety, uncertainty, a feeling that something overwhelming is going to happen; paranoia.
- BPM III: Full volcanic ecstasy of propulsion down the birth canal, marked by violence, explosion, dismemberment; Dionysian experience (how terrorists long to fashion a new world).
- BPM IV: Paradise regained, birth achieved—but in an uncertain external dimension, with periodic separation from the mother. Experiences of being cold and encountering strangers, among other new experiences. The associated dreams may vary from homecoming to exile—the stranger in a strange land theme.

Both of my aforementioned patients had recurring no-exit dreams wherein they were trapped somewhere in a terrifying situation and couldn't get out, or they were stuck in a tunnel or were underground, or being buried alive, for instance. This would identify these contents as corresponding to Grof's Basic Perinatal Matrix II, as described above.

Nightmares and Night Terrors

Nightmares and night terrors are two different things. Nightmares are fairly common events that may occur from the age of three to six, when the developing brain of the child starts to make sense of the world and the child realizes that there are real dangers and crises associated with it. Nightmares are scary dreams, commonly associated with the REM state and with a content the child can usually describe. The nightmare might involve being chased by a monster or being lost in a scary place. Usually the child can describe what is happening in the scary dream, and thus the parent may be able to intervene.

That said, for a concerned parent to tell their child, "It isn't real, honey; it's only a dream" may be the worst strategy for all involved. This is because, at this point, the scary dream no doubt feels very real to the child. The best strategy is an associative one—What did that remind you of? Does that monster have a name? The child could and should be allowed to talk about the events of the dream and, if possible, be given an effective coping strategy (see chapter 10, "Dreaming While Awake, Waking in the Dream," on lucid dreaming and active imagination).

Night terrors are neurological entities that are different from nightmares. They emerge from deep sleep typically from non-REM stage 3, and with no content; the child may be screaming, whimpering, thrashing, even sleepwalking. These fugue-like dissociated states often are understood to emerge from disturbances in the child's life. Examples of this would be trouble in the household or between the parents or the arrival of a new sibling, or sometimes even a change of residence or sleeping in an uncertain or anxiety-producing place.

According to Stanford University, the following are common characteristics of a night terror.

- Your child is frightened but cannot be awakened or comforted.
- Your child's eyes are wide open, but he or she does not know you are there.

- The episode lasts from ten to thirty minutes.
- Your child often does not remember the episode in the morning.

According to some of the most reliable psychological sources, the best strategy is to soothe the child and coax it back to sleep. It is not unreasonable to ask the child, "What was that about?" But the adult should realize that the child probably does not have content from the experience. If anything, the cause of a night terror *is a deep, dissociated state of emotion*— "fearful," by definition. The presence of night terrors might invite the parent or caretaker to inquire into basic issues involving the child's safety and security or the presentation of fearful stimuli through real or symbolic content (movies or video games with violent content, for instance).

Approximately 30 to 60 percent of children may experience occasional nightmares or night terrors. If they are frequent or regular there is cause for some concern. Again, the child may be engaged in a conversation about the nightmare (because they have content) or even asked to draw or make up a story about a monster, zombie, animal, or whatever describable intrusion is disturbing the child's sleep. Sometimes sandplay* or another form of symbolic enactment can help to introduce perspective (the child is larger than the symbolically represented monster) and even bring humor into the situation. (See the discussion on the "Cookie Monster" and therapeutic intervention in chapter 8.)

Adults may also experience nightmares or night terrors, but they are rarer—and can usually be traced to some kind of actual disturbance in the environment or the larger world. In Stephen's archives are dozens of therapeutic examples of end of the world, tidal wave, or fire catastrophes, as well as terrorist attacks. It is wise neither to dismiss these totally (considering the world we live in) nor take them as literal predictions. The best result for adults having nightmares (or, more rarely, night terrors) might be to discuss them with a psychotherapist or sympathetic friend or group.

---

*Sandplay is the therapeutic technique derived independently by Margaret Lowenfeld in England and Dora Kalff in Switzerland, which often has profound therapeutic effects.

In ancient times, disturbing or bad dreams could be prognostications or omens, but also—from ancient Egyptian to Shakespearean times— simply attributed to indigestion or some kind of other physiological disturbance. We might consider the very natural reality that when physiological problems occur while we are sleeping or dreaming, they disturb our dreams. These could be respiratory problems as in asthma or sleep apnea; gastrointestinal problems, including having eaten overly rich food (or improperly prepared or otherwise toxic or allergenic food), or something as simple as restless leg syndrome (often due to standing too long or walking on hard surfaces, or a magnesium deficiency). The author has frequently noted that encroaching infections such as flu or fever make their

Fig. 2.1. "Troubled Sleep and Nightmares," plate 11 from William Blake's Illustrations of the Book of Job (1825), captioned "With dreams upon my bed thou scarest me and affrightest me with Visions."

presence known in sleep disturbance or restless dreams (that sometimes verge on nightmares). More encouraging is the ability of neurofeedback to help both children and adults with nightmares or night terrors.

Dreaming and Rapid Eye Movement (REM)

The association of dreaming with REM was discovered in 1953, in the laboratory of psychology professor and researcher Nathaniel Kleitman at the University of Chicago. Along with the discovery that the eyes moved during relatively brief (ten-minute) periods five to six times during the night, there were simultaneous disturbances of the EEG. Out of the deep sleep characterized by large rolling ocean waves (0.5–4 Hz delta) emerged these paradoxical periods in which eye movements were accompanied by waking-type brain waves. It would seem simple to say that "the dreams that blister sleep," to use Joseph Campbell's phrase from his book *Hero with a Thousand Faces,* coincide with those periods of disruption, for we now know that dreams may occur throughout the entire sleep cycle, but they are less vivid and less memorable than those that occur during REM.

While deep sleep is accompanied by slow (0.5–4 Hz delta) rhythmic activity, the onset of REM or dreaming seems to be accompanied by desynchronized, even chaotic, complex activity resembling (but not the same as) waking states. This has led researchers to define dreaming as a state that is neither waking nor sleeping but is instead a curious third state—neither this nor that.

REM periods of about eight to twelve minutes are more frequent in the early part of the sleep cycle, and more frequent, and longer, in younger people (about sixty to seventy minutes apart). In older people, and later in the sleep cycle, the periods between REM are eighty to ninety minutes. There is debate among researchers about whether REM is the same as dreaming. At this juncture, the consensus is that *it tends to appear at the same time without being identical;* that is to say that REM is often, but not always, associated with dreaming. The more vigorous the REM, often the more lively is the elicited content of the dream. At the same time as gross motor activity is inhibited (during REM or dreaming) there is more activation of fine or subtle motor activity (those *little* twitches we see in the dreaming dog or cat).

In various studies that will be discussed later in this chapter, Harvard psychologist Alan Hobson has drawn analogies between the eye movements in REM and the saccadic movements involved in normal vision—where tiny, unconsciously programmed movements of the eyes allow us to form a complete picture of the environment.

It is definite that our waking concerns permeate our dreams (as we will see in chapter 9 on creativity in dreaming). Studies have also shown that humans learning repetitive tasks use REM sleep to enhance performance. In some cases, this off-line practice session seems to be just as good as practicing the experience when awake. Tests have shown that both rats and humans perform a recently learned task better after a period of sleep and that activation of a little organ called the hippocampus is crucial to the formation of memories. These memories might also permeate dreams that take place in familiar environments. The hippocampus may also be responsible for allowing us to have vivid memories of people who have passed on and those whom we haven't seen in many years.

What is less well-known is that dreams may, in an anticipatory way, permeate and configure our waking consciousness. I dream, for example, of bleak urban slums, endlessly extended, and then fail to notice how everything the following day is tinged with a certain futility, a little depression. (We will not say that the dream caused the depression; however, the emotion—or affect—has permeated both the dreaming and waking states, for reasons we will not postulate.) Alan Hobson has affirmed that dreams may, ontogenetically, prefigure the affect of our waking experience (more on this later).

The Hard Problem

Dare we say it, humanity is just now beginning to realize that consciousness (or the lack of it) is implicated in everything we do. Heisenberg's uncertainty principle of the twentieth century has shown us that con-

sciousness cannot be disentangled from the most important inves-
tigations of matter that the best minds among us are conducting! In
philosophy, science, and the philosophy of science the relationship
between physiological processes and consciousness is called "the hard
problem." And why is it so hard?

Because no one has yet solved it! (Nor have we even been able to
define what consciousness *is*!)

We humans seem to love to *alter our consciousness* and see what
happens: we ingest that first, second, or third martini; that joint of
purple haze; that LSD; those mushrooms . . . And the species is divided
on how best to modulate consciousness. There is the tribe of coffee,
cocaine, amphetamines, and workout highs. Then there is the dreamy
tribe who love alcohol, barbiturates, opiates, THC in all its inflections,
and all downers. (Some modern folk flirt with or flit between both
tribes, depending on the direction they want their consciousness to take
in any given moment.)

An experienced mental health professional knows that
self-medication is a form of self-regulation and tells us whether we are
overactivated or underactivated. People who crave speed are lethargic
and slowed; people who crave sedation can't stop themselves (from
thinking or acting). The above metabolic proclivities are present awake
or asleep, by the way, and so the pharmaceutical market is crowded
with the Ambiens and Lunestas to help us sleep when we can't, or the
Ritalins and the Concertas to help us when we can't achieve the maxi-
mum brain activation that the waking world requires. Nothing about
the psychology of modern culture is as salient as its dependency upon
chemicals and pharmacy to achieve some sort of appropriate balance in
our consciousness.

In general, our endogenous neurotransmitters rule waking or sleeping; they activate *epinephrines* for waking and dreamy
acetylcholines for sleep and dreaming. These chemical inundations
also cause characteristic forms of activity to occur in the brain. The
consciousness of our waking state is clearly fitted to the kinds of per-
ceptions and problem solving we exhibit in the waking world. The

problems of dreaming are different but comparable in a curious way: we have to find something or someone, we have to get somewhere, and we have to overcome obstacles that may be in our path. Even the landscapes of sleeping and waking are similar: we negotiate a complex subway system, climb a mountain, weather a sudden storm at sea, or contend with a bear in the yard. True, dreams juxtapose elements in ways that waking consciousness does not: there are monsters or torturers in my familiar basement; my window looks out on a European city; I fly an airplane without a license or knowing how to do it; and/or my backyard becomes an Amazon jungle!

Some researchers have pursued why we don't remark on the anomalous, irrational, or unlikely elements in our dreaming, which also seems to relate to the way dreams unfold in the brain.

Learning from Brain Waves

In a waking person's EEG or brain wave profile, usually all of the ranges of the possible spectrum are visible: delta (0.5–4 Hz), theta (4–8 Hz), alpha (8–12 Hz), beta (which comes in three ranges from 12–28 Hz: low, medium, and high), and gamma (28–40 Hz). (Hz, or Hertz, is a frequency measure of cycles per second.)

In addition, there may be brain waves nested within other brain waves, as when chirps of beta or gamma appear along with delta or theta. Here we discover the clues to anxiety driven depression or seizure disorder. (So when we talk about which brain wave characterizes a state, we are talking about which range is salient—also called "the dominant frequency.")

Electroencephalography (EEG for short) was discovered in 1924 by Dr. Hans Berger, a relatively isolated researcher with an appointment at the University of Jena. It gives us an extraordinary, irreplaceable, window on consciousness. EEG is not at all the same as the physical evidence revealed by a CAT scan or MRI; rather, its display shows the dynamic, moving properties of the brain as it passes through states that we also call "states of consciousness." A good qEEG, or quantitative

EEG, map of the brain can tell us many things: how it is functioning at the moment (too fast or too slow, or just right), for instance. It can also tell us much more: what is going on in what area, whether there is brain injury, and how one part of the brain talks to another. (You can find examples of qEEG at Robert Thatcher's appliedneuroscience.com or qEEG pro, http://qeegpro.eegprofessionals.nl, a European site.)

Poor Hans Berger, discoverer of the EEG, died lamenting that the science of the time (the 1940s) had failed to make use of his amazing discovery (that the brain is a rhythmical organ) except to declare clinical death or seizure proneness. Following discoveries involving transistors and microcircuitry, it has taken an entirely new generation of brain research to make relatively simple machines to show how every discernible change in brain frequency is accompanied by a change in consciousness and how operant conditioning of brain waves (and other forms of neurofeedback that we will discuss) can have profound effects upon behavior—as in the amelioration of ADD or ADHD, for example.

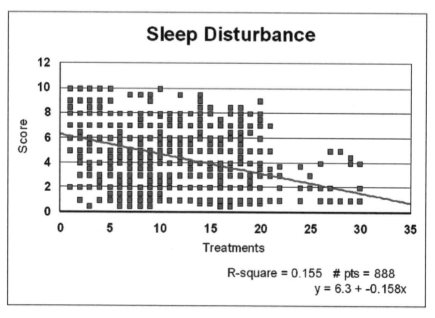

Fig. 2.2. Scatter graph showing the cumulative benefits of neurofeedback (FNS/LENS) on sleep disturbance

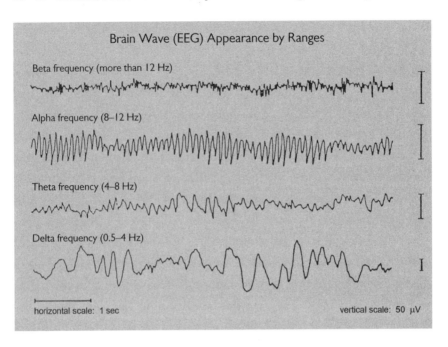

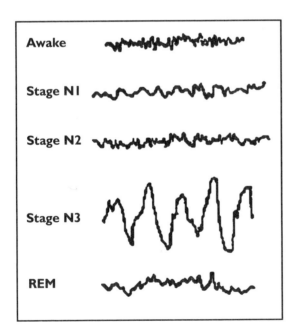

Fig. 2.3. Top image: Brain waves and states of consciousness. Bottom image: Brain waves and stages of sleep.

In 1953, it was changes in the EEG, monitored along with measures such as EMG (electromyography) and GSR (skin conductivity), that allowed researcher Nathaniel Kleitman at the University of Chicago to discover rapid eye movement (REM) sleep as a condition that is discernibly different from deep sleep. Up until that time there was really no science of sleep to speak of nor stages of sleep to be associated with different conditions or problems a patient might experience; hence, no sleep labs.

Nor was the enormous relevance of sleep to overall health, especially mental health, very well understood! Since the EEG, we now know that there are three stages of sleep that are passed through during the night, repeatedly. (Previously four stages of non-REM sleep were recognized; in 2007 the American Academy of Sleep Medicine consolidated stages 3 and 4 into stage N3.[4]) Each has its own function and action relevant to the sleeping organism. Broadly, stage N3, deep sleep, is associated with physiological recuperation and the activation of digestive, endocrine, and metabolic functions. Stage N2 involves some metabolic recuperation, and stage N1, the lightest sleep, leads to rapid eye movements and (not gross, but subtle) activities of the body, represented by small muscle twitches and those rapid eye movements that give REM its name.

It was psychologist William Dement, intrigued by the implications of Kleitman's research, who in 1953 conducted the studies that

Waking	REM Sleep	NREM Sleep		
		Light Sleep		Deep Sleep
Stage W	Stage R	Stage N1	Stage N2	Stage N3
Eyes open, responsive to external stimuli, can hold intelligible conversation	Brain waves similar to waking. Most vivid dreams happen in this stage. Body does not move.	Transition between waking and sleep. If awakened, person will claim was never asleep.	Main body of light sleep. Memory consolidation. Synaptic pruning.	Slow waves on EEG readings.
16 to 18 hours per day	90 to 120 min. per night	4 to 7 hours per night		

Fig. 2.4. Stages of sleep

answered the question: What, if anything, happens if you deprive some-one of dreaming? By that time REM and dreaming (not identical but closely associated) were understood to be correlated. So if you had a sleeper in a laboratory who was hooked up to a dozen or so electrodes (not always a pleasant experience for the sleeper, by the way), you could tell when the period of REM and subtle muscle activities began. Then the sleeper was awakened, talked to (among other things) to find out if he or she was dreaming, and allowed to go back to sleep. This was repeated periodically throughout the night as the person went through the regular cycles (stages N2 and N3, then up again through the stages, and periodically into REM).

Generally, if a person was awakened in stages N2 through N3 they would have dim recall, or none, of any dreams. However if awakened during or shortly after stage N1 or REM periods, they would have fairly good recall of dreaming. It is here that I wish to say a few things about the physiological properties of dreams as revealed through the EEG and other subtle measurements, which are not at all alien to science.

The activation/synthesis theory of Hobson and McCarley, first pub-lished in 1977 in *The American Journal of Psychiatry,* rocked the world of traditional psychiatry by seeming to turn some of Freud's pet (psy-choanalytic) theories on their head. The underlying forces that produce the dream, the investigators said, are physiological, not psychological (involving a chain of activity beginning in the pons of the reticular activating system, moving through the geniculate—previsual—nucleus, and reaching the occipital area, hence the primarily visual character of dreams). The acronym for the sequence is PGO (pontine-geniculate occipital).

Freudian psychoanalysis had dominated psychiatry for the first half of the twentieth century, and the alleged interaction of id, ego, and superego, and the psychosexual defense mechanisms of repres-sion, distortion, projection, sublimation, are known to most psychology students. As well, Freudian psychoanalysis constituted an orthodoxy of the genesis of dreams for many psychodynamically oriented clini-cians.[5] If you'll pardon the metaphor, Hobson wanted to stick it to

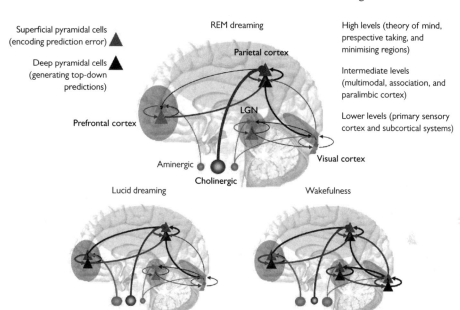

Superficial pyramidal cells
(encoding prediction error) ▲

Deep pyramidal cells ▲
(generating top-down
predictions)

Prefrontal cortex

REM dreaming

Parietal cortex

LGN

Aminergic

Cholinergic

Lucid dreaming

Visual cortex

Wakefulness

High levels (theory of mind,
prespective taking, and
minimising regions)

Intermediate levels
(multimodal, association, and
paralimbic cortex)

Lower levels (primary sensory
cortex and subcortical systems)

Fig. 2.5. Hobson-McCarley model (from Hobson, Hong, and Friston, "Virtual Reality and Consciousness Interfere in Dreaming")

psychoanalysis, claiming it to be opinion rather than science, and actually holding hostage legitimate scientific inquiry into dreaming and unconscious mechanisms by its prevalence and its orthodoxy. (After all, Freud's Pulitzer Prize was in literature, not science or medicine.)

Hobson was the first to show that neurochemistry changes rather profoundly from sleep to waking and back again. (To reiterate something mentioned earlier, during sleep, the neurotransmitter acetylcholine predominates. In waking, it is the epinephrine or adrenergic-related activating neurohormones that predominate.) The shift from one to the other explains why it is so hard to remember dreams upon waking—we are instantaneously awash in different chemicals. While Hobson has been resented and his work resisted for almost forty years by the psychoanalytic establishment for reducing dreaming to an epiphenomenon (by-product) of physiological processes, his own perspective has been continually modifying to keep up with changes in neuroscience and increasingly sophisticated computer modeling.

THE AIM MODEL OF CONSCIOUSNESS

1. Activation of the brain (measured by hormones or electrical activity).
2. Input: Is the generated energy internal or external? (See "day residue" discussion on page 57).
3. Modulation: Which neurochemicals are prevalent—adrenergic, cholinergic, or a hybrid—as in lucid dreaming where the person is seemingly awake while dreaming?

Important to Hobson's more recent ideas is that waking consciousness is a neurodevelopment that followed from dream consciousness—and in some ways rests upon it. Dreaming begins intra-utero and continues as the predominant type of consciousness through infancy. By dreaming, he says, the brain learns how to construct virtual reality free from the tyranny of sense experience. Thus it uses its own innate plasticity to model increasingly accurate versions of what outer sensory experience may require.

We get a preview here of the main theme of chapter 10, both that our waking lives are dreamlike and that we may bring waking concerns into the dream in the hybrid form of lucid dreaming. This is an area that Stanford's Stephen LaBerge has brought to scientific and public awareness and respectability.[6]

In what seems like a refutation of his earlier, mechanistic (activation-synthesis) model, Hobson seems to have arrived at a perspective in which "mechanisms don't trump meaning" and "dreams are not without psychological meaning and function."[7]

Based on the neurophysiological reality of pruning, in which the brain reduces its own redundancy, and neuroplasticity, in which new growth follows new learning, Hobson and McCarley have integrated their theory to include that dreaming is as necessary for cognitive development as waking experience. Hobson says, "Our point here is to explore the idea that both waking and dreaming are leaders and followers. Indeed one might argue that 'not only are all dreams experiences, but in a way all experiences are dreams.'"[8]

In an Internet article on Hobson's latest thought, dream researcher Ryan Hurd says, "Whenever someone suggests that 'dreams are random nonsense,' remind them that view is twenty years out of date!"[9] Personally Hobson has grown considerably, perhaps by associating with dreams as intimately as he has. Hurd says, in the same article, "In real life Hobson is a dream enthusiast and is reputed to have over 100 volumes of personal dream journals."[10] Hobson acknowledges that he has come to appreciate the approach of Jung, who says that dreams reveal more than they conceal, rather than Freud, who sees dreams as full of misdirection and concealment.

A Paradigm Clash (Wherein the Authors Weigh In On Ghosts in the Machine)

Are dreams merely the outcome of biological processes occurring in our physiologies or nervous systems? Are they the outcome of psychosexual (and culturally forbidden) dynamics? Are they the voice of our ancestors, our deep archetypal imagination—as Carl Jung suggests? Are they creativity, medical intuition—as in Edgar Cayce's work? Or even God, speaking in our psyches, as Morton Kelsey declares? The authors submit that an unbiased investigation of dreaming invites us to consider each and every one of the paradigms active in our psyches and in our time. (Learn them all, and then put them to one side when you truly "stand naked before the dream," which we will discuss further in chapter 5.) The new psychology of dreaming must include awareness—but not prematurely cede primacy—to any one of these perspectives!

Each has been investigated and promulgated by sincere thinkers. Each has a basis of its own—starting from the beginning—as in our chapter 1 wherein we discuss shamans who used dreams to navigate a perilous physical world, including how to find food or escape danger, and relayed their findings to the whole tribe. The prophets of the Hebrew and Christian scriptures used dreams to guide people through a wilderness, free them from captivity, and/or find a world savior. The Therapeutae of the cults of Apollo or Asclepius in ancient Greece and the alchemists of the Middle Ages asked dreams to help them in their "chymical" processes. The Renaissance dream-vision writers from Dante to Shakespeare wove dreams and history into their epics and dramas. They were the cultural creatives of the Age of Enlightenment, whose dreams opened completely new ideas and directions for them. The psychoanalysts of the nineteenth and twentieth centuries used dreams as "the royal road to the unconscious." Edgar Cayce, believing that dreams were indispensible concomitants to life and health, in his dreaming state was able to diagnose illness and give health-related advice to thousands of people. The lucid dreamers of the 1960s and 1970s believed that you could wake up in the dream and take charge of its symbolic unfoldment, and thus take charge of your life in an unexpected and powerful way.

Dreams are indispensible to life and have always accompanied it. Their importance has been acknowledged, and, since times of old, they evoke the paradigm of a human species that is very much in the stages of becoming. We are moving through developing fields of knowledge and expertise and inexorably toward a future that may involve the beautiful next stage of growth and creative unfoldment—or destruction and the unraveling of our (fragile) species. As we do so, our continuing dreams involve everything that we humans are about.

The new psychology of dreaming cannot leave any moiety out—that is to say, Human beings have studied and grappled with this (perennially interesting) subject since time immemorial. And we are studying a living process, no less important than metabolism, digestion, hormonal regulation, sex, or thinking!

In fact, because dreaming goes on every night, for every person in every community on Earth, we would be fools not to give this perennial form of immersion in the depths of our own consciousness our most serious attention. As noted earlier, there is a (we could say dumb) prejudice that says, with no further examination, "Oh, that was just a dream!" And so on we go. We think consciously and intentionally, not knowing that the (silly, childish) state that says, "just a dream," is itself just a dream!

Day Residues and Unsolved Problems

Early (1960s) dream researchers Green, Ullman, and Tauber, in an interesting paper that draws both from the physiological and the psychoanalytic perspective, point out that the sensory, and hence visual-symbolic, dimensions of the dream often refer to experiences from the previous day (juxtaposed against other previous experiences from the recent or even long-ago past).[11]

In an addition to this synthesizing discussion about unsolved problems they also hypothesize that the effect may be amplified by the unsolved problems in the entire culture in which the individual resides. This, of course, includes that culture's mythology. The mythology may work psychodynamically in the dreamer either in a direction of support or anxiety. Support would include life-affirmative and meaningful dimensions of the mythology that comforts the individual and makes him/her belong to the culture's symbolic universe. Anxiety producing ones would include dimensions where the individual may feel he or she has broken a taboo or somehow is in conflict with the culture's underlying assumptions.

There is a fascinating conversation going on in the field of cultural anthropology about whether dreams can be interpreted cross-culturally—that is, without knowledge of the cultural values and mythology of that culture. Psychoanalysts and psychohistorians speak in the affirmative, but cultural anthropologists are quite dubious. (This controversy involves complexities that are beyond our discussion here, but it does allow us to weigh in on a fundamental value that will be brought out in chapter 5, "Standing Naked Before the Dream.")

Dream analyst Edward Whitmont would weigh in strongly for an accurate understanding of the social and symbolic context before even hazarding a guess as to what the dream might mean. That is to say, any interpretation must exhaustively investigate the associations of the dreamer, which would of course take into account those social and culturally contextual memories and symbols. A simple example of one symbol would be that of a horse appearing in the dream of a Mongolian nomad—

who uses the creature to go everywhere in his world—as opposed to the horse of a city dweller who has never ridden one or that of a family that is addicted to horserace betting and whose favorite pastime is the racetrack!

Throughout this book we shall return to the paradigm clash between dreaming neurology and the content or meanings of the dream, and the authors will show again and again that there need not be a clash but that both or all dimensions or perspectives are useful. Of course the dream is produced in a brain, but the brain is located in a human person who dwells in a certain culture, has a certain learning history, and experiences a complex and idiosyncratic outlook on the world—if such can be elicited in the psychotherapeutic discussion.

Ullman and Krippner, who worked together at the groundbreaking Maimonides Medical Center dream lab in the 1960s and '70s, point out that all of the frequencies observable in the EEG are simultaneously present in both the waking and the sleeping brain; they are seamlessly continuous. That is to say that literally and physiologically we are dreaming while awake, and some of our sleep brain waves are simulacra of waking ones—particularly when REM is present and the body has to be (neurobiologically) paralyzed to keep us from acting out the dream. Likewise, in the phenomenon of daydreaming, which every schoolteacher and every psychotherapist or psychoanalyst knows about, dreamlike reveries permeate waking consciousness.

It is known, of course, that when internally produced fantasies predominate in consciousness, the person becomes as if "autistic" and unresponsive to signals from the outer world. This relates in a very specific and interesting way to brain wave theory and the widespread cult in the modern world of putting schoolchildren on stimulants such as Ritalin and Concerta.

The stimulants, of course, speed up the frequency of the brain waves so they are less dreamlike (theta) and more like healthy attentive brain activity in normal people (beta). In fact brain scientist Joel Lubar has devised a brain discriminant based on the ratio of beta to theta. The less of the former and the more of the latter, the more likely the child is to be in the ADHD population. Lubar believes, as do many biofeedback and neurofeedback practitioners, that neurofeedback, which leaves no drug residues in the child's system, is preferable to the pharmaceutic approach, which leaves drugs that stay in a child's system for an indeterminate period and have global effects on that child's functioning, including problems such as insomnia and irritable/explosive behavior as the drugs are wearing off.

There really need be no paradigm clash in dream psychology, because it is not about either/or, but both/and!

Neurofeedback has some excellent contributions to make to dream theory for the following reasons (which are strangely unknown to mainstream science, either psychology or neurobiology).

- The character of dreams often is related to the stage of sleep as measurable through EEG. For example, night terrors and sleepwalking, and some nightmares occur, not usually in REM, but in deeper stages of sleep, including stage N3. Subjectively, as reported in psychotherapy or experienced, these dreams are murky, vague, and sometimes very difficult to remember. (These would be dreams occurring mostly in delta sleep.)
- Dreams in REM are far more lively and colorful than non-REM dreaming; they are likely to contain day residues and in fact may resemble waking problem-solving. These dreams are relatively easy to remember if awakening takes place right in or just after the REM period.
- The real difficulty people have remembering their dreams has been attributed by psychoanalysis to the defense mechanism of *repression*. According to Freud, the latent dream is so horrifying or unacceptable to the person's sensibility that it has to be symbolically distorted into the (perhaps bizarre) events remembered in the manifest dream. The neurobiological explanation is much simpler: if you wake up during slow-wave sleep too long after the dream there is almost no recall (remembering that sleep and dream are associated with cholinergic dominance and waking consciousness by epinephrine neurotransmitters).

- Remember that almost all brain wave frequencies are present in the raw EEG at any one time. The proportion, however, is very different depending on whether the person is awake and concentrating or daydreaming. Where the power lies can be determined by the dominant frequency of the power spectrum, measured in Hertz or Hz cycles per second as well as the amplitude, measured in microvolts (millionths of a volt). When awake, your dominant frequency will probably be alpha or above. When asleep, you are likely to be producing delta or theta (unless in REM). How can we transport an image that may be clear or vivid in the dream from one frequency to another? (Think of the problem of someone intoxicated trying to remember what he just said.) Memory works differently in different frequency ranges. In fact, there is a definite kind of amnesia when we shift from one range to another.

- Hypnagogia (leading into sleep) and hypnopompia (leading out of sleep) states are liminal (between realms). They are often characterized by theta (4–8 Hz); they may be hallucinatory, even delusional. (We introduced the idea of cittavritti—a dynamic mind-substance from yoga—in the last chapter.) Suffice it to say here that all of our experiences, whether generated from within or without, must be transcribed or encoded onto the living stuff of consciousness itself. To move from sleep to waking, waking to sleep, we pass through this liminal realm, which can either add to, or take away from, what we are able to be aware of.

- Brain frequencies may literally show up in the imagery of dreams—as ocean waves or ripples on ponds, as storms or hurricanes of fierce centrality (depicting, perhaps, a seizure focus), or quiet, rhythmical music in a sacred grove. The rhythms, like real music, can range through the rhythmical modes of musical time. Some people have heard complex, exquisite symphonic music in their dreams, as discussed in Jim Robbins's book *A Symphony in the Brain: The Evolution of the New Brain Wave Biofeedback*. In these cases, as the metaphor implies, all instruments are present and the timing is different but connected among them.

Symphonies in the Brain

In Jim Robbins's classic book on neurofeedback mentioned previously, the metaphor of a symphony seems apt. Not a rock band, nor a string quartet, nor a baroque ensemble—for only a full-on symphonic orchestra can even begin to do metaphoric justice to what happens in our brains. Most music is mediated by the right cerebral hemisphere; words and mathematics (of most kinds) are mediated by the left. A good friend of mine by the name of Michael Schacker, a composer and musician, suffered a massive stroke that took out almost his entire left hemisphere. This involved damage to the part of his brain known as Broca's area (an area of speech origination primarily), but he could still sing—and the songs had words that he couldn't speak but only sing. Why?[12]

Spoken language and musical language come from different parts of the brain. While Michael's spoken language was occluded, his musical language was intact. In fact it was glorious. I know this because I used to sing with him in therapy sessions, before he could speak again.

I remember my mother, Mabel, looking me in the eye in her last (one-hundredth) year of life and telling me, "Stephen, I have heard the most glorious music—it is not like anything I have ever heard before." She teared up as she was talking, as if the emotions she was experiencing were far more articulate than her words could ever be (in certain respects they are!). I myself have indeed heard music in my dreams, perhaps not quite like what my mom described, but pretty wonderful nonetheless.

Many composers—from Mozart to John Lennon to Bob Dylan—report that the themes and compositions of their most immortal works have come from dreams. Rhythm, frequencies, and themes repeated and elaborated are part of our dreams and the brain rhythms on which they ride. In chapter 9 you will find the tale of the genesis of "Yesterday," the widely popular song by the Beatles. Sometimes attributed to John Lennon, its actual composer was Paul McCartney—who was obsessed by the tune in a dream before the well-known words were finally written.

This story takes us back to the topic of the rhythms of the brain.

They are not only rhythmical, they are also musical, and exquisitely so! In the dreaming state, free of the constraints of daytime concerns and ego trips, they break forth in wonder, in beautiful melody and harmony. Our only task may be to remember them, in whatever form they take. (Play them, write them down, hum or sing them—and then if you are willing to add perspiration to inspiration, find the right words for them!)

When my wife, Robin, and I were in the Brazilian Amazon at a village sacred to the Santo Daime tradition called Mapia, we discovered something amazing! To drink the entheogenic (psychedelic) beverage called ayahuasca, hundreds of people gathered in the great teakwood cathedral that was the heart of the village. During ceremonies they would sing together hymns that had been received in their dreams. While we were there, a young girl of about thirteen heard a song, or a *hino,* in a dream. It was very beautiful, and she couldn't get it out of her mind. By that evening, as we all drank the Daime (specially prepared ayahuasca) in the great church, everyone was singing her song!

There it was: the phenomenon I had written about in *The Shaman's Doorway*—how one person could have a dream and communicate it to the entire community! (I called this "the enactment of vision," and in 1976 said, "This is how a *mythologically instructed community* does things.") Much of the great art of our civilization has come from our dreaming— and our willingness to share the dream—that is, to write it down, sing or hum it, transcribe the poem or the incantation, and/or write the equation.

So there it is: the brain is a rhythmical and rhythm-seeking organ. Think of an orchestra tuning up (a familiar cacophony). Probably most of us are like that most of the time. But what happens when the conductor lifts his baton? It truly involves a symphony, for there are many different instruments playing their different roles, and yet our lives, waking or sleeping, are a harmony (or a disharmony—a symphony in the brain!).

Neurofeedback and Dreaming

Len Ochs, who has been one of my teachers over the years, alerted me to the phenomenon that neurofeedback enhances (and modulates) dreaming. He was completely right, but I have discovered much more: neurofeedback (see my books *The Healing Power of Neurofeedback* and *The Neurofeedback Solution* for more) is a brain-stimulating and balancing technology. It cannot only end years of dream deprivation for some people, it can also do away with night terrors and nightmares. To be sure, my remarks are based on clinical experience rather than controlled studies, but I have done informal studies on the hundreds of clients whom my students and I see in therapy. I have found that neurofeedback, as it stabilizes and balances the brain, not only restores normalized sleep patterns (it is known for that) but also brings relief from disturbing dreams to both children and adults.

A recent example is a seven-year-old afflicted with nightmares and night terrors. His family is relatively intact but has had its challenges over the years, including PTSD from their house burning down. The child, Chris, we will call him, was afflicted with very restless sleep. He suffered from anxiety attacks caused by any changes or disruptions of his routine. He also suffered from car sickness (on any trip over an hour or so he would vomit copiously). His parents were thrilled when the latter symptom subsided after only four or five neurofeedback treatments. But then almost simultaneously his nightmares and night terrors dwindled, first to about half of their former frequency and then disappearing altogether.

At this point, as his therapist, I probed for the complexion of his dreams. He could remember a few—they seemed to be about ordinary things—but again, his nightmares had completely ceased. (His attention in school also improved, and his daydreaming decreased.) After his having undergone about ten treatments, we now had a happy family (the mother, a professional therapist, was astonished as well as being very pleased).

A not uncommon visitor to my practice is the perpetually stoned teenager. He (more usually than she) is languishing in school, stays up late, and is hard to arouse in the morning. These kids tend to sleep very late on weekends and may also neglect personal hygiene. Needless to say, parents are very concerned whether "Jesse" will still be at home on the couch at the age of forty (which is not at all unknown). When I take on such clients I offer no promises. The allure of marijuana and psychedelics is ubiquitous and supported by peer culture. (Of course, none of us can deny that this drug use takes place in a culture that seems to have no roots of its own and has otherwise lost its bearings.) I have tended to be on the more liberal side of legalization over the years, but experience has forced me to reconsider. Furthermore, there are experimental chemists, not always certain of what they are doing, who ensure that the black market has an ample supply of psychedelic (or hallucinogenic) drugs, as well as trafficking pharmaceutical downers and uppers.

Recent studies have swung the balance away from my earlier liberalism, showing that there *are* long-term neurological affects from the chronic smoking of marijuana (not to mention other drugs) between the ages of thirteen or fourteen up to the age of twenty-two (at which time the brain has largely developed).[13] These changes affect the white matter tracts that undergird memory and intellectual development—and can cause what very well may be irreversible damage to memory, attention, and the executive functions. One of the most salient symptoms is an almost complete amnesia of dreaming. (In fact, I include the question on clinical interviews from the very first day: Do you remember your dreams?)[14]

A couple of cases illustrate that there is definitely an oneiro-suppressive effect from daily marijuana use. This was demonstrated in individuals who stopped smoking it and who began neurofeedback. Their dreams came rushing back in—as if to make up for lost time! I will cite the case of one young man of sixteen, who had been smoking pot for at least four years. As well, he had been taking other drugs such as alcohol, barbiturates, "molly" (MDMA), and acid all at one time (which resulted in a trip to the emergency room). Other times he took various combinations of these drugs in formations of "unholy cocktails." When he finally detoxed and returned to see me, he reported that his dreams had come back in spades. The expression on his face and the wonder in his eyes told me that his straight experience, that of remembering his dreams, eclipsed any of his extravagant drug trips.

Two of my older clients had lived with years of nightmares. Brad, in his eighties, had grown up during World War II. Some of his male relatives had come back from the war wounded. Others just hadn't come back. One of Brad's earliest memories, from the 1940s, was of a funeral that was deeply upsetting to him. *He told me he had had a nightmare every night since he was a young man—a period of more than seventy years.*

After about four months of neurofeedback and psychotherapy, Brad told me that he had remembered his first dream that was not a nightmare. Then he told me about dreams of his that had been marked by frightening, nightmarish elements but that also contained magical and fascinating elements. In some of them a wizard appeared to give him help at crucial moments. Here is one such dream.

> *I am in a canoe going first through choppy water, then, it seems, up the Amazon. There are alligators on the banks. The wizard appears. I say, "Look at those alligators!"*
>
> *He says, "I'm not afraid of them." Up ahead is a giant serpent, towering over the trees. The voice says, "That is your father!"*
>
> *I say, "My father?"*
>
> *"Yes," says the voice. "Everyone's father looks like that to them."*
>
> *I am caught between fear and wonder.*

After undergoing five months of neurofeedback and psychotherapy on a weekly basis, Brad has switched to every other week. He feels steadier on his feet, more optimistic. His nightmares no longer occur every night. Instead he may have a couple of them a week. However, they are mixed with other dreams that he finds curious and intriguing.

Joe, a Vietnam-era vet in his midseventies had been traumatized many times and had suffered fractures of the spine and pelvis. When he first came to us, he had wall-to-wall insomnia, nightmares, and incessant pain. He couldn't sit straight in a chair, and he awoke every morning with dread. It took a full year to reduce his pain and insomnia. *The nightmares gradually were replaced by ordinary dreams.* Today his dread is less, and he has more optimism. His dreams are characterized by a workspace that grows increasingly nicer (as reported in chapter 7). He also reports being able to drive. He walks relatively upright, and his pain is about 50 percent diminished. His insomnia is reduced, and he remembers more dreams, sometimes of friends and of happier times in his life.

As the brain normalizes, dreams become normalized. The traumatic events of the past can never be totally erased, but they cease to obsess and control PTSD sufferers.

Our finding is that neurofeedback (also called "biofeedback for the brain") can not only heal but also balance the brain. It is the West's complementary method to Patanjali's elucidation of *AUM,* and people who have practiced it find themselves more balanced, whether awake or asleep. When we can find our inner resting point, through all the changing tonalities and rhythms of the brain, we learn to listen for the polyphony, the harmonies—the sounds of the separate instruments of our symphony in the brain.

Our next chapter takes a more practical turn. In it we will explore how we may remember our dreams, and how we may work with them to enrich our daily lives.

3

Remembering Our Dreams
(And a Few Tips for Beginning to Work with Them)

In the Words of Coauthor Tom Verner

Henry Reed, in his creative and useful book *Getting Help from Your Dreams,* refers to remembering dreams as an art. In using the word *art,* Dr. Reed acknowledges that he is partially "making a confession as to the mystery of the process" of remembering dreams.[1]

One of the most mysterious aspects of dreams reveals itself in the common experience of being in the grip of an intense dream, one that is vivid, powerful, and seemingly unforgettable. We awaken and within seconds the dream is gone, never to be known again. The way in which a dream can vanish suddenly tells us something of the perennial mystery of dreams and why it might be an art to remember them. In learning this art, we may, like the ancient Greeks, need to propitiate Lethe, goddess of forgetfulness. That there is a divine presence associated with forgetfulness itself lets us know that this act of recalling, this art of remembering something as delicate as a dream, perhaps has something sacred about it.

How to Remember Your Dreams

What follows is a step-by-step process to help you recall your dreams. This is a process we have found helpful; over time as you develop your recall abilities, you will come up with your own methods of recalling and recording your dreams.

Step 1: Motivation

Even though remembering dreams may be a sacred art, it is like any other art we wish to learn in that it requires motivation, skill, the application of various techniques, and a willingness to be persistent and patient. This may sound a bit circular, but we will be motivated to remember our dreams when we begin to experience the profound guidance they can provide. It is important to value and record whatever we recall, even a simple and silly-seeming fragment. We will soon discover what amazing benefits can be gained from working creatively with just such a fragment. As with any relationship, the relationship with our dreams will deepen and develop only if we pay attention to them and value what they give us.

Step 2: Actively Prepare Yourself to Recall Your Dream

When you are first beginning to develop your ability to recall your dreams, select days when you will be unpressured and able to awaken naturally without an alarm clock. Perhaps on a weekend or during vacation is an opportune time to begin learning the art of remembering your dreams. Before going to sleep, set your intention to recall whatever dreams may present themselves. Place a journal and pen or a voice-activated tape recorder on your bedside table. In your journal, jot down a few sentences about the day, including the important facts and feelings that were its highlights. A few sentences are enough. Carl Jung suggested that dreams often respond to the events of our day in a compensatory or corrective effort to bring about balance. So writing down these few facts and feelings about our day may prove immensely valuable when reflecting on the dream the next day. It may prove to be even more valuable weeks later when other dreams, what Jung called a "dream series," has accumulated, often around an unfolding theme.

Dreamwork can be understood as a dialogue between your waking life and the dream universe, between the known and unknown parts of yourself, and, as we will find, dreams may shed light on one another. After you have written a few facts and feelings about your day, write down the next day's date on the blank page of your journal. This will create a positive affirmation that you will in fact remember a dream the next morning. As you drift off to sleep, give yourself pre-sleep suggestions. Seed the unconscious by saying a few times, "In the morning I will remember my dreams and write them down." There are other ways to set your intention. For instance, each night before going to bed, in your dream journal you could write a question or simply note a dilemma that you're facing and ask for a dream that provides you with guidance about this dilemma.

These are the fundamentals of dream incubation, which we explore in detail in chapter 8. Remember Synesius's sage counsel: "You have an *Oracle* inside you without highly elaborated ritual or propitiation. It is there for everyman/woman. . . . It is there," Synesius goes on to say, as "a gift of God to each of us; something that we should not neglect; it is in fact, an inestimable aid on the spiritual path." As Synesius insists, "While we are awake we must listen to our fellow humans talking. When we are asleep, it is only God talking." If this description doesn't quite match your belief system, we can believe that we may be talking to ourselves in a unique way, one in which our deeper or higher self gets a chance to speak with us.[2]

PRESENT PERIOD LOG

Something that might be useful in getting a sense of what the dreams may be responding to is a journal-writing exercise developed by Ira Progoff called the "Present Period Log."[3] Deepening our understanding of dreamwork as a dialogue between the dreaming and waking aspects of ourselves can be extremely valuable if we develop a clear sense of what Progoff calls "this time in your life." If dreamwork is like gardening, working with a Present Period Log is like rototilling the garden, preparing the ground to receive the dream seeds, and deepen our understanding of what dreams may be trying to tell us.

As you ready yourself for bed, begin by quieting your mind and making yourself as receptive as possible. Allow a sense of "this time in your life" to emerge. According to Progoff, we live our lives in periods. When did this period, this "time in your life," begin? You may know the exact day, but certainly as you open yourself to this time in your life you will get a *sense* of when it began. Move around in your mind through this time, allowing the important people, relationships, events, works, issues, concerns, challenges, accomplishments, psychic experiences, big dreams, whatever, to come to you.

Now, with all this floating around in your mind, allow an image to emerge that captures this time. Complete the sentence "This time is like . . ." It may be like the calm before the storm; like a tree putting down roots by a stream; like standing at a crossroads, torn about which way to go; or like preparing to set out in a new direction. Jot this period image in your journal. You may also want to make a simple drawing of the image in your journal. Then complete the sentence "This is a time when . . ." Complete the exercise with the questions, "What are the main issues, themes, and questions facing me? What is life asking of me at this time?" Write a paragraph response to each question in your journal.

And now finally begin to write as much as you can about this time in your life, bringing in all those elements: people, relationships, and accomplishments that you came up with when you were imagining your period image above. When you have fully explored this you are ready to drift off to sleep.

Step 3: Upon Awakening, Recall and Record Your Dream

Upon awakening, lie as still as possible, allowing the dream images to float through your mind. Keeping your eyes closed allows the images of the dream to come to you. Often they come in reverse order, last ones first. This is a delicate and dangerous time for dream recall for the dream is still fresh in your mind and the thought *I don't need to write this down, I'll remember it* is one to which you might respond,

"Get behind me, Satan!" The idea of writing down your dream later is a temptation that should be resisted; it is important to lie still in that twilight state between sleeping and waking, recalling the dream but not falling back to sleep.

When you have a sense of the dream, begin to record it in your journal or on your recorder. It may be useful to move back and forth between writing and eyes-closed recall, moving back and forth in that twilight space as much as possible. There is some evidence that dreams are somehow encoded in the body in the position in which they were dreamed. Sometimes when we are unable to recall the dream, if we gently roll over, eyes closed, into a new position, the dream may come to us. Try this if you are having difficulty recalling your dream.

Remember to write down any image, no matter how insignificant it may seem at the time. Often, writing something down triggers other images, and even whole dreams. Throughout this book you will encounter numerous examples of working with simple dream fragments, thereby yielding immense guidance and meaning. Especially when we are just beginning to work with our dreams, it is important and a sign of respect for our dreams to record anything and everything we receive. As Jung might say, the Unconscious works only as hard as Consciousness. This is a relationship you are fostering, so record, work with, and be grateful for whatever you receive from the dreamworld.

Keeping a Dream Journal

Keeping a dream journal is a very personal and potentially creative undertaking. What kind of journal you use is a personal choice. Some people like a bound notebook or an artist's sketchbook. Others prefer loose-leaf pages in a three-ring binder. Some like to record their dreams on their computers. Each method offers its own possibilities. It can be very useful to take the notes you write down upon first awakening or in the middle of the night and copy them over in the present tense into a separate dream journal. If you record the dream in the present tense you will connect more deeply to the emotional tone of the dream's images.

This tends to bring the dream alive and connect you in a deeper way to the original dream experience. It's also advisable, for the same reason, when telling the dream to another person to tell it in the present tense.

The following is how we authors record our dreams. Tom keeps a regular journal and records his dreams in that journal and not in a separate dream journal. He found it was simpler to keep track of one journal. But he writes his dreams in red in his journal, so they are very easy to find. See color plate 4 for a sample from Tom's dream journal.

Tom writes the dreams down the center of the page leaving wide margins on either side. The first thing he does is give the dream a title as if it were a movie or a short story. Most of the time he gives a dream three or four different titles, naming it from different perspectives—from various viewpoints of different characters in the dream. A title may be serious or funny; perhaps using the name of a song will capture the sense of the dream. Both authors have noted that often their first response to a dream is one of total bafflement, for they may not have a clue about what the dream might mean. Giving it some titles begins to bring a certain kind of focus or attention to the dream—a way into the dream to begin exploring its many possible meanings. As James Hillman, Jungian scholar and founder of archetypal psychology, reminds us, any meaning we find in the dream is "only one among many."[4]

In the wide margins on either side of the dream text you can write associations to the images, draw pictures of odd or interesting things in the dream, and/or make connections to your waking life and perhaps to other dreams. Make associations to the dream images: What do they remind you of from your waking life, especially the last day or two? We will be sharing many ways of working with our dreams throughout this book. Recording, giving titles to, and making associations to one's waking life is a good way to begin.

Stephen keeps a smaller loose-leaf journal, 8½" × 5", so that he can carry it everywhere. He uses colored divider tabs for different sections (in the method he learned from Ira Progoff in the 1970s) for dreams, poetry, and creative ideas. In the dream section he records just the dream. In his daily calendar he records the events of the day. Other sections might

*Fig. 3.1. The dream journals of coauthor Stephen Larsen.
Sections include dreams, associations, poetry, free writing,
and creative projects/weekly planning.*

include poetry, hints about other things he is working on (like this book—in part coauthored by the dream muse herself!), building projects, and even how to make office procedures run more smoothly. If there are any health issues pending for him or a family member, sometimes dreams may have surprising input such as "I need more hydration" if water keeps coming up. Even a particular plant or homeopathic or herbal remedy might be hinted at. Robin has been keeping a dream journal at least as long as Stephen has, and she often receives her artistic inspiration from dreams (see the color insert, plate 3).

In this discussion of dream journals, we have given but two of many possible formats for recording your dreams. Some of our friends and students have a tape recorder by their bed, which they use to record their dreams. Later they listen to and transcribe them. It's not a bad idea to use a voice-activated recorder if you have one available, so you don't have to do anything technical in the middle of the night when you may no doubt be in a thetalike state. These days, voice-recognition software is easier to use and competitively priced, ranging from programs like Dragon Naturally Speaking to the simpler applications commonly available on iPhones and other smartphones. Those most effective for dreamwork should type out what you say—and may require minor editing later, or resaving into a dream file. What you will probably find, if you use this method, is something that we are increasingly going to emphasize in this chapter: The more times you go over your dream, the more associations and meanings will jump out at you—it's guaranteed!

ROBERT JOHNSON'S FOUR-STEP PROCESS

A good, clear process of recording and learning how to work with one's dreams in a journal is presented by Robert Johnson, Jungian analyst and author, in his extremely helpful book *Inner Work: Using Dreams and Active Imagination for Personal Growth*. Johnson's four-step process of working with a dream is a wonderful way of beginning the practice of dreamwork by creating associations and connections to your current waking life and moving toward some interpretative sense of what the dream may be telling you. In the fourth step of the process, Johnson helps guide the dreamer in imagining how he or she might bring the dream into waking life; what the dreamer might do with the dream in their life by creating what he calls a ritual from the dream. Johnson's way of working with dreams is powerful for beginners and seasoned dream workers alike.

Other Little Tricks That May Aid in Dream Recall

1. **Set a timer** for an hour or half an hour before your usual waking time and keep your journal or voice-activated recorder nearby. You may just catch an REM cycle that customarily shows up at that time.

2. **Drink water** or some other beverage such as herbal tea right

before sleep. (The need to go to the bathroom later might help you "catch a dream.")

3. **Use a mugwort dream pillow,** for traditionally this common garden herb (*Artimesia vulgaris*) aids dreaming. (It's also called moxa, traveler's herb, Artemis herb, felon herb, muggons, old man, sailor's tobacco, and *Cingulum Sancti Johannis*.)

4. **Allow a dog to sleep in your bedroom** (an ancient Asclepian trick). He may bark at something unexpected, thereby waking you from a dream.

Things That Can Interfere with Dreaming and Dream Recall

1. **Sleeping pills.** For years it's been known that certain pharmaceutical sleep aids may suppress REM activity, so that while you appear to sleep soundly, the REM component, which provides psychological restoration, is missing. If you seem to sleep well but don't wake up refreshed, consider looking into whether any medications you are taking, either to aid sleep or to combat anxiety or depression, are inhibitory of REM activity. The usual suspects are benzodiazepines, SSRIs, and antipsychotics such as Seroquel and Respirdal.

2. **Marijuana.** Though this herb seems to induce pleasant reveries and excursions of thought for many people, it also seems to suppress dreams or render them so cloudy and obscure that they can't be remembered. THC seems to stay in the system for weeks, so it may exert an ongoing inhibitory effect on dream recall. (See the previous chapter in which Stephen and his clinical colleagues report many cases of young people with a daily marijuana habit who stopped smoking pot and began to have vivid dreams very quickly thereafter.)

3. **Alcohol (in all its many forms).** Although a nightcap of brandy or whiskey can sometimes make us sleepy, as can wine, and in small amounts does not seem to affect dreaming much, drinking

several drinks right before bed seems to introduce a chemical distortion into the process, so that dreaming is turbulent and confusing. Also, when the consciousness that is trying to retrieve the dream is drunk, it doesn't do such a good job of sorting things out. (Perhaps this is the nighttime equivalent of "Don't drink and drive!")

4. **Sudden awakening to alarm clocks** and having a busy agenda. As discussed in chapter 2, "The Dreaming Brain," when we don't leave enough time to bring our nighttime activity through the portal of transition to waking, especially as a daily habit, the dreams are likely to not make it through. Or they may vanish as soon as they do, as the stars vanish when the sun shines brightly.

5. **Being dismissive of dreams,** or saying "It was just a dream" too often, or having a mental habit that dismisses one's inner processes as worthless or trivial.

Partners in Dreaming

Another method we will emphasize—with an understanding that not everyone has this wonderful luxury available—is to tell your dream to a sleeping partner or a good friend with whom you have breakfast or see regularly during the day. It's all the better if your sleeping partner is someone you love and trust and who has an equal regard or respect for dreams. The person you tell your dream to also may ask you clarifying questions such as "Was the dream clear or kind of murky?" Or "Where was it taking place?" If you have the time and inclination, friends can engage in much more detailed associations and amplifications of the dream, which is often very valuable. When a group is gathered together, as in one of Tom and Janet's dream retreats, or Stephen and Robin's regular dream groups, the effect we are mentioning is truly amplified.

One tool we use consistently in our dreamwork is a list of helpful points to bear in mind. We call it the Dream Portal Method. It may be printed out as a single page and distributed to your friends/

dreamwork colleagues; it is found in the appendix. Montague Ullman and Nan Zimmerman's marvelous book, *Working with Dreams,* has immensely helpful guidelines for starting one's own grassroots dream group. Another helpful work is Montague Ullman and Claire Limmer's *The Variety of Dream Experiences.*

For years on the commuter train from Connecticut to New York City, a group of interested dreamers would gather in a compartment each morning during the commute and share their dreams from the previous evening with one another. This brings to mind societies such as the Iroquois or the Senoi of Malaysia, for whom the recalling of dreams was woven into everyday life as a ritual. Being in psychotherapy or analysis is of course an aid to remembering and taking seriously what comes in the night, especially if your therapist is attuned to the value of dreaming or is a depth psychologist.

Both Tom and Stephen worked with Jungian analysts, as well as Ira Progoff, attending his intensive journal workshops and participating in his ongoing weekly intensive journal groups. Progoff worked a great deal with dreams in his journal work. These kinds of intensive practices of self-exploration using dreams—whether in analysis, an intensive journal-writing group, a dream retreat (which we describe in chapter 8), or a regular ongoing dream group—can teach you a great deal about yourself and about dreams. The authors both believe that they learned more about the power and possibilities of dreams through this intensive committed work than from anything else in their lives.

Journal as Place and Presence

Over the years, as you keep a dream journal in which you both record and work with your dreams, you begin to develop a sense of your journal as a friend and companion on your spiritual journey. Your journal is not just a lifeless book in which to record facts and information. This kind of journal can become a living witness and participant in the growth and development of your inner spiritual life. The kind of journal work developed by Ira Progoff and others (and strongly advocated by the authors) enables you to *experience your journal as a place and a presence*. Your journal becomes a place *to retreat* to, where you can work on your memories, dreams, and reflections. The most comprehensive presentation of Ira Progoff's Intensive Journal Process is in his book *At a Journal Workshop*.

Your journal becomes the kind of sacred protective place the ancient Greeks called a *temenos*. When working in your journal as temenos, you sense *a magic circle drawn around you into which you can withdraw* and explore your inner world in a safe and creative way. This kind of journal work is similar to yoga, meditation, or any other practice done for personal growth—it requires discipline and perseverance and needs time and nourishment to bear fruit.

Commit yourself to this process, a process that often takes place invisibly and without you knowing it. Once you do so, thereby bringing to it the needed discipline, your journal can become that companion walking beside you on your personal pilgrimage through your inner world. This is a companion who will keep your experiences alive for you; a friend to remind you what things you have forgotten and need to remember; a presence with whom you may speak and who will respond with needed words of guidance and healing.

Keep Writing in the Dark

We have presented but a few ideas about remembering your dreams and beginning to work with them so as to develop a relationship with this profound source of guidance, healing, and insight within us all. This inner presence seems to know more about us than we know about ourselves; it sends imaginative and healing letters to us every night. The hope of this book is that you will begin to collect these letters each morning and learn to read their mysteriously poetic language. As the Talmud says, "A dream that is not interpreted is like a letter that is not read." May the ideas and images we present in these pages help you to develop and deepen a relationship with your dreams, which begins with remembering and recording them. Denise Levertov invites us to do just that in her poem "Writing in the Dark":

"Writing in the Dark"

Keep writing in the dark:
a record of the night, or
words that pulled you from the depths of unknowing,

....

words that may have the power
to make the sun rise again . . .[5]

Other Dream Components

The Four Elements

One of the best ways to remember your dreams is to start an inventory of the traditional four elements in your dreams. Do your dreams feature earth, water, fire, or air? If so, what form do they take? Gaston Bachelard, one of the foremost symbolists of the twentieth century, instructed Sartre and Albert Camus at the Sorbonne. Richard Leviton writes of him: ". . . the elements of life—air, water, fire and earth—speak to him in every moment of being alive, freshly, vividly, metaphorically. He traces the life of images back to their organic roots in the substances of nature; our mind and the world as we see it are made from these."[6]

Let's explore some associations of these four elements as follows:

Earth: Think of "hardness." Become a miner, a troglodyte of your own dreaming. Even if you have nightmares of being buried alive, ask yourself, What is so substantial about this particular dream? Befriend the substance around you. Can you till your own soil? Won't you try to climb your own mountains? (All you have to fall into is yourself.)

Water: Think of birth and of becoming; think of riding on the flows and currents of your dreams; think of swimming in your own imagination—diving in your depths, slaking your own thirst like a greedy camel. Water is a guarantee that your dream life springs eternal. You can weather your own storms, surf on your own tidal waves.

Air: Here your imagination is most transparent, most capable of blowing through you. Your "airy nothings" can vary from a gentle zephyr to a full-blown gale; the atmospheres of your dream can wax from sunny to sultry. Mists and vapors allow you to brood, to see things indistinctly. What kind of a day is it where you are? Take a breath of air like champagne.

Fire: Become a candle-dreamer (try writing your dreams by candlelight). Bachelard writes, "I myself need no more than the image of a person at his candlelight vigil to begin the undulant movements of thoughts and reveries."[7] Meditate on a flame and you get "vertical food." The Chinese ideogram for a person is a house on fire. Fire can warm you or transform you in your own autos-da-fé. Do not fear the alchemy in your own soul—welcome it!

The Architecture of Your Dream

Basement: Basements can be spooky; they are the underworld, the subconscious. (*The Far Side* cartoonist Gary Larson writes that his brother would lock him in the basement and whisper through the door: "They're coming, Gary, they're coming . . ." It was enough to trigger a lifetime of macabre imaginings.) But basements can also contain wonderful closets, workshops, furnaces; what is yours like?

Attic: Attics can be as spooky as basements. What strange bats are in your belfry? What curious chests full of forgotten antiques? Do you climb a hidden ladder or a twisting staircase to get there? Do you need some storage space or a secret hideaway?

Living Room: Can you entertain guests there, or is it always cluttered? How, indeed, have you been living? Can you see out, and is there a view, or are you shuttered? Do you have a TV—an entertainment center? What about bookshelves, and what about moving some furniture around (permissible or impermissible)?

Kitchen: Can be warm, fragrant, a place for the most important conversations; an alchemical lab where wondrous creations are made and transformations happen. Do you have big handsome copper pots? Do you smell the coffee? Do you use a microwave? How do you deal with nourishment? Do you nourish yourself; do you nourish others?

Do you have a study, a library, a workshop, a garage, a sauna, a hot tub? (We leave you to figure out the symbolism of those!)

The Dramatic Structure of the Dream

Expect your dreams to come with a time-honored archetypal structure. While modern drama has emphasized the beginning/middle/end formula, we like the four-part, more textured approach a little better. It's from Greek drama—at least twenty-five hundred years old—and both Carl Jung and Edward Whitmont preferred it. It features four classical stages: exposition, development, crisis, and lysis. Gaining a sense of this structure not only can help us understand the dream more clearly as a dramatic, meaningful entity but also having this model in the back of our mind can aid in recalling our dreams. Following is the four-part structure and a brief description of each of its stages.

Exposition: First; where does the dream take place? Is the setting recognizable? Does it pertain to your past or present, or is it out of your ordinary time and space? Is it natural, supernatural, or exotic (a place you have never been, but having a definable quality)? Is it a place of torment or rapture, or indefinable quality—inexpressibly strange or like the dawn of a new creation? Most importantly, does it present overtly, or hint at, a problem—something requiring a solution? *The gist of the exposition is that it states or identifies a problem.*

Development: What then unfolds? Does it seem to lead to a journey, a discovery, a creative excursus, a meeting with remarkable men? Look at the dramatic structure carefully—is it seamless, or does it occur in parts, or subparts? (Do you save the wounded animal, or ignore it? Do you set out on a familiar path only to lose your way? Do you feel absolutely lost and then get help—or does help never seem to come?) *The development brings all the players on stage and identifies the resources and the nature of the problem.*

Crisis: Is some sort of crisis present? You have fallen into a well and the sides are slippery. You are chased by a monster whom you have no hope of overcoming. The enemy has breached the walls and you are surrounded. You are climbing a cliff, have lost all strength, and are falling, falling . . . (If it didn't contain these elements, it wouldn't quite be a crisis.) You have lost your way; life is threatened; hopes are dashed; you have lost your love forever; the community is being destroyed by aliens or enemies; the planet is engulfed in conflagration (you get the picture). *The crisis represents the pivotal dilemma that the dream exemplifies.*

Lysis: Does a resolution occur? Inexplicably, help arrives. You find your way; you remember the talisman you were given earlier; most importantly (per renowned Jungian scholar Marie Louise von Franz), the animal you saved or the beggar that you helped turns out to be your savior, your helper. Or, quite simply, you come home, having found your way. *Dreams that feel satisfactory, or other dramas, have this element. Otherwise the dreamer (the observer of the play, movie, or opera) may feel incomplete, or cheated: There is no homecoming.* By articulating this dramatic structure, we are helped to believe that each dream contains salvation in its *bourne,* in its bosom. In life, as the ancient Greeks understood it, and as we are coming to understand it, there is no crisis without a lysis. The elements of exposition and development lay the groundwork for the drama and give us hints about how the ultimate resolution might be achieved. Dream mimics life, and life mimics dream.

My Experience in Dream Remembering
In the Words of Coauthor Stephen Larsen

After fifty or so years of keeping a dream journal I thought I knew everything about remembering and recording dreams. That is, until January 2015. I knew this book was due in a year. I set my intention very strongly that this would be the best year of dream recall out of the past fifty. I underestimated myself! Usually I will record more than fifty dreams on a poor year, more than one hundred on a good year. In 2015, setting my intention and doing due dream diligence, I recorded 233 dreams—and in great detail! I charted the usual suspects: family members; friends both living and dead; persons unknown; and animals, both natural and strange (shape-changers or mythical beasts). I recorded settings: mountains; deserts; forests; lakes; watercourses such as brooks, rivers, cascades; caves, or vast caverns. If I dreamed of interior spaces in buildings I noted hangars, warehouses, basements, kitchens, attics, bathrooms, and/or living rooms. I referred to Gaston Bachelard's wonderful symbolic morphology of elements: fire, earth, water, air—each of them with a mythical or psychological message. I also referred to the rooms in a house: the scary basement, equally scary attic, and the warm and nourishing kitchen denoting alchemy, for example. Frankly, I admit that for all those fifty years I was just a little bit lazy and underestimated how dream recall may be turned in to an act of spiritual discipline.

As 2015 wore on, my dreams became more vivid, textured, and detailed. I could remember more of them. I trained myself to make dream recall my first priority of the morning, every morning, before coffee and before exercise. My journal got fatter than it had ever been. It was such an exemplary year that I set myself to recording recurring themes: How often did I go to that family camp in Maine? How often to my childhood home? I noticed recurring scenes and settings in many of my dreams: in the past mountains had often been present, but watercourses dominated this past year, emphasizing fluid transitions, baths, and coming clean. I charted dream parallels with those of my wife, Robin, with uncanny synchronicity.

"Did you dream of horses?"

"Mmm hmm, and they were kind of wild and beautiful."

"I spent a lot of last night looking for you in an Eastern European city."

"Yes, I was there, and couldn't find you, either!"

In my dream journal I record how often I find myself in a particular setting; how often particular characters recur; how many living versus dead people appear. Is my setting contemporary or far past—does it fit into normal calendar time, or does it seem to be in an ancient or mythical time or a "never where."

In this exercise I have perhaps enacted a small, personal replica of the famous statistical study of Calvin Hall, the exhaustive dream researcher who garnered his samples (perhaps the largest study ever collected) from thousands of subjects: college students, men and women, and people young and old.[8] Such studies are quite useful in a broadly based sense. They let us know what is the sociological texture of dreaming, in America, say, or a certain sociopolitical stratum of America. The difference between what I am doing versus Hall is that I myself am one of a kind. My sampling may not be so good for a statistical study at all—but could be noted for the quality of attention I have been able to give to dreams, as well as my respect for them, and a chance to range up and down the possibilities of content that occur for one dreamer over a year. Thus I think of myself as a kind of *pathfinder in the landscape of dreaming, with the idea that if I can do it, you can do it too.*

Put the quality of attention into this oneiric discipline that is possible for you, given your lifestyle and resources. For myself, not only did I find myself able to record more details and textures of dreaming than I ever had before, but I found that planting the dreamseeds worked in a variety of projects. I could, as Saint Synesius noted, enlist the support and advice of dreams in my conscious enterprises such as building an ornamental gate—or writing this book.

One of the gifts I received was a glimpse into the energy of Morpheus the shape-changer, or the cittavritti itself. Early one morning it revealed itself to me in its living and magical and metamorphic selfhood. I watched the profound restorative energy of delta deep sleep thin and melt into theta, where it seemed truly magical and protean (remember Proteus in chapter 1).

My own conscious-of-dreaming-self thinned and diffused in the dream environment, until I was part of the morphic medium in which I was swimming. However, I recognized that I had some unique privileges in that world: to be a source of phantasmagoria, nucleus of my own dream environment, witness of what came forth from my inadvertent creativity, and possible lucid dreamer. In this, I was the one with clarity both of *consciousness* and *agency*—the ability to make choices and decisions in the midst of the unfolding events—which I either *didn't like* (being tortured or attacked) or *did like* (being with a beautiful partner in lovemaking). What was exciting for me, in the context of this book, was how the psyche (anima, unconscious) and I seemed to be engaged in a complex dance—a pas de deux—whirling giddily and ecstatically on the dance floor of becoming.

This year, perhaps as never before, I recognized the partnership we are in with the deeper more autonomous parts of our beings. We each can partake of our own *Memories, Dreams, Reflections* (Jung's classic and groundbreaking memoir). Rather than go on in this chapter with more about what I discovered in that amazing year of 2015 in terms of landscapes, architecture, situations, and features of dreaming, I invite the reader to check out the website symbolicstudies.org and do a search to find "dream research." I also invite the reader to utilize the material found in the appendix of this book, "The Dream Portal Method," which my wife, Robin, and I utilize in the dream groups that we conduct.

Next we will move into a chapter that's designed to whet the appetite for dreamwork even more! It shows how the landscape of dreaming always offers to open out into horizon after horizon, moving from one's personal little surroundings and memories into mythological (hence archetypal) scenarios, life-changing experiences and insights, and realms that people describe as shaking the very roots of their existence!

4

What Makes for a Big Dream?

The breeze at dawn has secrets to tell you.
Don't go back to sleep.

....

People are going back and forth across the doorsill
where the two worlds touch.

....

Don't go back to sleep.

RUMI, "THE BREEZE AT DAWN"

The Naskapi people of Labrador talk about the million-year-old man, Mistap'eo, who is available to all of us. Only a fool would neglect one of the dreams that comes from the "million-year-oldness" of things! (It was the Naskapi tradition, in fact, that cemented for Carl Jung the idea that some dreams go way beyond others in significance.) Other indigenous peoples of North America, South America, Siberia, Australia, and Africa have no trouble with the same concept. The Great Spirit, the Manitou, Wakan Tanka, moves in our sleep, knows when we face life crises, and knows when we are lost or moving down the wrong track. Such messages change the course of a person's destiny and may pertain to the collective instead of just the individual. Among the Iroquois, big dreams indicated the most important of all wishes of the soul, and to neglect the wishes of your own soul could bring illness, madness, or disaster. (These perspectives clearly antedate the shallow modern one that says that all dreams are *merely* the result of a flooding of acetylcholine or the random firing of neurons.)

We remember the big dream of Pharaoh. It confounded him and all the wise men of Egypt until the Hebrew slave Joseph revealed that the dream wasn't for him alone; it foretold the future of the entire land. And we will consider the megalomaniac Babylonian king Nebuchadnezzar, who treated the visions that came to him in the night as life-and-death matters ultimately needing God's own elucidation through the mouth of Daniel (another Hebrew slave in captivity). The Hebrew Bible (or Hebrew scriptures of the Christians; the Old Testament as it is otherwise known) leaves no doubt that God (Yahweh, Elohim) moves in our dreams, making some of them carry quite a different imperative than others. The supplicants of the Asclepian temples suspended all other business for the god to come with a life-changing message or a healing.

Synesius of Cyrene, the neoplatonic philosopher discussed in chapter 1, says that the character of a big dream is unmistakable and it needs no interpretation. These are the *somnia a Deo missa,* dreams sent from God. They were, in fact, welcomed all through Christian history, through the Middle Ages until the present time, especially in the contemplative tradition. (However, author Robert Moss makes an interesting point in *A Secret History of Dreaming* that spells out how unwelcome big dreaming might be in times when the church was trying to consolidate its doctrinal authority. Who wanted visionary dreamers upsetting the theological applecart?)

The dreams presented in this chapter are almost in the tradition of holy dreams. They certainly were for the dreamers, who had little or no doubt that they were meant for *other people* in addition to themselves.

Big Dreams Recounted

In an interview with Stephen Larsen, dreamer Jim Marzano recounts, "I believe I had this dream when I was about three years old. There was no prelude leading into the dream. I was just suddenly aware that I was dreaming."

I feel light and airy and begin to realize I can fly. There's not much of a landscape; it's dark, almost foggy. I start rising up above a misty forestlike scene and want to go higher. As I cruise up through the clouds I become excited at the thought that I can fly; and I want to go up to heaven and find God. I immediately make that decision and accelerate my speed up toward a light in the clouds.

Upon my arrival, I feel like I've snuck in the back door. I feel this incredible wave of warmth from the light; it's extremely comforting. I feel as if I'm bathing in the warmth of God's unconditional love.

As God realizes my presence, I feel this rush of infinite knowledge. It was as if the floodgates of telepathic communication opened up for me. As God communicates with me, the light fluctuates with his words.

He's not happy that I'm there. He lets me know it isn't my time yet and that I must go back. I'm not happy to hear that; it's so warm and loving here. I don't want to leave, but I do. I go back to my body; a little, scared, odd, three-year-old boy.

It wasn't until I was over twenty-five that I discovered the work of Dr. Elisabeth Kübler-Ross on the near-death experience (NDE). At that point I called my mother and asked if I'd had any serious incidents when I was really little. She said I was very sickly as a kid, with severe allergies and asthma, which I hadn't known at the time. I pried deeper, and she finally recalled my first asthma attack at the approximate age of three. That would have made her barely twenty-two, with two babies in diapers. She said she had no idea what was wrong with me. By the time she got me to the hospital, I was quite blue. This, I believe, was the true nature of my first flying, lucid dream experience.

In retrospect, this dream molded my whole life. I came away having experienced the full power of God's unconditional love. After that I could never accept or believe all the fearmongering I heard in Sunday school. I instinctively knew there was no such thing as hell. God loved all his children, no exceptions.

I also knew that God had no ego and couldn't care less what name we called him by. That left me open to explore other religions as I got older. I came to love the notion of the Native American Great Spirit, Wakan Tanka *or Kitchee Manitou. After all, why should God, available to all humans, all cultures, be respected only when called by the name of our favorite religion!*

Eventually I fell in love with Taoism and the I Ching. (The I Ching never lies.) I also knew that I could fly in my dreams, and that was always exhilarating!

An Experience Recounted by Coauthor Tom Verner

This experience of my granddaughter Sangeeta, who was nine years old at the time, occurred within three to four months after my mother's (her great-grandmother's) death. And it was the only dream that Sangeeta ever shared with me unsolicited. In telling me the dream two or three times she would pause and say, "Beba, this wasn't a dream; this was real. Gram was in my house." Here is Sangeeta's dream, in her own words.

I was lying in bed looking at the card Gram gave me for my ninth birthday, and I started to cry. I opened my bedroom door, and there was a big glow that lit up my whole room. I was still crying, and I heard a voice say, "Come with me," and it was Gram's voice when she was young. She was not the age she was when she was down here with us. She was instead a young pretty lady, wearing a red dress, very long, and she had a halo on top of her head.

She had beautiful white wings with a sparkle on them spreading out from her back, and she said, "Take my hand, and I will show you where I live now." We went into the clouds, and she showed me her house; it was a huge cloud you could fly right into. It had pictures of Beba, Pat, Mira, and all the cousins, and me.

Grammy brought me over to another cloud, and I said, "Whose cloud is this?"

She said, "This is your great-uncle Jim's house." Gram then said, "Oh, Jim!" and he came out of a room.

He said, "Is this Geeta?"

Gram said, "Yes it is, this is Geeta."

Jim said, "We finally meet."

I gave him a hug. He was also much younger, maybe in his thirties. He said to say hello to Beba and Mira, and he then said he had already met Amaya [Geeta's younger sister] and, "She is going to turn into a bright girl, just like you are, Geeta."

I said, "It was nice to meet you, Jim."

And he said, "I will see you again sometime."

I gave him a hug and left with Gram.

Then Gram said, "It is time to go, you have to go back to sleep. Tell your mommy, and you know this yourself—I am watching Amaya grow up, just like you. Take my hand."

I took her hand, and it was a long way back to sleep.

On the way, Gram stopped to meet Jesus. Jesus said, "I am glad to have Grammy up in heaven; she is a very lovely lady." Gram took me back, a long way back to the bedroom, and I fell asleep in her arms and she tucked me in and kissed me.

In the last chapter of this book we will discuss further vision dreams that are characterized, like Sangeeta's, by a quality we call "felt presence," or the encounter with a "numinous other." This distinguishes these dreams from ordinary dreams that come in connection with major transitions such as death (our own or others whom we love).[1]

Next, in a discourse, we will detail a big dream that coauthor Tom Verner dreamed.

STEPHEN: Tom, can you tell me about a big dream you've had?

TOM: I had one dream in which the character Uncle Remus showed up and then kept recurring in my dreams over several years. I had the initial dream when I was about twenty-eight.

I am in a department store. I'm in the jewelry department, and on the counter is a black mat and on the mat, a beautiful gold ring. I pick it up and put it in my pocket.

I go walking toward the door, and as I'm getting close I feel a tap on my shoulder and I turn around. There is a person very much like Aunt Jemima, with her hair up in a cloth. I know that she is the store detective. She says to me, "You're going to have to come with me to the manager's office."

We go out the back door of the store, and we're at the bottom of a grassy hill out in the country. We walk up the hill toward a log cabin at the top of the hill. We get to the front door, and she says, "The manager is inside; just knock on the door."

I go up to the door, knock on it, and hear a voice say, "Come in."

I go in, and there is Uncle Remus sitting in a rocking chair. He tells me, "Come in and sit down." I sit beside him near the fireplace. He says, "You know, stealing that ring was not wrong because it's not yours. The ring is yours. It's wrong, because you didn't work for it."

Then he looks past my shoulder with a very concerned look on his face. He says, "There's a problem; you have to go for help!"

When I go outside the cabin, I see a group of redneck-looking characters carrying rifles, and I know they're coming after Uncle Remus.

The scene changes, and I'm coming up the hill with a bunch of armed men—we're going to rescue Uncle Remus from the rednecks. I'm looking across this valley at Uncle Remus on another hill, almost at eye level. The rednecks are moving toward Uncle Remus to kill him.

My own group of armed men and I aim at the rednecks and send a volley of shots. Up out of that valley come blood and bones—the rednecks. Through the blood and bones I see Remus on the hillside crying—for the rednecks and me. Once again I took a shortcut to the problem.

As I worked on this dream I came to realize that it brought up a question of *character*—a tendency to take shortcuts and perhaps to receive things I didn't deserve because I hadn't worked for them. Remus started showing up in my dreams over the next four or five years—especially in dream situations where I was tempted to take a shortcut. He would play a kind of bit part that reminded me of the way Alfred Hitchcock would put himself inconspicuously in his movies (only Hitchcock aficionados know the places where he is in his movies).

In my dreams I could be sneaking into a hotel without paying, for instance. There would be Uncle Remus across the lobby operating the elevator—he would look sadly at me and shake his head, clearly acknowledging that he knew I was doing something unscrupulous and letting me know that he disapproved of it. This happened at least a half-dozen times.

STEPHEN: Who do you think Uncle Remus was, and why did he show himself in this way?

TOM: In addition to underscoring my tendency to take shortcuts, I think that some part of me is really intrigued by the wise person who looks ordinary or less than ordinary.

While I was at the Catholic Worker in New York (the radical Roman Catholic movement and newspaper founded by Dorothy Day to promote social justice) a man who seemed to be homeless would come for soup. One day I served him a bowl of soup and noticed that he was reading Brecht's *Galileo*. We talked, and I asked him why he was interested in Galileo. I was a bit shocked and intrigued when this disheveled, homeless man said that he used to teach physics.

I got to know him over the next few months—his name was George. Once I saw him on the Bowery and stopped to chat with him. He had a letter with him; its return address was Yale University. It was from a physicist there who was corresponding with George. George would go to the library and keep up with the latest developments in physics. There was a whole lot going on behind the appearance.

STEPHEN: I think Peter Kingsley goes in to this and brings up something Robin and I have noticed throughout Greek mythology: the gods go around dressed as paupers.

TOM: My mom would say, "Be kind to the stranger." I believe she took this from Hebrews 13:2 (New International Version, or NIV), which states, "Do not forget to show hospitality to strangers, for by so doing some people have shown hospitality to angels without knowing it." There's a movie about the life of my old teacher Dorothy Day, called *Entertaining Angels*.

STEPHEN: It's like Odin going around in a stained cloak and slouch hat, testing mortals to see who's kind. But tell me more about what Uncle Remus means to you.

TOM: He's a storyteller, and wise and funny and a bit of a Trickster figure (I first saw him in the Disney film *Song of the South*). My father managed movie theaters when I was a child, and on Saturday afternoons I would often go to the movie theater with him. I saw *Song of the South* about Uncle Remus many times. In particular I felt Uncle Remus was really endearing—grandfatherly.

STEPHEN: Me too, and you know, for all the criticism you hear about Disney, that was, for most of us, the introduction to the mythic imagination replete with talking animals and various characters, and little families, cartoon towns, and situations.

TOM: Other associations to Uncle Remus include: My maternal grandfather and uncle were more present for me than my father when I was young. My uncle Jim was a chemist, and, every Sunday when they came for Sunday supper, he would bring me laboratory equipment, test tubes, flasks, liebig condensers, ring stands; I created an entire chemistry laboratory in the basement, and I made my own ink and kept my first journals there in that laboratory. There was a sign on the door, "Laboratory Keep Out." This was a secret, magical place for my ten-year-old self.

I also had a Dick Tracy crime detector kit, complete with cards on which you could take fingerprints—I learned about all types of fingerprints, whorls to the right and left, each unique. This was my very first exposure to typology, which I learned a great deal about years later when I studied Jung's elaborate system of psychological types. I went around the neighborhood, a ten-year-old boy, and took the fingerprints of all the neighbors. If a crime went down, I was going to be on the scene and dust it for prints. That laboratory in the basement felt like a place of magic, a place of transformation and discovery, an early introduction to Alchemy and Magic, my first place to "work and pray," which some say may be the root of laboratory, "labor" and "oratory," Latin for "work and pray." Amazing where associations to dream characters can take you. I feel I need to come back to Remus for a moment.

In working on the Remus dreams, I discovered scholars who

traced the Remus character back to a West African Trickster, a character named Legba who lived at the crossroads. In reading and reflecting on Legba and the symbolism of the Trickster at the crossroads (think of Robert Johnson's famous Delta Blues tune "Crossroad Blues"), I learned a lot from this marvelous character who clearly came from the "big dream" depths of the psyche, and in the process of this dreamwork I learned much from this trickster Remus about developing character and not cutting corners.

A Friend of Stephen's Finds Spirituality from Within

The call came just before New Year's Day 2015. The previous fall, in October of 2014, Tom and I had already decided to collaborate on this book. My wife, Robin, was undergoing a bout with cancer, and due to this, as well as work I was doing on another book, I had asked the publisher of this book, Inner Traditions, for a year's extension on the originally contracted submission date of 2015. They were kind enough to grant it, and the extension to the contract came through just at the beginning of the year, but now I knew we were seriously under deadline to successfully deliver the book by December of 2015! It was very clear at this point that Tom and I would have to really dig in—we definitely had our work cut out for us.

Out of the blue, with no idea of my private creative project, a friend, G.M., called up and asked to meet with me privately. He initially asked for confidentiality and privacy, but I quickly figured out this was not a therapy appointment, nor did he go through the customary protocol at my office. We are both busy men, and I don't often have time off, but I made it happen on New Year's Day 2015. We sat in my living room in the early afternoon, with the winter light streaming in the window. (The snow that would make 2015 one of the worst winters on record had not yet begun to fall.) We both like good wine, and so we shared a glass, along with some cheese and crackers. With the solemn revelation that then came, and that you will read below, with the "bread and wine" the occasion felt a little like a Eucharist.

My friend knew nothing about my work on this book, nor that it was in part about big dreams, but he had previously read my book *The Mythic Imagination*—quite thoroughly I might add—and came to think that I might be the one person with whom he could share his dream. As he began to talk, the synchronicity of it broke upon me with a frisson that traveled up the spine and ultimately left no cell untingled! (The numinous feeling had empowered work on the book for 2015 and was added to by the other big dreams that were shared with me in an equally synchronous manner.) The following is my friend's account.

In the Words of G.M.
My Dream: A True Life Experience

The following is an attempt to describe the dream I had in November of 1970, in Paris. Nothing in my life has even come close to this experience, both in its scope and in its effect on me.

I must preface this by saying that words are simply so inadequate to do this that I feel in the making of this effort a pang of betrayal to the reader, because as a result, what I write may be misleading, has to be misleading, as we are so attached to words and to the idea that it is possible (and good) to capture and encapsulate experiences, as words attempt to do in Western languages and culture, because this experience was so totally contrary to that. There is no way to reconcile this problem. One cannot look back through the dark mirror. That said, I will undertake to relate the events, if not their scope.

That night as I got into bed, I recall that I was in a state of sexual arousal and need. However, I purposely ignored that, without knowing why, I didn't recall having done that before—and instead I went directly to sleep.

I awake in a small room, on a thin mattress on the floor of a small, dimly lit room enclosed by Japanese sliding panels. It is otherwise empty except for the presence of two Asian girls, about 17, who are there and greet me as I awaken. They have long black hair and by all appearances are in a very happy state, obviously because I have arrived. Everything is so clean. They fuss over me and ask me if I'm ready. I affirm that I am, and assume that this is related to my sexual arousal, and that we are about to have sex. They seem very excited, but instead, tuck me back in under the soft covers. Again I go to sleep.

I don't remember waking up after that, but the next thing that I'm able to discern is a seated figure before me. I can't make out any features, but it sits in a lotus position and the energy around it is amazing, perfect energy. It's emanating the aura of perfection in a pervasive radiance. This energy has a high frequency of clarity in communication; any less and the possibility of doubt would be allowed, but here there is none. I feel an incredible joy.

The place in which we find ourselves is outdoors, clearly an appointed meeting place; the grass shimmers with energy. I'm aware that there are others also present and that this figure is only one among them.

The figure is full, Asian, rotund; he is silver like his robe. He begins to speak in English, in verse. His hands begin to move as well, illustrating what he is saying and adding to the story with another dimension, much like the hands of dancers of India whose hand movements tell stories. Soon both hands and speech illustrate and echo each other. But I don't remember words, because the communication was multidimensional; it had much the feel of telepathy.

It's not before he has completed the first two stanzas that I become aware of my own presence. As I do so it's with the deep certainty that at last, here is truth in a form that is connected to me, that I am part of, that I am connected with. I feel an overwhelming joy. The landscape, although not discernible, is also steeped in joy.

The hands and poetry continue to reflect each other and create a third element consisting of overtones that are the result of their combination; all is perfectly in tune; even the dissonances are perfect and perfectly woven into what is being told. The story that is being told has subject "The Present." I am woven into it, hearing, listening, understanding, completely open, and I am an intrinsic part of it. There doesn't even seem to be any "I." The experience is awash in overwhelming joy.

And the effect of the two elements combining to form the third has a remarkable intent. Instead of their combining to result in a context, the opposite arises: together they describe a continuous changing of form and shape surrounding an immaculate emptiness. It is as if much work has been learned to expose what is left after all else has been cleared away.

As this is taking place, I am acutely aware that there is only this one way for this to happen, that it is the result of one and one combining to form not-one, and continuing in a series of different absences that form an ascending path of comprehension and an intense, overwhelming joyousness. All this has somehow, somewhere, been learned, for I feel the work in detail and the sacrifice others have experienced to form this path that passes between everything. I feel hours and days and years of learning; with each flick of the fingers I feel there is only this one way. I feel endless years of sculpting to form this perfect nothingness. Only without impatience, only with an open heart, only with great determination can one access it. But this determination is created from an outside pull, a magnetic pull.

I am open; with any shred of doubt, or thought of profit or "self," the openness quavers and threatens to close. (I later discover these lines from Ramana Maharshi: "What exists in truth is the Self alone. . . . The Self is that where there is absolutely no 'I' thought.") A deep comprehension came to me then, not only that this was a time of complete expansion, totally opposite of any constriction, but that those two elements are as pervasive in our lives as gravity, as light. Everything earthly can be seen as having greater or lesser degrees of those two opposites. In the dream, I understand that there is no possibility of constricting, of telling myself anything, or any thought of gain, or enjoyment—I must remain open and without any contact with myself for it to continue. This is not a problem; I have no trouble doing it. Even later, I came across a text that described this moment and perspective perfectly: "The Great Way is not difficult for he who has no preferences; but make the slightest distinction and Heaven and Hell are infinitely set apart." This is part of a poem called "Hsin Hsin Ming," or Faith of Mind, by Jianzhi Sengcan, known as the Third Chinese Zen Patriarch, who died in 606 CE. The last verse of the poem is a virtual echo of my dream (see page 103).

What makes this even an issue is the joy filling me of having arrived here, realizing that it is my inner language being spoken, from deep in my DNA, music from the pith of my soul, my amazement of having connected to this super-reality. It is the space-time mold that fits perfectly over my inner face; it is clicking in perfect time to my pulse. Here is what has been underlying any and all hope or faith I'd been able to feel leading to this event, although I'd been completely unsuspecting that anything such as this could be accessed. There is a certainty here that wraps and envelops me in joy.

As the story progresses, an actor appears close by—more like a ghostly reflection, or a hologram. The story being told by the Asian figure is that of what happens to this man as life twirls around and through him, rippling over his particular character, his vicissitudes, his mistakes, his observations and conclusions, even the effects of his hapless circumstance; it is about the way in which he eventually becomes one with the flow of the present moment, despite all the diversions he focuses upon and believes.

Other characters appear briefly and disappear, each acting his or her role in his life. Events flash by, take form, and then evaporate like smoke. Some make changes to the actor, in color, mood, shape; I feel his conviction that he must turn from this and toward that, perhaps only because of a sunbeam through a room, or the smell of a breeze. His footsteps, his failures, his changes through his life and time. One moment he is victor, the next he has upon his shoulders the confusion of centuries. It is a portrait of the chaos of Life. One moment he makes a decision, and in the next that decision is gone, but it has whisked him to a totally different place that is unrelated and illogical and yet somehow perfectly the result of his decision; it has taken him in a different direction, but higher.

His actions are now this way, now that, now his life turns itself inside out like a glove peeling itself off one hand to fit perfectly backward over the other, and although they are opposites, both forms are perfectly appropriate. This force, this river, this continuum, although very few of us seem to ever be aware of it, is the great force that underlies our wills.

It is clarified, amid all this, that elements of life on Earth, those things that matter and hold so much sway in our lives, work, war, justice, sex, religion, survival, self-analysis, art, love, sorrow, passion, feelings, thoughts, pride—all these things are earthly, and compared to this ecstatic ether engulfing me and the endless, ecstatic ocean of knowledge around me, they are as so much dust. How can this be? Simple: the ecstasy is infinite—it pulls you out—there is no constriction or expansion—so, there is no cause for all those things. In a place of exaltation there is even no basis for humor. How to let go? One must turn away from trying and allow that to happen. Paradoxically, it takes incredible determination, but it can't be realized by doing.

At the end of his life, this character's final glimpse is of his life, of his times and labor and haste and work, as one would look at a far-off chain of mountains, with the tops caught in the sun, those tops representing the moments of joy, of utter loneliness, and moments in which his life, for reasons unknown, penetrated a higher harmony, accepted and conjoined a nameless surreality of connectedness to unfathomable cosmic energy. His eyes are blinded by the light from these peaks, and as his heart gives over, it is only from this brilliant light that he may draw the power to ascend.

In the end, the solution, moral, and conclusion concern themselves in direct proportion to every detail of all that which, evident or not, has received the emanations of the will and purpose of this character. The form of the actor now represents the culmination of a life, but his body has disappeared, and I perceive him now as an outline, a ring of light-blue flames around an upright oval of darkness, of perfect emptiness, but made of a living non-matter, which is filled with endless meaning, endless possibility and potential, and consisting of utterly pure radiance.

As the story ends, I remember only the last line uttered by the figure: "In the name of the Rama and the Lao-tzu bell." The words are accompanied by the tinkling of a small golden prayer bell.

As I removed from the scene, I remember that a three-verse poem was recited to me that I wish to god I could remember—the words did not make linguistic sense, but it was so perfect, and so perfectly comprehensible.

The next moment I awake again in the room with the two Asian girls. They have been sitting, watching me, and waiting for me to awaken. They welcome me back joyously and are very excited, wanting to hear about my experience. They press me for a word, wanting to know what I remember. I apologize; the energy of the experience is still *flowing through me like an electric river. I manage to say, "In the name of the Rama—" and they say, excitedly, ". . . and the Lao-tzu bell!" and they giggle and are just so happy they can't contain themselves. They know where I've been, and we share the perfection of that union.*

And that was the end of the dream.

The effect of it was so universally ingrained in me that I had no thought whatsoever of doing anything about it. Again, this was way beyond any "doing." A full year passed before it even occurred to me to write down what I remembered about it. Nor did I feel moved to search to get back to it, nor to follow any course of Asian study, nor did I feel it necessary to seek anyone who could tell me anything further about what I'd been through.

I did feel a number of things that I describe as eminently unremarkable. But these were long-term changes in my outlook and my decisions from that day on. It was as if I understood something now that I couldn't explain, but that had placed me in a different, invisible river in my heart, and with a sort of unending abundance and with the latent possibility of solutions, or compensations, for everything.

The dream minimized the importance of any events that happen as part of earthly life that might shock or hurt, but I still felt I belonged to that experience, and I didn't seek to change that. I did begin to develop a kinship, however, to those things that reflected the essence of that dream and its feeling, and I started noticing things in my life that echoed its sentiments. A book here, a line about something there, and sentiments expressed by people who were outside of the constriction or expansion mode when they said it. For example, when I read Nietzsche's postulation that whatever happens out of love happens beyond good and evil, it was with a mixture of personal earthly experience hand in hand with the effect of the dream that I saw the ultimate truth of that statement. It's not all good, from our present point of view—if one kills another for love, this statement would appear to condone that. It's simply a paradox, and we have to deal with it; neither logic nor language help. Giving comfort to a person who is being persecuted for a crime appears to condone that crime, but the compassion is still more important, and truer, than punishment. It became evident that contradictions, or rather our perception of them, are earthly, period.

Before this dream, I had never been completely sure of how to steer my intentions between the shoals of the situations that I had to navigate in my personal life. I had to deal with all kinds of people making all kinds of demands on me, including myself. But when should I be angry, when should I be willing to stand my ground, and should I seek to do unto others before they do unto me? This question had been prevalent in my adolescence—I didn't know how to feel; I was rudderless about that. The dream forever oriented me against that, showed me that aggression and revenge, et cetera, were manifestations of constriction, and that the only right way was away from that, through expansion.

I was certain now that compassion is the most important of our motivations, in all considerations regarding how to interact with other humans. The manner in which I had been gifted convinced me of that beyond any possible doubt. And it was enough. Whether or not others were aware of it, I must always act with compassion in deciding my actions. In that way I would render what I consider to be my service to my species. I'm no saint, god knows, but now when I come across a person whose actions or attitude offends me, I try to walk around that reaction and put myself in that person's place and circumstance, since none of us are above being there, whatever the case may be. I'm not always successful but when I am, I can speak to that person in terms that could dissuade them from that offensive behavior—empathy brings peace.

I found that I was still the same in my character as I was before, but completely changed in what underlay my person. I was still the human I'd been, with all the propensities and proclivities and bad habits, but it all had a basis now, a meaning. The energy of the universe that tapped me that night dwarfed the dramatics of my world to such a degree that I no longer wanted fame and fortune, or any power whatsoever over others, and I've spent a good deal of energy since then in sidestepping those things. It's not that I couldn't have them, it's just that now my feeling was that I'd much rather be one tiny grain of sand, but an enlightened grain of sand, than to be king of the world. There is such joy in that lighted grain as to sustain all my heart's aspirations forever. What the hell is that? I asked myself, laughing. I knew, and I didn't know. But so, one year later, I sat down and wrote about my dream.

In the many years since I had this dream, I've never met anyone else who has mentioned having had it or one like it. Yes, I was curious; I am still convinced that I was brought to that place, that I was shown and told and taught; but why me, I'll never know. I know it was far beyond my imagination to concoct such a thing, with all the details and all the power—and I could never conceive of such ecstasy, let alone find the way to it. Yet, incontrovertibly, it all happened in my head. To me that can only mean that there must be a center of the mind that I got near to, a source of spirit within each one of us that connects us with the eternal. Is it possible that normally I'm living with a degree of awareness somewhat equal to some debris on the outer rings of Saturn, and for that one time, for an unknown but definite reason, I got to come much closer to the planet, so as to be illuminated by it, with some of that illumination remaining permanently, and then was spun back out to the rings again? If that's true, is there a way to get closer again?

I couldn't help but feel that it went against the nature of what I was taught: to always look for more meaning than what had been given me. I had plenty of occasions to do so. Besides, how would I go about looking, put an ad in the classifieds? For how many years? How many detours, how many goose chases? I suppose it doesn't matter to me. As long as I can bring that light into my life to improve the way I affect others, that's enough. But it won't hurt to spend some time now finding others who have some knowledge or personal experience about what I went through. I have met people who have those same beliefs, without having had the dream. Then I connect, and it feels like stepping back into a warm river from home. Being ready to empathize, to encourage those in doubt, to act in such a way as to show how much I believe that Nature takes very good care of us, for the time being—that's the compassion, and when I see it in other people,

I salute it, and it makes me smile and reach out to join with it. It has happened to me, to connect with someone with a simple look into their eyes, followed by a very intense embrace. It's not the past or the future, it's the present that matters; that's where life is happening, and "the readiness is all."

I again apologize to the readers of this account. I assure you that it is a failure, only a poor, useless offering, a glimpse into an experience so immense that it had no beginning and no end—no stillness, no description.

Every time I read this poem, my heart and mind taste the dream again.

"Hsin Hsin Ming"
(Final verse)

Emptiness here, emptiness there,
but the infinite universe
stands always before your eyes.
Infinitely large and infinitely small;
no difference, for definitions have vanished
and no boundaries are seen.

So too with Being and non-Being.
Don't waste time in doubts and arguments
That have nothing to do with this.

One thing, all things,
move among and intermingle without distinction.
To live in this realization
is to be without anxiety about non-perfection.
To live in this faith is the road to non-duality,
because the non-dual is one with the trusting mind.
Words!
The Way is beyond language,
for in it there is

no yesterday
no tomorrow
no today

JIANZHI SENGCAN
(TRANSLATION: RICHARD B. CLARKE)

Stephen Larsen's comment: The effect of this dream, in the recounting, was so powerful that I couldn't resist the urge to ask my friend for more amplification, reluctant as he was.

How Did the Dream Change Me?

To explain how I was changed is difficult for a few reasons. The effect was so ethereal that, like air or water, it seeped into everything. In a general way I can say it changed nothing, but everything, because my eyes were changed; although the world hadn't changed, I saw things in a new way. I had knowledge and awareness I hadn't had before. I did feel a great happiness about it, but it was so vastly spread through me that it didn't occur to me to be outside of it so as to be able to write about it, until a year later. It was that basic.

One result from this event was a new understanding of the word "faith." The experience established a faith in me that, without any trace of dogma, is absolute and unshakable. But I have no language in which to speak about it—language being one definition of religion, I therefore have no religion. How odd! I really feel that I have nothing to question about it; it's as sure as the air I breathe, yet it is so much larger than everything. The only thing that comes close, in religion, to speak to me about it is what Taoists call "The Way"—all they say about it is so excellent! How true that it has no name!

The dream gave me a larger perspective but did not change me in a way that I see myself above life. I know that if I lived among hunger and disease, or in circumstances more dire than life in New England, in which I had to kill to survive, I don't know what I might not do and I don't think I'm above doing whatever it would take to survive. I don't doubt for one minute that, given certain circumstances, I could be just as evil as anyone. Or, I don't know, maybe it would prevent me from succumbing to it, because now I know it's all up to me. That's a good lesson to ponder.

I became more aware of the commonality of peoples. I will usually talk to anybody now (which was not the old me), and I seek out what I can learn from each person I meet. I know that I care more now about other people and am more willing to accept, however grudgingly sometimes, our foibles. There is more awareness about it than ever, but it isn't awareness that I would call my own; it's just there, it's more accessible to me. It's not even me, the world simply seems more open than before. I no longer wonder how to see with my heart, I just do. As for my role, the least I can do with this peace is to share it when I can and try to console others, which, when I do, in large and small ways, has an unmistakable sameness, an unmistakable oneness with my dream experience.

Something I believe I gained from my dream and that has made me a better person is a new propensity to see myself in others. Life is the same as ever, as pedestrian, shocking, disappointing; I'm still in the thick of it, and my efforts to meet it with terms we can all live with have not resulted in any markedly improved results. For all my amazement about the dream, I see that the world has not changed, nor has my character. But some of my feelings have. I feel an incredible organic violence inside myself when I see brutality, which I think is normal, but I couldn't help but notice that I felt an incredible new compassion inside me when I see someone who is hurt, even if it's an aggressor. This feeling was greatly reinforced later when I had children. When I saw someone doing wrong, I began to project the thought "What if that was my child?" into it, and I tried to act accordingly. But I don't always succeed.

For all this new empathy toward others and truer appreciation for what life brings and for the very bringing of it, I don't think I stand out because of it. I have met many people who do better than me in this regard who have not had this dream experience (sometimes I ask). I could have taken a road upon which I would expend all my energy fighting all that which I think prevents access to that deep, endless peace, try to be a knight of sorts. But that would have gone against the lesson—the dream expressed strife as normal life, to be expected, to be lived, to be unresolved. It just told me to be natural, and so I would liken that to accepting being in a cocoon or a similar stage—whatever it is, it has to be lived out.

Yet if I stay focused upon the new perspective that was given to me, I run the risk of appearing complacent—I don't like that in others and have tried not to be it myself. Focusing on the experience should only be done in meditation. I cannot reach it, I cannot teach it—I can't float upstream. So, because what truly lives always has movement, I work to come to terms with proportion in how I distribute my energy. I have more of an attitude through which I try to meet others on a platform of providing help; this is certainly something that I did not have or felt licensed to do before the dream. But I wouldn't say it's help that I bring; it's more like the ability to recognize when help is needed, and providing it when it will be accepted from me, and knowing when to refrain. Or maybe that's just what growing up is.

Another direct connection to what was given to me in the experience is in the case of what is meant by the word "strained" in the following passage from Shakespeare.

> *The quality of mercy is not strain'd,*
> *It droppeth as the gentle rain from heaven*
> *Upon the place beneath. It is twice blest:*
> *It blesseth him that gives and him that takes.*

There was no question anymore about this—the mercy I felt was universal. I feel the quality of mercy is even bursting upon us, if we can just turn around, look up, and accept it. There is nothing we, as a species, want more than compassion; and my dream experience confirmed, as has the testimonies of many others' over the ages, that giving it will lead us to receiving it a thousandfold.

Lastly, I see everything that occurred prior to the experience as having been spent wandering in darkness, as though wearing a blindfold. Sometimes lucky, sometimes not so lucky, and not lost, really, but aimless. I believe that tendrils from this enormous spirituality were stretched out to me in earlier times, although I didn't know it, and even if I had, what would it have meant to me? Not as much, without the experience. But because I remember this, I feel a great gratitude to every person who ever took an interest in me, and looked me right in the eye, who talked to me earnestly, and entrusted me with and appealed to my right thinking, and put their hope in me.

Stephen's Epilogue to These Dream Accounts

Knowing my friend as I do and reading his words so graciously offered, I reflect upon my own blessings. Those that come from dreams do almost seem to drop like a "gentle rain from heaven." This book feels to me like a blessed enterprise, given that so many people have freely volunteered what means so much to them—that which is hardly ever spoken of, in contemporary, secular, practically, and economically driven life.

I know that I am in the presence of something blessed when I realize that my friend Jim's three-year-old self met God, which changed his life, including his theology, forever. I also sense this presence of something blessed when my friend and coauthor Tom, the grandpa of little Sangeeta, tells me a story about his mother and his granddaughter that streams the tears down both our faces. And when my friend, unsolicited, tells me the exquisitely profound dream recounted above, just when I was in the early stages of this book.

The dream analyst in me could not refrain from asking my friend this question: What was going on in your life when you had the dream?

He answered nonchalantly (considering the depth and power of what he had revealed) that he had been in Paris, as a young man, to attend his father's funeral. His father, a member of the French Resistance, had been captured and tortured by the Nazis as a young man—and eventually he had succumbed to his many injuries.

There was no direct interpretation by my friend. However, I couldn't help myself from musing that the blessing of this dream came as a compensation for the evil to which his father had been subjected and ultimately died of—but left him with a *something*, where otherwise there might just have been a bleak *nothing*.

"Vacillation"
(Verse 4)

My fiftieth year had come and gone,
I sat, a solitary man,
In a crowded London shop,
An open book and empty cup
On the marble table top.

While on the shop and street I gazed
My body of a sudden blazed;
And twenty minutes more or less
It seeemed, so great my happiness,
That I was blessed and could bless.

W. B. YEATS

5

Standing Naked
Before the Dream

In the Words of Coauthor Stephen Larsen

The year is about 1985. I can still see Christopher standing in front of us, Yoda-like, his eyes blazing with intensity. Seated with me are a couple of psychiatrists, a clinical social worker, and a college professor on her way to becoming a Jungian analyst. We are all fairly competent, adult professionals who have worked with dreams. Dr. Edward C. Whitmont ("Christopher" to those who know him well), is small, definitely not green, and his ears are fairly normal human ones; but his eyes are like the Jedi master's and the Force is clearly with him.

"You have no right to know what someone's dream means!" He says this emphatically, looking, I think, at me in particular; me the apprentice mythologist, who he knows has also sat at the feet of the redoubtable Joseph Campbell for many years. He knows that for me to listen to a dream, without out a crowd of mythical associations cropping up, is almost unbearable. He tells me pointedly, "Those are *your* associations, not the patient's. You are here to help *them*, not impress them with your knowledge!"

I am an experienced psychotherapist of some twenty years, a psychology professor, and a martial artist with a black belt, but I quiver with anxiety before the little Austrian Jewish analyst who is a couple of inches shorter than I am. I look around and see that the other apprentices are similarly chastened. Most of them have, at one time or another, been in personal analysis with this director of clinical training at the Jung Institute, which means that they too have had the sensation of being delicately, incisively, dismembered.

Each one of us was given to understand that we dragged the "long bag of our personal shadow" around with us (as in Robert Bly's picturesque metaphor). If any of us had a hidden agenda, or some unconsciously self-serving attitude, Christopher would remind us not only of the dirty laundry that was in each of our bags but, in fact, how it smelled!

We knew, therefore, that the Force indeed was with him, because if anything could be said about the process of being analyzed by Christopher, it was never exactly "nice." Every week you might have the experience of knowing you were paying very high analytic fees to have your nose rubbed in it—again and again. *But there was never the experience of deadly stagnation of which I have heard so many people in psychotherapy complain.* And he used dreams in the process, sometimes mercilessly, to show you your inflation, your egotism, your willingness to jump to the cheap or shallow interpretation of something.

I now want to tell you my story of how I got to him in the first place!

The Shadow of the Great War

I was born on the eve of World War II and was nine months old when Pearl Harbor was bombed. Europe was already crisscrossed with trails of blood, and the Holocaust was careening into its horrific apotheosis. Adults spoke in hushed voices about the war, and the echoing voices over the radio (for there was no TV to speak of yet) among the cheerful jingles and situation comedies rang with a strange apocalyptic urgency.

No wonder little boys had nightmares! Mine were of being inescapably caught in a great haunted house. I ran and tried to crawl between rooms, but there were strange, evil, puppetlike beings in every room—every time I thought I could escape, I found I was trapped all the more.

Perhaps I was trapped inside the zeitgeist—the world of my time—or inside Jung's collective unconscious. Much later, reading

Jerzy Kosinski's book *The Painted Bird,* I realized that much of Europe of the time was like my dream. There was no safe place. Evil, fascistic informers, life-threatening peril, lurked on every side. Though my home in America seemed an island of safety, the whole world seemed to be in a battle for its very life.

The child mind cannot wrap itself around the nightmares that sleepwalking adults wreak in the world that we inhabit together. One of my earliest memories was during a blackout. Blinds and shades were not enough; blankets had to be hung over every door and window so that enemy planes could not see where we were. Everyone talked in hushed voices, as if that phantom, night-flying enemy could hear, as well as see us, somehow, from thousands of feet above.

The nightmare recurred many times, until I had my first experience of another archetype: *the helping animal.* He was a comic-book character from the 1940s called Oswald the Rabbit. Oswald showed me the way out—*away from that claustrophobic house of haunted rooms.* It was down a beautiful spiral bannister that we slid, into a peaceful garden that was outside. (To this very day, I always feel a freshness and a burst of optimism when I go outdoors . . . and a—seemingly mindless—affection for rabbits!)

As a teenager during the 1950s I was still trying to reconcile my maturing mind with what had just happened to the world. My high school in Northport, Long Island, moved across the road from the VA hospital, and I was face-to-face with the consequences of that war: the amputees in wheelchairs or on crutches—shattered hulks trying to chain-smoke their memories away—made a profound impression on me, as did an older cousin whom I was fond of, who returned, broken and alcoholic, from the war.

My puppets returned in the form of hypnagogic images that would dance around in my brain as I was trying to fall asleep. I think it was my first experience, aside from dreams, of the independent life of the mind-stuff (cittavritti). Making early forays into meditation, I glimpsed that our minds are only partially and only rarely in our control. These insights help me to this very day as I work with children with attention deficit disorder (ADHD) or autism. They are extreme examples of a universal condition—the wild, alive, mind-stuff on which all of our experiences are imprinted. Memories, or any kind of experience for that matter, are like writing on sand at the sea's edge—trying write or carve into a constantly changing dynamic field. It's a wonder we can remember anything at all, but the deeper levels of our nervous system remember the stuff that is emotionally significant—or instrumental to our survival!

I came to believe that psychology must hold the answers to these riddles: If my mind was so wild and ungovernable, wasn't everybody's? Psychology must be the most important subject in the world, for only it could explain the illusion-producing dynamics of the mind, or such monumental, incomprehensible events as wars. At sixteen, I found Sigmund Freud's *Interpretation of Dreams* in the high school library and couldn't put it down. The same thing happened with Shirer's *The Rise and Fall of the Third Reich*. Then Erich Fromm's *Escape from Freedom* became a bible of sorts. How could people so easily be swayed to turn the world into a nightmare?

At Columbia College, to help me answer my questions, I decided on psychology as a major. I set out to learn about that mysterious body of knowledge called depth psychology. But the psychology department was steeped in behaviorism, and all freshmen were assigned rats at the beginning of the year. The unfortunate rodents were reinforced, punished, then destroyed at midterm—because they had lost, at our hands—their naïveté! (They had perhaps learned too much about humans.) A new generation of naive rats or pigeons would come in for the second semester of operant conditioning (unaware of the fate of their unfortunate predecessors). The great event of the year would be the visit of B. F. Skinner, down from Harvard, to see what his followers at Columbia (Keller and Schoenfeld) were doing in New York.

I had various clashes with my psych professors when I would bring up topics such as dreams or (heaven forbid) the unconscious mind. To even think about finding a meaning in life was anathema. In fact, to get a course that covered the thinking of Freud and Jung, I had to go to the English department, and indeed found a wonderful course called "Metaphor, Symbol, and Myth" taught by professor Robert Gorham Davis. (This would prove to be a great experience, because it also introduced me not only to depth psychology but also to the work of Joseph Campbell and his book *The Hero with a Thousand Faces,* which truly changed my life.)

I kept thinking that there must be more to psychology than reinforcement schedules, and that creativity, depth, and meaning could be a legitimate part of human psychology. These clearly unacceptable desires sent me, a lonely, socially awkward, existentially tormented twenty-year-old, to the C. G. Jung Foundation in Manhattan. (I had learned in Davis's course that Jung was less reductionistic than Freud and more open to the creative dimension of the psyche.) Now I regard it as a serendipity, or life-changing synchronicity, that landed me at the foundation in 1961, the year of Jung's passing.

At the Jung Foundation, I learned that dreams could not only be taken seriously, but maybe they also contained some of that wisdom for living I felt so in need of—the inner dimension that was such anathema to my psychology professors! During the 1960s the foundation would meet in a hall across from the United Nations—a block or two away—where talks and presentations would ensue. In those days, even though our audience was merely thirty to sixty people (depending on the appeal of the presenter), we thought we were the real thing (the *psychological* United Nations). The political, extroverted, UN across the avenue was clearly misguided—*we were in touch with the deep interior* of whatever was happening in the world.

The foundation's programs in the 1960s featured notables such as Marie Louise von Franz, M. Esther Harding, Alma Paulson, Edward Edinger, Robert Johnson, Ross Hainline, Werner Engel, June Singer, Edward Whitmont (and as a guest, the nonanalyst presenter Joseph Campbell). I liked almost all the speakers I heard, and particularly the "wild" younger analysts: James Hillman and Arnie Mindell—who were on loan from Zurich. (Personally, I felt like such a mess that I knew I had to find an analyst!)

An audible hush (if I may call it that) would fall over the assembled company whenever Dr. Whitmont took the stage. It was now twenty-some years since he had arrived in America, and he spoke a soft, musically inflected, perfect English. One knew as he talked that German was his native tongue, but he was near fluent in all the European languages and had also, like Jung, studied Greek and Latin. Listening to Whitmont speak, and realizing his depth (yes, "depth psychology"!), I made my choice and have never regretted it.

Becoming Initiated

I entered analysis with Dr. Whitmont in 1964, at a much higher fee than I would have paid a younger trainee at the institute. Why would I go to an expensive senior analyst with the reputation for raking you over the coals; why would I do that?

Looking back at the trajectory of my life, it is probably because *I needed to be raked over some coals.* At twenty-three years old, I felt quite crazy. I had been raised in a politically and morally conservative religious family. (My father was a public school gym teacher and trainer of World War II commandoes, who then had, after a midlife crisis, become ordained as a minister. He could become quite authoritarian at times.)

I graduated high school almost a year early, at seventeen. I applied for and was granted a full NROTC scholarship to attend Columbia College. Later on, studying with social psychologist Otto Klineberg, I think I must have been in culture shock! On Wednesdays, I marched around campus in a uniform, saluted senior officers, and said, "Yes, sir!" The rest of the week I was reading beat poets (having known Jack Kerouac as a personal friend while I was still in high school), studying deconstructionism in my college courses, learning to drink in the West End Bar, and talking wisely about Nietzsche.

The first dreams in my (now brittle and old) dream journal of 1965 (exactly fifty years ago almost to the day that I am writing the first draft of this chapter) captures my world of that time.

I am in my father's church in Orange, New Jersey, and some of my snide and arrogant city friends are there, laughing and making fun of the church and some of the parishioners. "What a bunch of losers you people are!" they say. I am trying to defend some of the curious and eccentric people whom I have known for most of my life, but my (new) friends are merciless.

I had already lost the handed down faith of our fathers, probably starting in high school, but much more so in college. Most of my Columbia professors looked down their noses at anything resembling conventional religious beliefs. Somewhere along the line, I had decided that, like most of my friends, I too must be an atheist.

The times, they were a-changing, and I was caught right in the middle. I think I had begun to experience in my soul what sociologist Emilie Durkheim called "anomie"—rootlessness, disaffiliation, and an empty desperation. Psychologically, I had overflowing anxiety, panic attacks, and self-esteem problems—and here I was, a psych major.

To make things worse, I was courting a beautiful and intelligent graduate student at NYU, Robin Searson, and not a few of the men in my social peer group were already hitting on her. Could I, with my existential angst and self-image problems, keep up? Did my newborn relationship have a chance? It was as an emotional basket case then, that I came to see Dr. Whitmont. I told him my sad, sad story, expecting, I suppose, some comforting. But that was not what I got.

From the very first session, he was not easy on me. He probed, excavated, and analyzed all of my attitudes and all of my relationships. He would not join me in blaming those whom I sought to blame (my parents, my teachers, my rivals) *but threw it back on me.* I was, after all, a child of privilege. How had I allowed myself to become a victim? And where did I fall short of the destiny I should aspire to? No miserable excuses, thank you very much! *You are responsible for it all*—grow up, please!

Then he asked me for a dream.

The first, really memorable one, went as follows:

I am caught, imprisoned, in a kind of cage or trap. It is made of wood. Around the trap are stern and uncompromising men. If I make one false move, a thorn mounted on a tensioned piece of wood will be released and will pierce my heart.

After eliciting all the associations I could think of (but not too many; the dream seemed way out of the ordinary to me), Dr. Whitmont informed me that I was caught up in an initiation crisis. (It wasn't until years later that I found the exact image from my dream in a photographic image from an Australian initiation—see fig. 5.1, below.)

Fig. 5.1. Australian Aboriginal initiation rite

There was another early dream, rather embarrassing to tell (literally) in which

I am in a primate tribal gathering of sorts. I'm not sure if we are chimpanzees or australopithecines of some sort, but we are crawling around in a jungle clearing, and there are males, some of which are clearly dominant and some of which are clearly subservient. Dr. Whitmont is with the dominant group; I am among the peripheral or subservient ones, and he mounts me.

Ouch! At the time I thought this was an extremely crude, shameful, Freudian type of dream. After all, wasn't I looking for redemption through (idealized, Jungian) *archetypes of the collective unconscious*? (And here my dream shows me in an uninvited sexual position with my analyst—and *neither* of us is gay!)

When I told Dr. Whitmont this dream, he laughed (I was very humiliated). "I get it!" he said cheerfully.

What seemed like a *small* shameful dream was actually a *big* and, in fact, definitely *archetypal* dream. Both Whitmont and I are physically small. During my military career I was often the object of humiliation by bigger, senior-ranking men, particularly sadistic Marine Corps sergeants. (Anyone who thinks that primate dominance hierarchies do not translate into the doings of higher animals—*Homo sapiens*—should spend some time in the military or, for that matter, in a men's locker room!) One of the ways that primates establish dominance (but also unequal affiliation), Dr. Whitmont reminded me, was through mounting behavior.

Then he told me a story: Whitmont (née Weissberg; he had anglicized his name on coming to America) had fled Vienna with nothing more than his medical degree in hand, narrowly missing the Nazi *anchluss*. (The same thing had happened to the much older but already famous Sigmund Freud, who subsequently found refuge in Britain, where he had a strong following.) In contrast, young Dr. Weissberg—with no following at all, a stranger in a strange land—arrived in wartime America impoverished and rightly scared by what was happening to

Jews in Europe. With his quaint accent, he usually was seen as either Jewish or German (who were indisputably the enemy at that time—maybe he was a spy!). At first he had tried to affiliate with the German-speaking anthroposophists (followers of Rudolf Steiner). But he came to find that though they sponsored a progressive model of education, they were also highly orthodox and hierarchical: "There was no truth apart from Steiner!"

Whitmont's interest in homeopathy, and preference for that healing modality over psychiatric medications, made him a maverick among his medical/psychiatric colleagues who thought psychiatric homeopathy must be an anachronistic joke of some kind.

At last he found his cultural and professional niche! Jung's philosophical depth had always attracted him. He applied for and began training (at the postdoctoral level) as a Jungian analyst. Initially he remained fairly low on the totem pole—but then an opportunity arose to have a session with Jung himself in Switzerland!

To meet the great master, one had to present a dream. Whitmont did not have a dream until the night before the scheduled meeting. It was probably as embarrassing for him as mine (previously mentioned) had been for me.

I am sitting in Jung's waiting room, but the great man seems to have forgotten our appointment. I wait, and call out, but there is no answer. Then I push open the door and go into his empty office. I hear a noise from a room behind the office, but I can hardly believe it: It is of someone having a mighty bowel movement! The effluvium is now everywhere!

The next day, Jung was actually in, at his office in Küsnacht, near Zürich, and with typical Swiss punctuality. But you can imagine the anxiety of the diminutive young Austrian Jewish doctor *required to tell this as his first dream* to the (looming and already world-famous) Swiss psychiatrist. The young would-be analyst did as required.

When Jung heard the dream, he laughed uproariously. "Wonderful," he said. "Now we can talk!"

If you have tended to deify Jung or put him on a pedestal, I highly recommend Deirdre Bair's thousand-page biography of him.[1] This carefully researched biography will introduce you to the man himself (shadow and all). This is perhaps why he laughed so genuinely at Whitmont's dream—it enabled him and Whitmont to get grandiosity out of the way so that they could talk as equals, and go on to become colleagues.[2]

At one point I loaned Whitmont my prized and beaten-up copy of *Gestalt Therapy* by Perls, Hefferline, and Goodman. (Ralph Hefferline had been my academic adviser at Columbia, and I had taken weekend workshops with the brilliant and curmudgeonly Fritz Perls.) Whitmont kept the book for a month and then gave it back to me without saying much. It wasn't until a year or two later that I learned that Dr. Whitmont was (a little) in trouble with the Jungian hierarchy (mainly the great M. Esther Harding) for using Gestalt techniques (rather than Jungian) in therapy and beginning to do group therapy— unheard of in Jungian circles. I was sympathetic to his innovative approach, and told him so.

"Now do you understand why Jung said, 'Thank God I am Jung, and not a Jungian'?" Whitmont asked me. We laughed together. From this point onward he was no longer "Dr. Whitmont," the male at the top of the (Jungian) dominance hierarchy, but simply "Christopher"— as he really preferred.

I remembered that Freud had urged his followers, "Stay away (socially) from those big babies who are our patients." But according to Jung, "Every successful analysis I have had turned into a friendship." Not only do I prefer Jung's approach to this issue but I think that becoming friends with our mentors as well as those we mentor helps our maturation.

Thus do dreams lead us squarely into what Freud called "the transference" in the doctor-patient relationship: the fact that, in the cure, the patient projects figures from his own past onto the doctor—parents, teachers, superior officers—and in therapy one must now work through all the psychological and emotional problems that those figures represent. But in my analysis, Christopher showed me that there was even more: I would try to project my own power—the Force in *Star Wars*—onto other figures rather than have the boldness to embody it myself.

Much of my anxiety had been an unconscious fear that, as in primate societies, *a dominant male would steal my female.* (King David would kill his general Uriah by putting him in harm's way in a battle and take beautiful Bathsheba as his very own—things of this sort had already happened to me with previous girlfriends!) But Christopher nailed it: "What do you admire in this or that person—or for that matter, what do you admire in me? Now take that back and own it!"

Shortly afterward, Robin herself entered analysis with Christopher's office-mate at the time: Ann Belford (later Ulanov). Robin had her own growing to do, and she stayed with me, *not because I was a dominant male,* but simply because, she said, she loved me (for her, gentleness and whimsy trumped power). We married in 1964 and celebrated our fiftieth anniversary in 2014.

Fig. 5.2. Edward "Christopher" Whitmont and Stephen Larsen, circa 1985, Stone Mountain Center, New Paltz, New York (photo credit: Robin Larsen)

Dreaming While Awake

The following—and third big dream from my own early Jungian analysis—was *preceded* by the following dreamlike (real-life) event.

I was walking down Broadway during my lunch hour. I was an apprentice psychiatric social worker at the Upper Manhattan Aftercare Clinic—a very appropriate job for a would-be Jungian analyst. (While Freud cut his psychotherapeutic baby teeth on neurotic Viennese women, Jung made his foray into psychiatry treating psychotics at the Burgholzli Mental Hospital, also called the Kantonspital of Zürich. You can find a good representation of this in the feature film *A Dangerous Method*.) I had my own initiation into the world of mental illness with a caseload of forty psychiatric patients who had been in and out of mental hospitals most of their lives.

That day, I saw a strange, definitely mythological character bobbing and slinking and whirling through the street. He was short, oddly dressed, with a broad-brimmed hat, a red kerchief, Italian wraparound glasses, and a cape. He also had a police whistle on a chain around his neck, which he would blow suddenly and piercingly! When he had thus instantly seized the attention of everyone on the New York City block, he would do a piece of performance art wherein he would whirl and slink some more and then proclaim something like an incantation in a foreign tongue to his inadvertent audience. Then he would dart down the street and disappear.

Thus it was amazing for me to encounter this being's unmistakable silhouette slinking up the stairs to the second-story clinic where I worked. (I think he had put much of his costume into a bag.) And there he was, sitting quietly and demurely in the waiting room to see his psychiatric social worker (not me). HIPAA regulations were not well defined in those days (and we all mutually discussed patients in staff meetings), so my colleague handed me his file after the man had left.

For hours I read the saga of José, the man I called "the Fleagle." Like the character Evil-Eye Fleagle in Al Capp's comic strip *Li'l Abner*, he had a magical (maybe incestuous) relationship with his mother. If you haven't ever seen the comic strip, Evil-Eye Fleagle is only four-and-a-half-feet tall and wears a broad-brimmed hat and a zoot suit. His special magic is called a "whammy"—I saw José doing those on passersby. In Capp's mythology, a single whammy can knock out a dozen men. A double whammy (you often hear people use this phrase, without knowing the reference) can make the stone head of Teddy Roosevelt on Mt. Rushmore cry; the dreaded triple whammy can melt a battleship—and don't even ask about the quadruple whammy. (You wouldn't want to know!)

Unfortunately, even a mere double whammy tires out the Fleagle for a whole day (due to the immense energy required); a triple for a week. The Fleagle himself cannot perform a quadruple. Only his mother—from whom the original magic seems to come—can do one of those!

I knew very little, at the time, of this peculiar comic-strip mythology, until later, when I researched it and saw exactly how José had modeled himself on the character. Then I encountered his letters (they were somehow copied into his file) to his mother. Though José was diagnosed as being schizophrenic, his letters were relatively normal in most respects, and hauntingly emotional and vulnerable. They revealed that he had never found a woman to match up to his mother.

Fig. 5.3. The Evil-Eye Fleagle, a figure from Al Capp's Li'l Abner *comic strip*

José was amazingly bright and articulate for a "mentally ill" man with a high school education.

Now back to my own psychological process. After the hours and hours reading this man's psychiatric history, I was empathically moved—not only by his humanity but also by the mythic journey he was on. At one point I read how, like Diogenes in his jar, he sat obdurately in a bathtub in the ward of the mental hospital, surrounded by staff trying to persuade him to come out. Finally the supervising psychiatrist was summoned, and a very interesting dialectical moment ensued. Fleagle (José) did not for a moment succumb to the doctor's undisputed authority. He questioned him and called the good doctor on the carpet for his own evident, personal flaws in an uncanny way—his "whammy," I suppose. It was an extraordinary moment of truth in a psychiatric setting, one that may happen many times in the various mental institutions around our land, but seldom is it immortalized. (Eventually, I think, José was removed by force!)

The net effect of this reading was that I went home to bed, exhausted, and fell into a deep sleep. I then had the following dream.

Robin and I are in a dark, shadowy place. Suddenly we are surrounded by strange, eerie beings. They are like puppets, or puppetlike characters. (I have experienced these before in many dreams.) They all are trying to take my wife away from me. They are pawing her over, and I am trying to fight them, but they are insistent and omnipresent.

The analysis of the dream was as follows—Christopher guided me to it. "You yourself are like the schizophrenic, but conditionally more 'together.' You both *have many parts to your personalities* (we all do), but the Fleagle has chosen his persona, his mask—the strangely charismatic one—you first encountered.

"You yourself are still a work in progress; you are neither this part of you nor that—sometimes you're an anxious fool, and sometimes a cocky self-assured savant; sometimes you're a child, and sometimes a wise man. 'Robin' is your soul, your anima, and she is 'up for grabs.'

The man you saw has made his choice—fascinating, *but very socially compromised*—and *what will be your choice?*"

It was, I soon came to realize, the third big dream—after the Aboriginal initiation and the dominance one. It contained the elements of my fear: having to protect my young wife and keep her for myself—so we could maybe even one day have children and a family. *But it was about much, much more.* It was about my struggle to find my own soul.

It wasn't so much that Christopher analyzed my dream; rather he *guided me toward my seeing what it was really saying; what it was really about!* It wasn't simple, it wasn't easy, but it was real! And it wasn't just about Robin, it was about me!

A personality is a composite, a "collection of masks" if you will (my puppet creatures). *Persona* means "mask" in Greek, and we all are just that; plural creatures who are not by any means a finalized "person"— nor should we be, because we are works in progress. We have one mask to wear with our family of origin, another with our friends, another for our teachers or our workplace, another when we are alone and facing ourselves in the mirror!

Who are we, where are we going, how do we put together our partial selves? These questions have haunted me for the fifty years that have ensued following the dream—and that is how I now know, indisputably, that this had been a big dream. Since that time Robin and I (and Tom) have led many mask workshops to help people deal with and relate to these part-selves of which we all are made up—the personas, the masks, that all have to be assembled to make a personality. See figures 5.4 and 5.5, and see plate 4 in the color insert.

As a practicing psychotherapist, this dream and the insights that came from it helped me understand schizophrenics, multiple personality disorders (now called "dissociative identity disorders," or DID), and even how very "normal" people are sometimes frightened by their own inner fragmentation.

Throughout our early years of analysis, Christopher always asked for a dream with which to begin things. In fact, he wouldn't let me kvetch

Fig. 5.4. Tom Verner forms a mask on Merlin Larsen during a mask enactment in Burlington, Vermont, in the midwinter of 1986. (photo credit: Robin Larsen)

Fig. 5.5. Mask workshop. Stephen directs a dialogue between participant and mask in a mirror in Burlington, Vermont, in the midwinter of 1986. (photo credit: Robin Larsen)

about this or that situation, or person, without a dream to comment on it. Then he would show me, through work on the dream, what was really going on. By the time that I came to be a psychotherapist in my own right I would always do the same.

After fifteen years of teaching abnormal psychology and practicing as a clinical psychotherapist I decided to return to Christopher for both personal and training analysis. (In the latter process you bring your patients' dreams to the training analyst, and both he/she and you are on the line for analysis.) This wasn't easy—I had to drive an hour and a half each way to see him twice a month only to have my all-too-easy and facile assumptions brought on the carpet, time and time again. Training analysis requires analysis of *both the patient and the therapist*. (As mentioned, Whitmont was for many years the training analyst at the C. G. Jung Institute in New York.) The associations and personal dilemmas of both therapist and patient are brought to the spotlight, compared and contrasted: history, assumptions, belief systems, distortions. It is a sobering process and one that disabused me of any illusions I had about being the charismatic or psychotherapeutic genius my grandiose parts liked to entertain. (This coming to self-knowledge must be worked through by any would-be therapist receiving the godlike projections of the patient.)

"Sit humbly, watch and wait, and see what the dream brings!" was Whitmont's infallible prescription—oh, and by the way, *We both know what distortions and illusions you yourself bring to this process, right?*

Right.

You wouldn't try to be some kind of God-substitute, would you? Not only do you *not know* what the dream means, *You don't tell people how to live their lives, right?*

Right!

It was enormously important advice, which I have lived by ever since. So if you don't offer people *your good idea of how to live their lives,* what is a therapist *supposed* to do?

Of course you elicit dreams, but you work with them only according to the following formula: *You ask far more questions than you make declarative statements* or pretend some kind of authority. Following is a brief summary of the types of questions that a psychotherapist who had been trained by Whitmont would ask.

1. What is happening in your life right now?
2. When did the dream come? (Before or after what events—or other dreams in a sequence?)
3. Where does the dream take place? (And what does that place remind you of?)
4. Who is there? (If characters occur whom you don't know, who does that figure remind you of?)
5. Ask for associations to each element or event: include animals, plants, and inanimate objects—and even further amplifications to those.
6. As these questions are asked, observe body language, nuances of facial expression, tone of voice.
7. As people work (play) with the dream, ask, "Where does that resonate in your body?"
8. If a figure appears whom we still haven't figured out would you be so good as to play (indwell) that figure (a strategy Christopher got from Fritz Perls)?
9. How did you feel as you awakened from the dream?
10. Can you think of anything you would like to do (creatively or in a problem-solving manner) with this dream?

The good dream therapist *always asks questions before anything else.* The locus of the meaning of the dream lies within the dreamer—not just in the realm of archetypes—though the serious study of myth and dramatic literature enables us to identify the roles and characters. "All the world is a stage," the bard wrote in *As You Like It*—and as James Joyce seconded in *Ulysses:* "We walk through ourselves, meeting robbers, ghosts, giants, old men, young men, wives, widows, brothers-in-love." It is a danger, though, for us to simply choose exciting or good roles within the drama rather than realizing that we ourselves are the whole drama played out nightly—if not over the course of a whole life. Whitmont's Dramatic Structure of the Dream, which uses the four-part archetypal framework of exposition, development, crisis, and lysis, gives us further guidance to understand the transformative meaning of the dream (it is described in more detail in chapter 3 on page 81). The dream, confronted honestly, offers us, in Goethe's words, "the becoming," as opposed to the "become and the set-fast." Every night the dream enacts exquisitely, and challengingly, that human beings are verbs rather than nouns.

Authentic psychological growth comes from a kind of inner alchemy. While we have within us all kinds of masks and all kinds of voices, the radical who pursues a fanatical agenda, the demagogue, the righteous ayatollah, or even the Fleagle character created by José, has sold out becoming to "having become"—not the endless task of "becoming." It is this never-ending synthesis of ingredients that brought Jung to study alchemy, or that had Whitmont title one of his deepest books *The Alchemy of Healing*.

TOM'S COMMENTARY ON "STANDING NAKED"

When reading this section of Stephen's on the human being as a collection of masks or personalities, a multiplicity of selves, this "polytheistic sense of psyche" that James Hillman speaks of so eloquently, I was reminded of the poet Walt Whitman when he said, in "Song of Myself" in *Leaves of Grass*, "Do I contradict myself? Very well, then I contradict myself, I am large, I contain multitudes."

I was also reminded of the great Swedish poet Tomas Transtrommer's poem "Romanesque Arches," translated by Robert Bly, in which the poet beautifully combines this sense of us being a multiplicity of selves with another idea Stephen presents in this section:

> "Inside you vault opens behind vault endlessly.
> You will never be complete, that's how it's meant to be."[3]

What a contrast to Freud's belief that "where there is *id*, there *ego* shall be." Rather than trying prematurely to get it all together, the dreaming psyche seems to be inviting us to fall apart, to crack up, to become aware of that inner commune of selves that we are. The dream invites them all to sit around the table of our life. These are what Jung called "the little people of the psyche." This is not multiple personality disorder; it is the many-faced, many-faceted, many-peopled world of the human psyche. Each night our dreams invite us into this world of opposites; contradictions; many-gendered animal, mineral, and vegetable worlds of possibilities. When we see all the characters—all the plants and animals, all the people, all the many atmospheres and weathers, all the images in a dream as parts of ourselves—the multiple meanings, the new perspectives, the sense of who we are, sometimes humbling, sometimes grand, slowly reveals itself.

When some jackbooted Nazi shows up in our dream, we may have to acknowledge—as does Prospero in *The Tempest* when beholding the uncouth scurrilous Caliban—"This thing of darkness I acknowledge mine."

This is how we grow, by living in and through and with the many people that we are, the selves that our dreams so elegantly, so terrifyingly, so creatively introduce us to every night. Thus, like Whitman, let us be large, let us contain multitudes. Inside each of us, "vault opens behind vault endlessly," and we "will never be complete; that's how it's meant to be."

The Dreams of Joseph Campbell

A day came that I never thought I would see. It was in 1974 in Kentucky at a mythically inspired conference titled Council Grove East (an offshoot of the conferences in Council Grove, Kansas, that had been going on for some years). Robin and I were participants, and Joseph Campbell was the keynote speaker. The conference conveners invited me to lead a dream group for the attendees, and Joseph was among them. I had already done my basic early work with Whitmont, and yet here was the great Joseph Campbell, *in my dream group!*

Fig. 5.6. Circa 1980, two mentors teaching together. Top: Robert Bly (left) and Joseph Campbell. Bottom: Campbell shown in a Mandarin robe and, as such, is seen as "the Sage."

The dream Joseph presented was recent—and fairly simple:

I am in an underground chamber—it's kind of nightmarish: I'm facing this tangled ball of poisonous snakes all biting each other. Now they are coming after me—there's nowhere safe. I've got to get out!

I started in on my questions: "Does this remind you of anything in your life?" It was like an explosion rocked the room.

Joseph became very animated. "I know just who they are!" he exclaimed. "It's those damned Freudian-Marxists at Sarah Lawrence. It's just like the dream said: 'I know they're after me!'"

He wasn't wrong, but it would be a couple of decades for the dream to unfold in the outer world. (It came to mind vividly after Joseph's death, when in 1992 a member of the Bronxville community, who had pretended to be a personal friend of Joseph's, attacked him for anti-Semitism on the basis of remarks supposedly made in private. However, Joe couldn't defend himself, or say what he really felt! I wasn't the only one who said, when these public slanders happened, "What a snake in the grass!")

The dream association with the Freudian-Marxists at Sarah Lawrence and the snakes was obviously affect-loaded for Joseph, but I held my ground and gently probed him for the inner level. (This was in group process, with maybe twenty people present, so I do not feel I am disclosing anything said in confidence.) Had the political intrigues gotten under Joe's skin? Were the snakes "in his bed," so to speak? Thus came the healing moment, and Joe laughed ruefully, confessing he had been suffering from insomnia. When he tried to sleep, he would ruminate; his "reptile brain" was restless. The psychological interpretation had hit the mark.

Joseph could have pulled rank as the grand mythological scholar who knew everything, but in that moment he deferred to where I was going and acknowledged his own vulnerability. I later learned that his insomnia—after being brought to the light of day through the dream-work process—improved!

At this point in the conference—sharing the same space at the Carter Caves State Resort Park in Kentucky for a week—Joseph and Robin and I shared a lot of personal issues and consolidated our friendship. We came to realize that for all his seeming extroversion and charisma, Joseph Campbell was actually rather introverted and shy. The culminating ritual of the conference had us spending hours together in Stygian darkness in a labyrinthine cave-crypt—symbolically reenacting, from the ancient Babylonian myth, Inanna's descent to the underworld. As I look back on that time together, the whole event itself was decisively, intimately mythological in our lives, reminiscent of the Eleusinian Mysteries and the rite of the Pholarkos—laying down in a lair, like an animal, to receive the healing dream. Even the snakes in Joe's dream were like the Asclepian serpents in their tholos chamber. They came, not to menace, but to bring healing!

Private Myths and Public Dreams

Joseph Campbell would often say, "A dream is a private myth, a myth is a public dream!"

He had a lifelong fascination with all things pertaining to Native Americans. He wrote in one of his earliest journals, which we still have: "I early became fascinated, seized, obsessed, by the figure of a naked American Indian with his ear to the ground, a bow and arrow in his hand, and a look of special knowledge in his eyes."[4]

At around the same time as he recorded the above mythologem (when he was about thirteen years old), young Joe went on an involuntary vision quest: He developed a case of pneumonia, serious enough to keep him at home in New Rochelle for several months. His dream life and journaling definitely intensified. His journal records "being swallowed by a whale"—perhaps the illness itself—or an early firsthand experience of what German ethnologist Leo Frobenius (and Joe himself) called "the night sea journey." He began to read the New Rochelle Public Library's entire collection of things Native American—including the multivolume *Proceedings of the American Bureau of Indian Ethnography*—not usually

HE WAS CROUCHING AND CLOSELY SCANNING THE GROUND

Fig. 5.7. A mythologem of Joseph Campbell's youth: The Native American pathfinder. From the 1921 book The White Wolf, *by Elmer Gregor. Frontispiece art by D. C. Hutchinson.*

considered fare for young readers! Finally his parents, realizing the previously active and athletic teenager needed a "rest cure," decided to send him to Sa-Ga-Na-Ga, the rustic cottage they owned in Bucks County, Pennsylvania.

Here began one of those serendipities—as he would later call them—those times when external life becomes like a waking dream. The neighbor whom his parents appointed to look after the teenager was a man named Elmer Gregor, an author of books for young people about—guess what?—Native Americans and the adventures of growing up on the American frontier. Down the shore of Wolf Lake from where the Campbell cottage was situated was the encampment of Dan Beard, one of the founders of the Boy Scouts of America, an avid woodsman and reputedly a dazzling storyteller, as was Elmer Gregor. They named their evening storytelling pow-wows around the fire "The Feast of Dreams" after the Iroquois midwinter ritual known by that name. There can be little doubt, as we later wrote in *A Fire in the Mind,* that Joseph hatched and incubated his considerable storytelling prowess in these early years. (After an event in which he was temporarily blinded by Citronella oil—for mosquitoes—Gregor changed Joe's Indian name from White Beaver to Throws it in his Eye!) His athletic prowess began to return, and soon he journaled about feats of swimming—including rescuing a drowning girl, and after two more months of country living, outrunning everyone in the neighborhood.[5]

Because of their special programs for Native Americans, Joseph's first choice for a college was Dartmouth. But he quickly tired of fraternity life and winter festivals and wrote home that he missed his family—so he began Columbia College as a sophomore. Here another waking dream occurred—although it seemed at first to be a tragedy. Naturally athletic and a fast runner, he joined the football team at Columbia. But on the very first day of practice, Jackson Schultz, later an All-American halfback, broke Joe's ribs, and the doctor suspended him from the team.

Hindsight, as they say, is twenty-twenty. In those days (1924) there was very little awareness of the fact that football, often leading to traumatic brain injury (TBI), could be bad for your health. The protective gear of the time was woefully inadequate. As an aside, before he got into baseball, Lou Gehrig, the famous American first

baseman, was a Columbia halfback. Today, one of my clinical special-
ties is the sequelae of head injury. I have written elsewhere that this
is also known as Lou Gehrig's disease and is based on recurrent TBIs.
In this case, what was formative was that Lou Gehrig's disease was
actually Chronic Traumatic Encephalopathy (CTE) left over from
Gehrig's football collisions.

Now here's the serendipity! Had Joseph Campbell followed through
with his original plan to play college football during the 1920s, I doubt
if he could have had his illustrious intellectual career. Nor could he
have mesmerized millions of people when interviewed by Bill Moyers
in what some said was the best piece of educational TV ever made in
America: *The Power of Myth* series!

I could go on and on with the waking dreams, as Mary Watkins
wrote about, or synchronicities, as Jung and Pauli called them, that
characterized Joe's life, but I would rather refer you to the detailed
accounting we give in *A Fire in the Mind*. That said, the gist of what
he felt was summed up in the quote from Arthur Schopenhauer that
he had memorized—it was one of his favorites: "Looking back over the
course of one's own days, and noticing how encounters and events that
appeared at the time to be accidental became the crucial structuring
features of an unintended life-story through which the potentialities of
one's character were fostered to fulfillment, one may find it difficult to
resist the notion of the course of one's own biography as comparable to
that of a cleverly constructed novel, wondering who the author of the
surprising work might have been."[6]

Who indeed? And do we have a glimpse here, not only of the way
that myth and dream might play into our lives but that, in fact, "the
author of the surprising work" seems to take account of our needs,
even when we ourselves are unconscious of them? I keep asking myself
this ultimate question—is the universe a friendly place? Guiding
dreams and the unexpected coincidences that befall us when the universe becomes dreamlike or mythic seem to say a resounding "Yes!"
La vida es sueño lo que ayudarnos (life is [like] a dream), which helps
us out (to paraphrase Calderon)!

Mentee into Mentor

Now in my midseventies, most of my own mentors have passed beyond this bittersweet mortal realm—"the place of becoming," with its loamy forests, mountain grandeur, and sparkling waters descending into rolling, salty oceans. Christopher, in his last year of life, returned to his beloved Alps, Joseph to the rolling seas of Hawaii, and Tom to his beautiful Vermont mountains. I am in my rock-girdled Shawangunk valley, with its forests and tumbling waterfalls. All of us seem to have become graybeards to whom others come for counsel.

Even so, it is a little startling. Speaking for myself and Tom, I know that neither of us feels like that finished product—the wise old man— of whom Jung wrote so compellingly. Tom's mentors too are gone: James Hillman a few years ago; Robert Bly in his nineties, to retirement in Minnesota. Tom continues his dreamwork, teaching, and studies, and with his wife, Janet, artist and La Fleur the mime, travels the world with their organization, Magicians Without Borders, bringing love, laughter, magic, and hope to many forgotten refugee and orphan children. We both juggle, and, in fact, we joked recently how many balls we each have in the air while we were finishing this book. I stayed closer to home, but see up to forty patients a week, help my wife with our not-for-profit Center for Symbolic Studies, ride horses and mountain bikes, and cuddle grandchildren.

The mentors whom I have most valued, and I think Tom seconds me, did not accept any kind of "wise old mantle" (if you can accept the pun), but pointed beyond themselves. Christopher said, "Listen to your dreams!" and Joseph said, "Don't listen to me; go to the myths!"

6

Archaeologist of Morning, a Digger of First Things

In the Words of Coauthor Tom Verner

"Magic Song for
Those Who Wish to Live"

Day arises
From its sleep
Day wakes up
With the dawning light.
Also you must arise,
Also you must awake
Together with the day which comes!

THULE INUIT

I was born under the sign of Aquarius in a small Irish Catholic, western Pennsylvania coal-mining town called Castle Shannon. St. Anne's Church and parochial school were the heart and soul of the town. The Angelus bell rang every day at noon, and for a few moments most people stopped what they were doing and silently bowed their heads in prayer. From the age of ten I was the head altar boy at St. Anne's, and one of my responsibilities was to serve six o'clock Mass every morning.

The mile or so walk each morning through the dawn light,

through the just-waking world, taught me to become what the American poet Charles Olson calls "an archaeologist of morning, a digger of first things." I learned to love that in-between world, that twilight time (Middle English for "two-light" time, the light of night and the light of day) between night and day. I slowly walked through the "crack in the world," when the air is fresh, the birds are awakening with their dawn chorus, rabbits are up and about, and a few lights are on in some of the homes where other archaeologists of morning are padding about.

Those morning walks got deep into my bones and for more than fifty years I have risen early and taken walks through this dawn world. Often I begin in the dark and feel the world awakening around me. The love of this in-between world, the world of dawn, is deeply connected to my love of dreams and the secrets they have to tell us.

"The Breeze at Dawn"

The breeze at dawn has secrets to tell you
Don't go back to sleep . . .
People are moving back and forth
Across the doorsill where the two worlds touch,
Don't go back to sleep . . .

RUMI

I left home at thirteen to join a monastic order. It was a complicated and unusual decision, but not all that strange in my traditional Catholic town. I spent seven years in that monastery, a world that, in many ways, was unchanged since the thirteenth century. We chanted five times a day in Latin, took solitary walks, spent many hours in silence, meditated and prayed, celebrated the liturgical year with great pomp and circumstance, and spent a good deal of time working on what we called our inner lives. We had a master who was our spiritual director, guided us in spiritual matters, and helped us map our inner world. At the suggestion of the master, I began keeping a daily journal filled with my thoughts, hopes, doubts, and dreams. Along with my early morning walks, keeping a journal has remained, for these fifty years, an important part of my life.

Out in "the world," as we called it, the "times they were a-changin'." The world of the 1960s was in full swing, and even monastery walls couldn't keep it out. The church herself was deeply affected by the transformative energy that was in the air around the world in those turbulent times. Pope John XXIII called the Second Vatican Council to "open the windows of the Church, and let in some fresh air." Many of us left the monastery through those same open doors and windows, answering a new call to be part of the social revolution that was rocking the planet.

The day I left the monastery, filled with fear and trembling, excitement and hopes for a new life, the master handed me a book and said, "This will help you move from this world of the monastery to the world you're going to, because the man who wrote this book had a foot in both worlds." The man was Carl Gustav Jung, and the book was his autobiography—*Memories, Dreams, Reflections*.

Jung's autobiography is one of the half-dozen books that changed my life. All those early morning walks, the journal writing, the silence and solitude, the world of ritual and community, all these prepared me to hear Jung. His amazing words, as the master said, come to us from that in-between world, the world between night and day, between the dreaming world and the waking world, the place between the inner and the outer worlds, the place between Time and Eternity.

Along the road that I entered as I left the monastery there have been many teachers who helped me understand what Jung was talking about in that autobiography. I have returned to that book again and again. Yes, I found Jung, but more importantly, I found myself. I still own that very copy the master gave me the day I left the thirteenth century. Now the book is literally held together with rubber bands. It's no longer just a book, but an object, a totem, a touchstone that I literally have taken around the world and read again and again. To this day whenever people ask me where they should begin their study of Jung or their study of dreams, I point them to *Memories, Dreams, Reflections*.

In many ways, after I left the monastery, I followed a path some-what similar to Jung's by entering the philosophy program at Duquesne University in Pittsburgh, Pennsylvania, and immersing myself in the world of those big questions that Jung entertained all his life. Jung once said that one of the differences between himself and Freud was that Freud immersed himself in the world of nineteenth-century science and medicine, and Jung immersed himself in the world of Kant, Nietzsche, Schopenhauer, and the great philosophers. The philosophy program at Duquesne focused on existential phenomenology and was very inte-grated with the Existential Humanistic Psychology Department. My philosophical education was always deeply psychological. A wonder-fully exciting and slightly humorous aspect of the existential philosophy I read while at Duquesne was the fact that all the books I was forbidden to read in the monastery were now *required* reading, by authors such as Jean Paul Sartre, Albert Camus, Martin Heidegger, and others. I felt like I had died and gone to heaven; some of my fellow monks back in the monastery might have felt that I had died and gone to hell!

Another important part of my work at Duquesne was studying poetry with the marvelous Lebanese-American poet and founder of the International Poetry Forum, Samuel Hazo. While in the monastery, a small group of us became passionately interested in poetry and would meet regularly to read it. We read both our own and that of contem-porary poets like Dylan Thomas, T. S. Eliot (we even put the "Hollow Men" to Gregorian chant), Allen Ginsburg, Lawrence Ferlinghetti, Brother Antonius, and many others. We had created our own dead poets' society there within the monastery walls. My work with Samuel Hazo at Duquesne continued and deepened this love of poetry.

Poetry has always played an important part in my understanding of dreams. For almost fifty years, I have had what I felt were two separate loves: poetry and dreams. However, over the years I have come to real-ize that there is really only one love, and that is what Carl Jung, James Hillman, and Robert Bly have taught me to think of as the *mythopoetic* nature of psyche. I think my love of poetry has deepened my way of understanding and working with dreams, and my work with dreams has

Fig. 6.1. Coauthor Tom Verner performs magic for noted Jungian psychologist James Hillman in the summer of 2010 at a gathering held at James Hillman's home in Thompson, Connecticut.

deepened my appreciation and understanding of poetry. I also directly use poetry in working with dreams. (We'll explore the relationship between poetry and dreams, and detail how I use poetry in dreamwork, in chapter 11).

My two greatest teachers have been Dorothy Day and James Hillman. One of Hillman's critiques of psychology is that it has made us too me-centered, too personal, too focused on oneself at the expense of the world. The title of his book *We've Had 100 Years of Psychotherapy—And the World's Getting Worse* says it all. Dorothy Day, the great Catholic social reformer and founder of the Catholic Worker Movement, established many houses of hospitality across the country that housed and fed the homeless casualties of our capitalist culture. The years I studied at Duquesne, I lived in a Catholic Worker house by the name of St. Joseph's

House of Hospitality, in the Hill District of Pittsburgh. This constant balancing of the philosophical, the psychological, and the concern for social justice has been my life's work and is deeply connected to my way of understanding and working with dreams.

As I was growing up in Castle Shannon, my first great teacher was my mother. She was head of an organization at our church called *The Christian Mothers.* One of their tasks was to bring food and clothing to the poor miners who were out of work due to the fact that the mines had been emptied of coal. For one reason or another, of the three children, I was the one my mom chose to accompany her to deliver baskets of food to the out-of-work miners and their families. The conversations that we had in the car were often lessons about poverty, gratitude, dignity, and the call to serve those less fortunate.

My work with dreams and Hillman's archetypal psychology are always balanced with a commitment to make the world a more just, compassionate, and loving place. When I hear the word *dream,* I always also hear Martin Luther King Jr. saying, "I have a dream . . ." and I envision his dream of a more just and peaceful world. The inner and outer . . . the monastery and the world . . . having a foot in both worlds is the real work of our lives. Jung often would ask, "What is the ethical demand of this dream?" How will I bring this dream into the world and make the world a more conscious place?

I have always brought this deeply rooted sense of spirituality, literature, philosophy, and psychology to my understanding of the dream and how to work with it. I love the statement attributed to Freud: "Wherever I go in search of the psyche, I find a poet has been there before me."

Freud is also said to have responded to the question, "Who are the three greatest psychologists," by saying, "Shakespeare, Dostoevsky, and humility forbids me to say who the third greatest one is." In this rare moment of public humility, Freud acknowledges that poets, playwrights, and novelists are the ones we need to look to for information and inspiration about the dreaming psyche.

Since 1982, I have attended the annual Conference on the Great

Mother, begun by the poet Robert Bly as a weeklong gathering to explore the intersections of poetry, Jungian psychology, spirituality, story, music, mythology, and art. We meet in a rural camp setting on a lake and spend the days listening to many of the great poets, psychologists, thinkers, and storytellers of our time, circling around a particular theme each year. Often the conference centers on a particular story that is told throughout the week and embellished through mask, movement, and theater.

In addition to Robert Bly, some of the conference's teachers have been James Hillman, Joseph Campbell, Gioia Timpanelli, Marion Woodman, Robert Moore, Stephen and Robin Larsen, Coleman Barks, Robert Creeley, Galway Kinnell, Sharon Olds, Etheridge Knight, Michael Meade, Edward Hirsch, Tony Hoagland, and many others over the years. The mornings are spent on a presentation of a piece of the story, and then usually a lecture is given that speaks to the theme of the conference. The afternoons are spent working with the theme through visual arts, writing workshops, mask making, movement, music, and meditation. The evenings are for music performances and poetry readings. This is summer camp for mythopoetic adults and has been an annual source of soul work, learning, and nourishment for me over the decades.

For Jung, our psyches are always moving toward balance and wholeness. When our lives become too one-sided, as Jung would say, too unbalanced in one direction or another, the psyche sends dreams and/or events to balance this one-sidedness. I was asked to give a talk on how I came to Jung in my life. As I was preparing the talk, I realized in a very profound and startling way that Jung had come to me. This calls to mind the old adage that we don't find books, but books find us; or the Zen teaching, when the student is ready, the teacher appears. This was certainly true when Jung's autobiography, *Memories, Dreams, Reflections,* found me as I was on the threshold of leaving the monastery. Since Jung came into my life, I have immersed myself in his way of understanding the inner and outer worlds. I know there is a profound interpenetration of the inner world of dreams and the world of the so-called waking world.

A Dead Jung

As we begin working with our dreams, we may start to sense a dream-like quality to the waking world. The boundary, the veil between the dreaming universe and the waking world, gets thinner and more transparent. As James Hillman would say, we begin to see through the moments, the people, the seemingly random happenstance events in our life and see through to an archetypal pattern, a purpose, a calling beneath and behind the seemingly quotidian events that we find ourselves in the middle of.

The following is a brief story of one of the ways Jung came to me and revealed this thinning of the veil between the waking and the dreamworlds.

I have worked at a small liberal arts college in Vermont since 1979, mostly as a professor of Jungian and archetypal psychology, but sometimes I held administrative jobs. The college had only been in existence for a few years when I arrived, and there had been only one academic dean since the college's founding. A few years after I arrived, the dean left to enter an Episcopal seminary to become a priest. The dean and I had a very good relationship, and we felt very much like kindred spirits. He asked me if I would take over as dean, because he thought I would do a good job. We shared a similar philosophy of education, and he felt that I would provide needed continuity for this still young and emerging college. With some reluctance, I accepted. There were a few things about the job that I enjoyed, such as the creation and development of curriculum and the mentoring of faculty. But for the most part I found the position, with its endless hours of meetings and committees, tedious and boring. Because of all my administrative duties I was also only able to teach maybe one course each semester, and teaching for me was not just a job but a deep, soulful calling. As dean, I felt like my soul was drying up.

At this time Jung came to me in the following dream.

I am in a hospital, and Jung is the patient. I have been asked to monitor his IV, to make sure he is getting the fluids he needs. I become

*distracted and stop paying attention to the IV tubes, and Jung dies.
The amazing thing about that moment when I realize Jung is dead is
my casual reaction to it. I say something like, "Oops," as if something
very minor had just happened, like I had maybe just dropped my pen
on the floor.*

*I go out of the hospital room to head for the nurses' station to
let them know that Jung is dead, and a young, very alive, redheaded
woman is coming toward me down the hospital corridor. She is very
excited, and I know—the way you know in dreams—that she is going
to see Jung. She flies right past me and goes into Jung's room. I turn
around and head back to the room, wanting to be there when she finds
Jung dead. When I enter the room, Jung is up, and the two of them are
very much alive, talking excitedly to each other.*

At that point I wake up from the dream.

The next day I drove another faculty member, Shams Mortier, into
Burlington. He also taught courses on Jung, mythology, and archetypal
psychology. I told Shams the dream about Jung, and we talked about it
a bit on the way into Burlington but got distracted by other more mun-
dane matters related to the psychology program. We did not get too far
with the dream.

A few days later something happened that, in retrospect, was very
much one of those events when the waking world and the dreamworld
overlap. As the poet Novalis (1772–1801) writes, "The seat of the soul
is where the inner world and the outer world meet. Where they meet,
the soul is in every point of the overlap."

I live an hour's drive from the college, in the rural mountains of
Vermont, and the commute was often difficult in the winter months.
A young social worker from a nearby town, to supplement his meager
income, started a little bus service with a twelve-passenger van. I took
his bus as often as I could during the snowy winter months. It was very
convenient, because he worked close to the college and picked me up
right at its front entrance.

After a particularly grueling day of nonstop meetings, grant writing, and search committee interviews, I was standing outside in the five o'clock, snowy, already winter dark, waiting for the bus. I was looking forward to sitting in the very back next to the spare tire, talking to no one and maybe sleeping for the hour drive home. The van stopped, and I tried the side door but it was locked. The friendly young social worker was already opening the front door, inviting me to sit in the passenger seat next to him for the ride home.

As we drove around Burlington picking up his ten passengers, I was quiet and sitting with my eyes half closed. As we headed out of town with everybody on board, the cheery young social worker asked me what I was teaching that semester. I responded by saying that I was teaching an introduction to Jungian psychology. He said, "I remember hearing some things about Jung in my psychology courses but not very much. What's Jung's psychology about?"

I had hoped to spend the ride relating to nothing more than the spare tire, not talking, and maybe sleeping after my dreary day of boring meetings. To answer the question, "What's Jung's psychology about?" seemed like a daunting, impossible task to my exhausted body and mind at that moment, but I launched into some thoughts about Jung. The young social worker kept asking "beginner's mind" questions, those simple, profound questions only a beginner's mind, an open mind, a wondering, not-knowing mind, can ask. His questions awakened something in me, and our conversation caught fire and became lively. I started to enjoy it very much.

The hour ride home through the winter dark flew by. As I was walking toward my truck, one of the passengers, a young woman student from the University of Vermont, approached me and said, "I couldn't help hearing your conversation about Jung. I'm a psychology major at the university, but I hate it; and it's too late now for me to change my major. But I just wanted to tell you that when you were talking about Carl Jung and all that he is concerned with, I got so excited that I was reminded why I wanted to study psychology. That love for what I thought psychology was has died. But at least tonight I remembered why I wanted to study psychology, so thank you very much!"

Plate 1. The Egyptian Dream Book is a hieratic papyrus dating from the reign of Rameses II from 1279–1213 BCE. ©The Trustees of the British Museum

Plate 2. This colossal head of Asclepius from a cult statue from the shrine of Asklepios at Melos originally had a metal crown that is now lost. Blacas Collection. (photo credit: Marie-Lan Nguyen, 2011)

Plate 3. Robin Larsen's art from dreams. The empty mandala is a "Spirit Catcher,"
and after the dream the full image emerges. From the series Alchemical Tryptich II.
First image: Spirit Catcher 1, "Waiting." Second image: "Rising."
(photo credit: Linda Law)

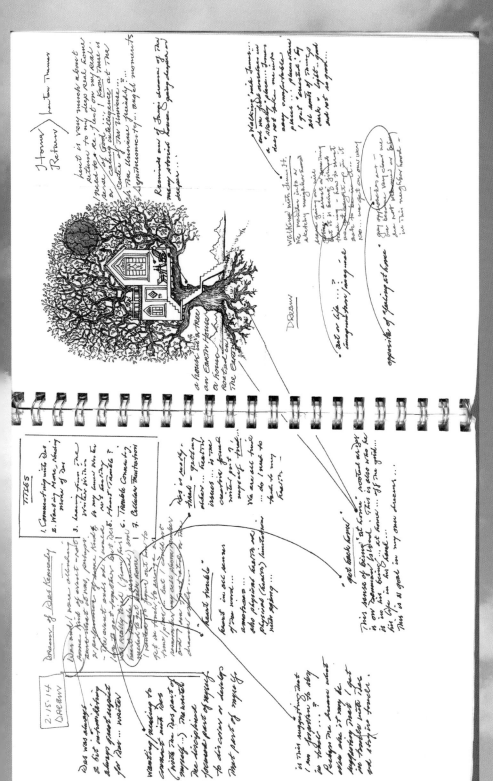

Plate 4. The dream journal of coauthor Tom Verner

Plate 5. A mask enactment, undertaken with a partner, in Burlington, Vermont, in the midwinter of 1986 (photo credit: Robin Larsen)

Plate 6. This wood engraving, by an unknown artist, appeared in Camille Flammarion's *L'atmosphère: météorologie populaire* (1888). Color added by Heikenwaelder Hugo, 1988.

Plate 7. Hildegard dictating to her scribe
(illustration from the Liver Scivias)

Plate 8. "Tartini's Dream" (1824) by Louis-Leopold Boilly, illustrating the legend behind Guiseppe Tartinit's "Devil's Trill Sonata"

Plate 9. Dante Gabriel Rossetti's painting *Dante's Dream at the Time of the Death of Beatrice.* Oil on canvas. First version created in 1871; this photograph is of the 1880 version.

A Dream

Once a dream did weave a shade.
O'er my Angel-guarded bed.
That an Emmet lost it's way
Where on grafs methought I lay.

Troubled wilderd and forlorn
Dark benighted travel-worn.
Over many a tangled spray.
All heart-broke I heard her say.

O my children! do they cry
Do they hear their father sigh.
Now they look abroad to see.
Now return and weep for me.

Pitying I dropd a tear:
But I saw a glow-worm near:
Who replied. What wailing wight
Calls the watchman of the night.

I am set to light the ground,
While the beetle goes his round:
Follow now the beetles hum,
Little wanderer hie thee home.

Plate 10. Blake's image, "A Dream," is one example of the visionary quality of his work.

Plate 11. *The Dream,* 1883 painting by Puvis de Chavannes-Orsay. In his sleep, the dreamer is visited by three women representing love, glory, and fortune.

She gave me a big hug and walked off into the snowy night. I got in my truck and began the five-mile drive home. About a mile into the drive, I just started crying, thinking of all the young people, all the psychology students across the country, who feel so betrayed and disappointed by psychology, like the young woman I had just met. I felt heartbroken for the field of psychology and so grateful that Jung had come into my life.

A few days later, I was driving Shams into Burlington again, and I told him about the young woman on the bus and how sad I was about her and the state of psychology. Shams immediately responded by saying, "So you met the woman from the dream [about Jung dying]." That felt so right when he said it. We then had a profound conversation about the dream, about how my life was feeling dried up with all my duties as dean, and how Jung was dead for me but alive for the fiery, young, redheaded feminine presence in my dream and for the young woman student on the bus.

It seemed as though the dream was trying to tell me this, but I hadn't paid attention. Thus did the psyche send the young woman in the dark bus and the eager young social worker, asking me beginner's mind questions and my colleague, Shams, to create a dreamlike event. They awakened *my* beginner's mind in relation to Jung and my own inner life.

Within a few months I resigned as dean and began teaching and working with Jungian psychology again full time. Leaving that job and returning to the country of my soul may have been what Jung meant by the ethical demand of the dream. "What are you going to do about this dream?" "How are you going to live this dream in your waking life?"

Dreams That Can Cross Continents

I underwent analysis for a number of years with the Jungian analyst Dr. Renée Nell, founder of the Jungian residential treatment center, The Country Place, in Litchfield, Connecticut, where I later worked. What I learned from Dr. Nell in analysis—from working at The Country Place with residents, from countless supervision sessions and staff meetings, and from many hours of informal conversation—taught me more about myself and the world of dreams than did anything else in my life. Dr. Nell had been a pupil of Jung's in Switzerland (and, in fact, an analysand of Dr. E. C. Whitmont, Stephen's mentor) and was herself a master of dreamwork.

From my own experience and the testimonies of many others, the best way to learn about dreams is to work with your own dreams, with a person as knowledgeable of the dreamworld as Dr. Nell or Whitmont. My thought on this is that every dream is always about dreams and dreaming, like every good poem is about poetry. No matter what other meaning we gather from the dream, we can learn about the nature of dreams from the dream itself.

As a result of our working together on so many levels, Dr. Nell and I developed a very close relationship, and I felt a deep gratitude and indebtedness for all she gave. I left The Country Place after a few years and moved to Denman Island, British Columbia, to start a community with old friends with whom I had spent years in the monastery. I continued to work on my dreams. Early one morning I was awakened by a dream that forever changed my understanding of the power and possibility of the dreamworld.

I am in the small conference center on the grounds of The Country Place where Renée Nell taught courses on dreams and Jungian psychology. I am standing at a distance watching as Renée is about to begin a seminar on dreams. She is in a circle with approximately a dozen students. Just as she is about to begin, Joni, the cook at The Country Place, comes out of the kitchen and says, "You have an important phone call, Renée." Renée gets up and goes to the kitchen to take the phone call. I somehow know that the phone call is about the death of her brother, her only living relative. A moment later, Renée comes out of the kitchen and I walk up to her as she heads back toward her chair. I say, "I am very sorry to hear about your brother's death," and I give her a warm hug. Renée heads back to her chair and begins the dream seminar.

I had the feeling that the dream woke me up, rather than that I woke up after the dream. I immediately wrote the dream down, which was not unusual; recording my dreams was something I did regularly. The dream stayed with me. I reflected on it and wrote about it in my journal but made few connections and got little from the dreamwork I did.

A few months later, I went back East to visit family and friends. When I was in Connecticut, I gave Renée a call and we decided to have dinner together. At some point during dinner Renée asked me if I'd had any interesting dreams lately. This was not an unusual question. It was a question she had asked me many times over the years we'd worked together and dreams were very much at the heart of our relationship.

At that moment I remembered the dream I'd had of her and the phone call about her brother's death. I took my journal out of my shoulder bag, which I carry with me all the time, and found the dream and told it to Renée. When I finished she asked me what the date of the dream was. I told her the date, and she pulled out her appointment book, looked at me, and said, "That's exactly what was happening that morning at the conference center. Just as in your dream, I was about to start the dream seminar, and Joni told me that I had a phone call. And the phone call was about my brother's death. But what I find most interesting about the dream is that as I came out of the kitchen I planned to tell the group I could not continue with the dream seminar; I needed to take a break and think about the difficult news I had just received. But somewhere between the kitchen door and my chair something happened. I received some kind of strength, and I knew I could continue teaching. Now I know where that strength came from; it came from you."

Renée got up from her place at the table and came around to my side and gave me a big hug and said, "Thank you very much."

I do not know how to explain this experience. Nor do I know what the answer is to questions like "How can you be in British Columbia and see something happening in Litchfield, Connecticut?" or "Is this an out-of-body experience?" or the many other questions that come from an experience like this. I am not inclined to explain it, for any explanation seems less powerful and inspiring than the experience itself.

Mary Oliver in her poem "Snake" says: "There are so many stories, more beautiful than answers."[1]

That night in the restaurant, while Renée and I continued with our dinner, we talked about the dream. I remember saying to her that it reminded me of those scenes in the Superman movies. Clark Kent is walking along the street minding his own business, and he picks up somehow that someone is in trouble somewhere in Metropolis. He then runs into the phone booth, or ducks into an alley, changes into his Superman outfit, and flies off to rescue the person in need. I remember saying to Renée, "The way I think of it is you gave me so much, you helped me so much in so many ways, I owe so much to you. It was as if in the dreamworld, my antennae somehow picked up that you were in need, and I flew to bring you help."

We spoke of the many implications of the idea that we can help others in our dreams. "Does that mean if there is white magic," Renée said, "there is also black magic; can we harm others in our dreams?" We talked of soul travel and out-of-body experiences and many other things. But when all was said and done, my only conclusion from this dream experience was that there is more going on than meets the eye, and the dreamworld is full of mysterious and powerful possibilities.

This experience was one of the most powerful and instructive events of my life. In the literature on psychic phenomena and dreaming, there are thousands of stories similar to this dream of mine in which I seem to be, in some mysterious way, in two places at the same time. These dreams in the literature range from dreams of a person waking up in the middle of the night from a dream of a burning house and calling her daughter a thousand miles away to find out that the daughter's house is on fire. The phone call awakens the daughter in time for her to get herself and her children out of the burning house, saving their lives. These are dream miracles, and I am in awe of what they tell me about the power and possibility, the magic and mystery, of the human psyche. (We discuss this in more detail in chapter 7.)

Our psyche, our consciousness, does not seem to be contained or restricted by the envelope of our physical bodies. Our psyche, *the soul, does not appear to be inside me,* as the good sisters of St. Anne's parochial school taught me those many years ago. *Rather, I seem to be inside the soul.* Once again, and it bears repeating, as the poet Novalis writes, "The seat of the soul is where the inner world and the outer world meet. Where they overlap, the soul is in every point of the overlap."[2] Dreams are one of the most eloquent and creative voices of our soul. They come to us every night, inviting us into this mysterious and magical landscape to live our lives from that endless depth of soul that Heraclitus (circa 535–475 BCE) wrote about when he said, "You could never discover the limits of the soul, even if you traveled every road to do so; such is the depth of its meaning."[3]

Guidance from the Dream World Heads Off Possible Inner and Outer Tragedy
In the Words of Coauthor Stephen Larsen

At one point Tom worked with a woman on a frightening dream of hers. When I heard the dream and the dreamwork he undertook to do with her, I was struck by how closely Tom simulated the Dream Portal Method that I had learned from Christopher and that Tom had probably learned from Renée. I was also impressed at how Tom interpreted the dream in such a way so as not only to benefit but also perhaps to actually save, the woman's life.

We'll relay this woman's dream and the ensuing dreamwork and conclude with a dialogue between Tom and Stephen.

> *I am coming down an exit ramp from the highway and my brakes fail. It is a dangerous situation because the exit ramp makes a T with Sigourney Street, a busy cross street in the city. I am going too fast and feel out of control as I careen toward the crossing traffic. I wake up frightened.*

Tom: So, how's your car?
Dreamer: [The dreamer laughs.] Good, so far as I know.

Tom: On a very practical level, the dream might be saying that you should have your brakes checked.

Dreamer: They seem to be fine, but I am scheduled to have my car worked on this coming week and I will make sure the brakes are checked.

Tom: Okay, just interested in your safety, in case the dream is trying to also tell you something practical. But tell me about Sigourney Street.

Dreamer: Well, it is a very busy street downtown. It would be terrible to have my brakes fail right there!

Tom: Any other connections with Sigourney Street?

Dreamer: I exit there when I visit John, my boyfriend.

Tom: How is the relationship going?

Dreamer: Well, we have been going together for a little while now, and it feels great in many ways. We really like each other, but it feels like it's going kind of fast for me. [*The dreamer says this without making any connection to the dream.*]

Tom: Feels like it's going kind of fast?

Dreamer: Yeah. We both really like each other, but I always seem to get into relationships and I get serious too fast and then I feel overwhelmed and out of control, and then I end the relationship because I feel too much pressure. This happens over and over.

Tom: Well, how long have you been feeling that things were going too fast?

Dreamer: Awhile now. But it's been hard to talk about, because we really do like each other and I'm frightened that he will feel that I'm saying I don't like him and he will want to end it.

Tom: It might be hard to put on the brakes on this thing, because of its forward motion and all of your conflicted feelings. Maybe you could just try talking to him about how you do this going too fast thing in relationships, and you don't want to blow it this time. Think that might be possible?

Dreamer: That would be hard for me to do, but I think it would be good for me and I might not have to run away this time.

Tom: What would it mean if you put on the brakes and slowed things down a bit? Do you feel frightened, like in the dream? Out of control and frightened?

Dreamer: [She laughs at the words I'm using as she understands the connection to the dream.] Oh . . . I get it! [*She then becomes very emotional—ambushed—it would seem, out of nowhere, by intense emotions.*] I do really love him, but we need to talk, and take our time, or I'm gonna crash like almost happened in the dream. I really want this to work this time. We really need to talk. [*At this point she is sobbing.*]

Tom: I think that might be one of the things the dream is asking you to do.

At this point the session ended, to be resumed the following week. The following week, the session continued.

Tom: How are you?

Dreamer: [*She has a funny look on her face.*] I'm okay. I had that talk with John; it was very helpful! We're going to back off on the relationship a little. Not end it, just slow it down a bit. Funny thing, he was feeling the same way. He was a little frightened by my getting so serious so fast; feeling pressured and wanted to talk about going a little slower. But you know what else? I took my car in to be checked out and asked them to check the brakes like you suggested. And you know what? The brakes weren't okay at all. The guy said, "They're not safe to drive with—metal on metal, there are no pads! You might have a brake failure. They need to be replaced right away!"

Tom: I only suggested that you have them checked because the dream seemed to be suggesting that. You are finding out that the more you work with your dreams, there seems to be someone inside you who is looking out for you in lots of ways. Let's talk about you and John and that going too fast and being out of control business.

The rest of the session, and many other sessions with this woman, were spent working on her relationship issues.

In collaborating on this book, we coauthors often sit and look at each other with mutual respect and not a little humor. We have spent many hours of many days speaking about dreams and dreaming over the long years of our friendship, and we certainly have had many marvelous conversations. The following is an excerpt from one of those conversations, in regard to the Sigourney Street dream.

STEPHEN: So did you save her psyche or her life?

TOM: Neither. It was the dream that did it!

STEPHEN: Yup. Good that you were *listening* [laughter between two old friends] to the dream!

TOM: The dream can speak to us on different levels at the same time. That is part of its creativity. I'd known about this for years, but had never seen such a clear example of it. Try to imagine the dream creation process (during the sleep time that leads up to the dream) as a group of story editors sitting around a table coming up with ideas for a film.

Here's how it might have gone with this dream.

The person at the table who thinks this dreamer's relationship with her relatively new boyfriend is the most important issue the dream should deal with might say, "We have to talk with her in the dream about her relationship with John because she's doing it again. She is going too fast, and she is beginning to feel out of control again and she will end another relationship."

The practical-minded one at the table might say, "If we don't get her to fix her brakes on her car, she won't have to worry about her relationship with John; she'll get killed. It's metal against metal with her brakes at the moment."

(The clock is ticking and it's getting closer and closer to the time the woman will begin her REM sleep—they need to come up with a dream!)

The creative one sitting at the table says, "Let's have her driving along Route 84 and get off at the Sigourney Street exit, the exit she takes to go to John's house. She'll come down that steep exit with the traffic light at the bottom, and then she'll go to put on her brakes and they won't work. She'll go speeding toward the cross traffic and wake up terrified." Here the creative and caring dream maker inside has come up with a dream that speaks to us on different levels.

On the conscious level the dream subject was going about her daily life, dealing with the things she had to deal with, but not thinking about the brakes. Instead, she was thinking about work or her relationship with John, or this or that; "highway hypnosis" we could call it. But each time the dreamer put her foot down, something wasn't quite right. Her foot "knew" the brakes were bad and this information came out in the dream.

STEPHEN: That is what the good Dr. [Freud] called *der unbewisst. Wissen* is the German verb for "to know something." It later made it into English translation and literature as "the unconscious," a noun, as if it was a place, instead of "all the things we're not aware of."

TOM: We're surrounded by things that we may not (that is, our ego-dominated self) notice, but *something* in us does. It notices, for example, that the brakes are not working well, even though "I" haven't consciously registered this.

STEPHEN: It's possible that the dream knows something we don't. It has access to that. This is why in "indwelling" a dream, we might have to take other perspectives than "I" or the usual ego. [This will come up again in chapter 10.]

TOM: Exactly. The dream also appears to have noticed that if I don't put a brake on this relationship, a crash is coming, and it may not be pretty, if not downright dangerous, psychologically.

STEPHEN: Is that what Jung talked about as the "compensatory" quality of dreams?

TOM: I would say so! It's all the stuff our little ego-awareness has missed, but it's there in the larger field of our "knowing." To be balanced and whole, not one-sided as Jung would see it and say it, we need to take these other perspectives, these other parts of ourselves into account. And one of the most creative and helpful ways these other parts of us speak to us is through the dream.

STEPHEN: This is a wonderful example, which I think will also speak to the readers of our book! And congratulations for your therapeutic acumen!

Postscript

This and the previous chapter, 5 and 6, are the autobiographical ones in this book. Chapter 5 chronicles Stephen's journey of becoming a dream analyst, and chapter 6 is Tom's: parallel lives in different geographies and culture zones. One author was raised Protestant, the other Catholic, but they arrive in friendship with a common respect for the dream and for the wise and living depths of the psyche. It is clear that the influence of Carl Jung on each author has been profound—yet they are in no way the same. Neither one of them is an officially shriven Jungian analyst. This could be seen as a tribute to Jung, for without an official structure or legacy, the ideas and the creativity of Jung live on in their work.

Our next destination steps off from some of the themes discussed herein that verge on the miraculous. Though our (mostly modern Western) culture has dismissed these elements that break through our contemporary prejudices, they are (and always have been) at home in the realm of dreams.

Part Two

Dreams Unite and Inspire Us

7

Precognition, Telepathy, and Synchronicity in Dreams

Signs and Wonders

In our opening chapter, "Ancient Dreaming," we looked at how dreams were regarded by our ancestors and the cultures in which they lived. Shamans in preliterate societies used dreams to track the movements of game or the encroachments of enemy tribesmen and the coming of storms or earthquakes (vital knowledge not available through ordinary forms of knowing).

In historical times, as far back as the Vedic, Egyptian, or Sumero-Babylonian worlds, dreams were expected to be oracular and prophetic, sent by gods or other supernatural beings to humans. Babylonian and Egyptian dreamers sought magical assistance to give baleful dreams better outcomes, or thwart the will of the demons in which their land abounded. Dreams could send a state to war or predict the outcome of it. This was true in Constantine's vision of the cross that read, "By this symbol you will conquer" (*in hox signo vinces*), and his dream of a radiant young man who encouraged him to go bravely against the numerically superior army of Maxentius the Usurper. Against all odds, he and his army did just that, and Constantine became the first Christian emperor of Rome.

In the Bible, both the Hebrew scriptures and the Christian scriptures contain more than seventy references to dreams. The two most famous instances are the Hebrew slave Joseph's interpretation of Pharaoh's dream, which had confounded Pharoah's counselors. The dream was of seven lean kine (cattle) devouring seven fat kine, and the same symbolic exchange reiterated with sheaves of wheat. Joseph, known for his youthful wisdom, interpreted that seven years of plenty would be followed by seven years of famine—Pharaoh, as ruler, was dreaming precognitively for the whole land of Egypt. The dream proved to be providential. Joseph would be recognized as a prophet and visionary and rise to high prominence in Pharaoh's court.

In a later captivity tale of the Hebrews, the Babylonian king Nebuchadnezzar was an even less-pleasant ruler than Pharaoh. Having a big dream in the second year of his reign that troubled him greatly, he summoned the magicians, enchanters, sorcerers, and astrologers of his land and laid on them a doubly difficult task. By extrasensory perception they first had to *guess his dream and then interpret it for him.* This story is recounted in the Bible, in Daniel 2 (NIV). The king said to the astrologers, "This is what I have firmly decided: If you do not tell me what my dream was and interpret it, I will have you cut into pieces and your houses turned into piles of rubble."

When the wise men of Babylon complained that "only the gods could do such a difficult thing, and they no longer dwelt among men," Nebuchadnezzar ordered them all put to death. Then Daniel, a man from among the Jewish exiles in Babylonian captivity, came before the king, told him he should not execute the wise men of Babylon, and claimed that God had not only sent him the same dream but also revealed its meaning. "There is a God in Heaven who has shown the king what is to happen in days to come."

Daniel then told Nebuchadnezzar his own dream (which has been famous for well over two thousand years).

Your Majesty looked, and there before you stood a large statue—an enormous, dazzling statue, awesome in appearance. The head of the statue was made of pure gold, its chest and arms of silver, its belly and thighs of bronze, its legs of iron, its feet partly of iron and partly of baked clay. While you were watching, a rock was cut out, but not by human hands. It struck the statue on its feet of iron and clay and smashed them. Then the iron, the clay, the bronze, the silver and the gold were all broken to pieces and became like chaff on a threshing floor in the summer. The wind swept them away without leaving a trace. But the rock that struck the statue became a huge mountain and filled the whole earth. (Daniel 2:31–35; NIV)

Daniel then interprets the dream for the king and praises him, the king, to be "the head of gold" followed by ever less valuable substances, as kingdom follows kingdom, down throughout history.

Nebuchadnezzar not only rewards Daniel for the miraculous interpretation but also falls at his feet, saying, "Surely your God is the God of gods, and the Lord of kings and a revealer of mysteries, for you were able to reveal this mystery" (Daniel 2:47; NIV).

A later dream of Nebuchadnezzar features a great tree that is cut down. Daniel is again summoned and plainly announces that this dream prophesies the demise of the king, which indeed comes to pass. "Immediately what had been said about Nebuchadnezzar was fulfilled. He was driven away from people and ate grass like the ox. His body was drenched with the dew of heaven until his hair grew like the feathers of an eagle and his nails like the claws of a bird. . . .

"At the end of that time, I, Nebuchadnezzar, raised my eyes toward heaven, and my sanity was restored. Then I praised the Most High; I honored and glorified him who lives forever" (Daniel 4:33–34; NIV).

Skeptics could regard this story as Judaic propaganda, but it is, after approximately twenty-five hundred years, very specific as to the sequence of events, the people, their characters, and the great *metanoia* (change of mind and heart) that comes at last to the megalomaniac Babylonian king. This story also exemplifies the didactic, or *anagogic* function of dreaming, as well as its paranormal dimensions (for which the book of Daniel is renowned), including Daniel's either telepathic mind reading of, or the clairvoyant seeing of, the king's dream.

Precognitive Dreaming in the Christian Era

The Christian scriptures of the Bible begin with the visitation of the magi to witness and worship the birth of the new world Messiah (Jesus). Led by a star, the Wise Men journey from their home (probably in Persia) to Bethlehem. The latter city is under affliction from Herod, a cruel tyrant-king who wishes to destroy the prophesied "king" who he fears will replace him and his dynasty. In a terrible paranoia, Herod orders the slaughter of the innocents, causing wailing and lamentation over all of Bethlehem and Judea. The magi had received a type of pseudo-hospitality from Herod, who suggested that, should they find the child Messiah, they should tell him so that he too could "come and worship him." Of course, Herod had very different intentions, which he concealed. But the Wise Men, "warned in a dream not to go back to Herod, they returned to their country by another route" (Matthew 2:12; NIV).

In about 168 CE, the Christian prelate Polycarp of Smyrna was sent a dream (by God, the text reassures us) that prefigured his own martyr-dom. In the dream, as he lay in bed, his own pillow burst into flames. He interpreted this to be a prediction of his own death, which was liter-ally borne out a short time later, when, because his Christian teachings were against the Roman State religion, he was condemned to death.[1]

First the Roman judge who was trying his case offered to have him torn apart by wild beasts, but Polycarp's faith was great, and, willing to embrace martyrdom, he said, "Bring them on." The judge became so angry that he condemned the prelate to be devoured by fire. Then something evidently paranormal happened. As they sought to burn him "the flames arched around Polycarp like a sail of a ship filled with wind and he would not burn. After some time, the command was given to the executioner to stab him with a sword, so he did. The result was that so much blood flowed from the wound that it extinguished the fire. The Judge, refusing to be dissuaded by these signs that he should not martyr Polycarp, the fire was rekindled and [finally] Polycarp's body was burned to ashes."[2] (Of course, the Christians who were present were strengthened in their faith by the forgoing wonders.)

Tradition has it that St. Augustine's eventual conversion to Christianity (after flirtations with Manicheism and other religions of the time) was prophesied in a dream to his mother, Monica. "By a dream, this devout woman was consoled in a time of anxiety," Augustine later wrote in his *Confessions*.[3] Augustine would record many dreams after his post-conversion period, saying that, in addition to knowledge derived through the senses (a la Aristotle), that "autonomous spiritual realities" showed themselves in dreams, such as angels delivering blessings or annunciations, on the one hand, and demons, luring the soul to infernal delights, on the other.

St. Thomas Aquinas, regarded as the great rationalist of the Middle Ages, who attempted a synthesis of Christianity and Aristotelian thought, was at work on his monumental *Summa Theologica* when a dream came to him in which he experienced the apostle Peter and the great convert, Paul, who came to help him to elucidate and clarify a theological problem that he had been having trouble with. This was followed by a vision, life-changing enough that he abandoned his work. "I can do no more," he declared. "Such things have been revealed to me, that all I have written seemed like straw, and I now await the end of my life."[4]

Remarkable Women Dreamers

As we researched clairvoyant women dreamers throughout history, we first came across the twelfth-century visionary dreamer Hildegard of Bingen, by whose music we have been inspired for years. We were intensely moved by her powerful story, which, for various reasons, we have situated in chapter 9, "The Cauldron of Inexhaustible Gifts." (The reader is welcome to jump ahead if you wish!)

Robert Moss, in a book both scholarly and groundbreaking—titled *A Secret History of Dreaming*—has performed a great service for us (the writer and the readers as well). He has recorded three wonderful stories of visionary women dreamers in historical succession. What is especially remarkable about each of the three is how their visionary and dream lives empowered them at times when women were severely disadvantaged in every social theater. We offer these stories to you in highly abbreviated form but suggest that you go to his thoroughly researched book (he began his academic career as a history professor) for the fascinating details.

France's Joan of Arc

The first story occurs a couple of centuries after Hildegard—who herself narrowly escaped being tried for heresy (for her creative dreaming)—to the legends and history of Joan of Arc, the Maid of Orleans, whom Moss refers to by her French name, Jehanne. The author promises, at the beginning of his chapter on Joan to present her free from the veils of propaganda and hagiography. He succeeds admirably in this, and much more, weaving stories of her dream life with those of her uncanny success as a visionary soldier and charismatic leader.

Jehanne herself, he writes, appeared in her father's dreams, even as a child, "riding off with men at arms. The father was horrified by these dreams, assuming that they meant his daughter was going to become a camp whore. Nice girls did not go away with soldiers, still less did they command them."[5]

The father told some friends that "if he had believed the dreams would come true, he would rather have drowned his daughter than see her shamed."[6] Nonetheless she was an obedient and modest child, regularly churchgoing—but, as Moss adds, "she also attended a church without walls."[7]

Jehanne later told judges of the Inquisition (who had put her on trial) that if she was in a wood, such as a grove of trees surrounding an ancient beech—the Lady Tree—she could hear the Voice that spoke to her clearly. Many times she perceived an angelic form that came to her. She later identified this form as St. Michael, the angel with the sword standing astride Mont St. Michel who rules the outcome of battles.

At the time that Jehanne arrived on the scene of the seemingly interminable and bloody Hundred Years' War, the English had used their longbows and greater battle discipline to easily rout the French (as they did in the famed Battle of Agincourt). But the coming of the Maid and the patriotic power of her visions began to swing the tide the other way. When she first visited the tough battle-hardened baron of Vaucoleurs, named Baudricort, Moss mentioned that he considered giving her to his men for sport. Instead he sent her back to her father for a flogging. A few months later she returned, this time with military intelligence of an event happening as she stood before him and of which she could not have known except by clairvoyance (or the whispering voice the Maid heard ceaselessly). She told Baudricort of another defeat of the French by the English Burgundians, which was borne out in exact detail when the news arrived a few days later.

When she persuaded the insecure young dauphin that he was destined to be a great king who would succeed his father (the second Charles), her charisma was great enough to enable her to be appointed the general of the French army. Moss says of the hard men who came to follow her, "she won them by producing military intelligence, they could not obtain by other means. This helps us understand how she persuaded rough soldiers and degenerate nobles to follow her."[8] She would live to see Charles crowned king and to win the battle of Patay (on June 18, 1429), which was decisive in dispiriting the English still further. This battle ended in the capture of one of the commanders, Talbot, and the disgracing of the other, Fostolf. (Moss speculates something no other historian has dared—that the sudden and unexpected appearance of the great stag that revealed the trap being set by the British archers, and ended the battle in favor of the French, was a paranormal event precipitated by Jehanne's charisma.)

Moss goes on to surmise that it was when Jehanne abandoned her visionary guidance and began listening to her human counselors that her fortunes took a turn for the worse. She was defeated in an attempt to take Paris, and following several other battles, her fate was sealed. History has meticulously recorded the unfair trial that led to her capture and her final execution at the stake—for the unforgivable crime, it seems, of wearing men's clothing!

Spain's Lucrecia de Leon

The sixteenth-century Lucrecia de Leon, the "dream seer," or *Vidente*, of Madrid, was so accurate in her clairvoyance and precognition that she was used by the Spanish government for political espionage, especially after her dreams not only proved true but also were perhaps relevant to affairs of state.

Moss writes:

> Like Jehanne, Lucrecia de Leon manifested her gift on the edge of puberty. When she was twelve she spoke to her family about a dream of a royal death. The location was quite specific. It was the town of Badajoz on the road to Lisbon that the king was traveling. She described the black-draped horses and the catafalque of the royal funeral. Her father, Alfonso Franco, a solicitor, was terrified. To dream of the death of the king could be interpreted as treason. And even though the girl thought the royal funeral in her dream was not for Phillip, the shadow fell close enough. So Lucrecia's father beat her and ordered her not to dream again. The news came two weeks later that a royal had died in Badajoz; not Phillip II, but his queen, Anne of Austria. Now the family knew that Lucrecia's gift was real, but this did not improve her father's attitude.[9]

An "Ordinary man" as she called him, showed up recurrently in Lucrecia's dreams, acting as a psychopomp, or dream guide. "On January 16, 1588, the Ordinary man told her that the Marquis of Santa Cruz, the man originally appointed to command the Spanish Armada, would die within weeks; the Marquis died on February 9, three weeks later. As early as late November, 1587, and again in mid-December, she saw the English defeating the Spanish Armada. When [against all expectations and with the intervention of a freaky, violent storm] that vision was fulfilled in the summer of 1588, a lot of people began to see Lucrecia as a prophet, and a cult began to grow around her."[10] Eventually, Lucrecia also ended up in the hands of the Inquisition; they did not burn her like Jehanne but instead flogged her severely for her (potentially very dangerous) dreaming and sent her to a cloister.[11]

America's Harriet Tubman

Just before and during the American Civil War, the woman we now know as Harriet Tubman—thrice disadvantaged by being female, being black, and being a slave in the slave-owning South—utilized clairvoyant dreams. Initially they were employed for her own escape. Later, on her peril-fraught missions, many of them were helpful in guiding other slaves out of the South to safety and freedom in the North.

Tubman has been celebrated as a culture-hero for her miraculous exploits, bringing well over a hundred (by various estimates) black slaves out of captivity on the Underground Railroad. Biographies that made her justly famous in her own time, beginning with the one by Sarah Bradford, have struggled with her paranormal abilities. "I scarcely know how to report the spiritual experiences of my sable heroine," Bradford wrote in 1886.[12] "They seem to enter into the realm of the supernatural, that I can hardly wonder that those who never knew her are ready to throw discredit on the story."[13]

Robert Moss, in his book *A Secret History of Dreaming*, devotes a chapter to Harriet Tubman. Titled "The Underground Railway of Dreams," it does not shrink from the task of letting those paranormal abilities speak for themselves, and even offers his interpretation of how they came to be. He notes, as we will in just a little while, how these abilities stay alive in a disenfranchised people such as African Americans. The use of these abilities were vitally inseparable from their own ability to survive in a perilous environment.

Born Araminta Ross, Harriet Tubman was also called Minty. She was probably descended from the West African Ashanti people, who were known as dream trackers and visionaries who could fly in their dreams. Her father was known for his ability to see the future and was known to have predicted the Mexican-American War before it actually came to pass. (Araminta took her first name, Harriet, from her mother and the surname, Tubman, through an unhappy marriage to which she

Fig. 7.1. Harriet Tubman: Civil War heroine and clairvoyant extraordinaire (photo credit: Seymour Squire, 1885)

tried to remain loyal, until her husband totally rejected her by taking another wife.)

But this wasn't all that qualified Araminta as a clairvoyant seer. She suffered a terrible head injury at the age of twelve, "coming between an angry overseer and a boy who was trying to run away, and she took a two-pound lead weight full in the forehead. She died and came back."[14] The injury left her with a disfiguring hole in her forehead, which she often covered with a slouch hat. This brings up a feature of ESP and clairvoyant and precognitive dreaming well known to students of neurofeedback and consciousness (also mentioned in chapter 2 and the latter part of this chapter on Edgar Cayce). Head injuries can crack the cosmic egg, so to speak, and let in the secret whisperings of the universe.

For much of her mature life, especially as she was leading the slaves north, Tubman would suddenly fall into what appeared to be a fit of narcolepsy. Evidently she would leave her body, flying over the landscape to find her way in places she had never visited before. Often, in so doing, she would find a safe passage for the runaway slaves whom she was conducting to safety.

She met and befriended abolitionist John Brown, whose incident of capturing the Marine garrison at Harper's Ferry was pivotal in precipitating the Civil War. Moss notes in his writings on Tubman that she, in a premonitory dream, anticipated the death of Brown and his two sons by hanging. When the event actually happened, Tubman was many miles away. Tubman, who felt Brown was inspired by God, felt a "flutter in her chest" and knew that John Brown was dead.

Tubman seemed to know that the Emancipation Proclamation (1863) was coming—and people were surprised by her puzzling lack of jubilation at the actual announcement, considering how hard she had worked for it! In his very interesting article "African Americans and Predictive Dreams," in *Dream-Singers: The African American Way with Dreams,* dream researcher and author Anthony Shafton writes, "[Tubman] . . . accounted for her calmness when emancipation was proclaimed . . . by explaining that she had already done her celebrating three years earlier. One morning in 1860, the unerring conductress had arisen singing 'My people are free! My people are free!' She came down to breakfast singing the words in sort of ecstasy. She could not eat."[15] The dream or vision filled her whole soul, and physical needs were forgotten.

Her friends and colleagues were doubtful that glorious day would ever come, even in their own lifetimes, but Tubman had felt that President Lincoln "would do the right thing." (Lincoln was to dream of his own death, an event recorded in many biographies, several days before it happened. He heard lamentation in the White House and came downstairs to see a casket and hear the terrible announcement: "The President is Dead!"[16])

Harriet Tubman's remarkable dream clairvoyance and precognition allows us to introduce a subsequent section of this chapter. This section will take up the topic of how, when the culture of white males decides that things such as paranormal and precognitive dreams are fictions, not only women, but also an oppressed class in its entirety—African Americans—remains more open to the precognitive dimension of dreams than do Anglo folk.

Science and Spirituality: The Cultural Myth

From the eighteenth-century Enlightenment on, science had begun to emerge as the dominant paradigm (alternatively, "cultural myth" in the West). The laudable emphasis on meticulous observation and the control of causal variables led to breakthrough discoveries in every department of science. But the mythologem of the big picture kept getting in the way. That is to say that, if science could explain so many things, it could, perhaps, explain everything!

As early as the seventeenth century, Renèe Descartes had come to Sweden from his native France and had become influential in the intellectual life there, including making an enormous impact on the way university courses were taught. The theology faculty at Uppsala (officially in charge of big picture issues) became incensed. They appealed to the King of Sweden to outlaw the new rationalism and secularism. The king, Charles XII, was a bit of an intellectual himself—and a skilled compromiser. He would finally rule that while science and rationalism could be taught in some courses, they had to have a hands-off approach to theological questions and big picture issues.

The issue would come to a head in the nineteenth century with the publication of *The Origin of Species* by Charles Darwin in November of 1859. No one could avoid the implications of the paradox (or the paradigm clash). Was the scriptural account correct? Did God create the world seven thousand years ago, or did it evolve over hundreds of millions of years—as the fossil record seemed to indicate? The Scopes Trial of 1925 in Dayton, Tennessee, was a poignant eruption of the paradigm clash that lurked beneath every school, college, and university. It filtered into churches and homes and families—it goes on today!

The issue is too large to be discussed here, but for the mainstream culture, ninety years after Scopes, it is pretty evident that science has won! (That does leave out theological strongholds and cultures outside of the Western mainstream.) What is seldom discussed, however, even today, is the psychological issue of how science functions as a myth in cultures and in individual minds. At its best, science is *methodology:* it teaches us how to observe objectively, conduct experiments, and measure outcomes. Charles XII was right: science still has no business commenting on big picture issues—such as, what is the ultimate purpose of the universe, of life? It also ran sadly aground when it decided it could pronounce on things psychological—and ultimately spiritual. Is there a soul—in humans, in animals? Is there anything that survives death?

More importantly for our purposes, is it possible that we can communicate invisibly with other minds? Could we dream things that happen at a distance? Could our dreams predict things that have not yet happened? (These questions have nothing to do with whether God created the universe seven thousand years ago or whether God even exists in the usual way of thinking.)

Ultimately our methodology, like it or not, affects our myth. And what science do we believe in? Is it Newtonian-Cartesian tenth-grade science that we were exposed to in public education? Or is it the post-Einstein, postquantum mechanics science of all matter is really energy, of charmed quarks, probability theory, and indeterminacy? Given that most people, of course, have neither the inclination nor the ability to read the new physics, nor think through its real implications, we stay on the materialistic, mechanical level.

Post-Enlightenment engineering successes had us portraying almost all manner of processes, the human body as well as the psyche included—*as machines and as mechanical processes.* (Cause and effect.) Medicine, to its ultimate detriment, is still beleaguered by this metaphorical error. Our pharmaceuticals make certain things happen while ignoring others. If something doesn't work, we double the dose or add more force. Then, if an organ doesn't work properly, we surgically remove it! There is little or no concept that we are working with exquisite, dynamic self-regulating systems that don't need powerful shoves and pushes.

In the realm of the psyche and the energy fields in which we all live and move, the effect is even more pernicious: Freudian psychodynamics operated by hydrological or chemical metaphors—suppression, condensation, displacement, sublimation—and so on and so forth. Dreams were portrayed as always distorted (because we can't stand the psychological truth represented by the primitive id—or the global censorship of the superego).

Hobson and McCarley (in chapter 2) seemed to pull the rug out from under this model—or myth, really—because it was *psychodynamically* based but *neurobiologically* naive. (No neurosurgeon has yet found the id, ego, or superego.) And while we commend the neurological sophistication of the activation-synthesis model, it too is dogged by the same materialistic fundamentalism. The higher centers are simply doing their best to make sense of the random firing of the brain stem or thalamic nuclei, with their own circuits. But, as we showed in chapter 2, this model lacks a systems theory approach in which the whole brain cooperates like a symphony to produce the dream. (Is it not a type of materialistic fundamentalism to trace all processes merely to physical structures?) Are we not enmeshed, like it or not, in a web of life that extends to other beings, human and nonhuman, and even other times and places?

We think you will have noticed by now that the authors of this book answer those questions in the affirmative. Immediately the scientifically socialized (or the officially skeptical) inquirers will say, "Nonsense, prove it!" Excuse us for what may seem a digression, but we will try to make it brief and to the point and, below, ask the question, "By what criteria shall we prove it?" (By most normal criteria, determining common sense and by the reports of thousands of sources—a relatively few of which are cited in these pages. Thus, the answer is: "The case is closed!") Humans have all kinds of ESP knowledge—information that *does not pass through the five senses*. What is sometimes called "paranormal," we think, should just simply be called "normal."

The Society for Psychical Research was founded in Great Britain in 1886. The world of that time, 130 years ago, was very concerned with the big picture conflict to which we have alluded. Many people were believers in a spiritual universe, prayer, psychic healing, mediumship, and the survival of the soul after physical death. Even the well-educated and scientifically oriented were, for the most part, Christian churchgoers.

With science came a way of thinking that directly seemed to contradict extrasensory perception of any kind. The difference between the narrative of the individual experience, on the one hand, and the demands of science—deliberately controlled circumstances, replicability, and statistical significance—on the other, have dogged parapsychological research since the beginning. Many people—including the British parapsychologists and the American William James, William McDougall, and J. B. Rhine—have all tried the latter methodology. (Let's call this "Trying to prove the works of God to man.") In the face of these attempts, the accumulated cultural-historical evidence, starting from what is sometimes called "idiopathic" (single, personal experiences), as opposed to "nomothetic" (replicable studies with large sample sizes), is just enormous—and simply irrefutable. (This is for anyone who cares to read the evidence with a clear mind and a trust that human beings, by and large, tell the truth about what they have borne witness to.)

It is true that humanity is a race given to storytelling and mythmaking, but not really intentional fabrication or pathological lying (with the possible exception of diagnosed personality disorders, or certain politicians or corporations with vested interests!). Yet the skeptical inquirers or materialistic fundamentalists among us have chosen to regard any accounts of the paranormal as deliberate falsification or propaganda.

Phantasms of the Living

In 1886, three of the founders of the Society for Psychical Research—E. Gurney, F. W. H. Myers, and F. Podmore—published their historic work, *Phantasms of the Living*.

Among the 1,300 pages of case histories, the book contains

149 cases of dream telepathy. Myers defined the term *telepathy* as "the extrasensory communication of impressions of any kind from one mind to another." These men, write Jon Tolaas and Montague Ullman, "were astute investigators and were very exacting in their search for evidentiality."[17] They were professional parapsychologists and knew, even at the end of the nineteenth century, that their work would be scrutinized closely. Whether or not it met modern standards may be beside the point when you are dealing with the large number of people with these experiences that these men found. Among the 149 cases were the following common patterns.

- More than half of the dreams concerned the theme of death.
- Another large group was concerned with the occurrence of an emergency.
- A smaller group focused on trivial matters.
- In the majority of cases the agent-percipient pairs were either relatives or friends.
- The percipients generally had no special psychic experiences or abilities before the dream in question; these dreams were rare and puzzling experiences for them.

We began this chapter with examples of paranormal dreams through the ages. What you will read next are relatively recent cases only a century old, not several centuries old. However, both the single cases reported by or about those fortunate enough to be remembered by history meet the same criteria. They involve the imminence of death or catastrophe (the tragedy criteria) and/or are marked by connections between family members or good friends (the intimacy criteria). The authors would like to state that these criteria are resonant with the idea that the roots of telepathy may be found in the intimacy between mother and child.

To answer the criticism that skeptics might raise that this is due to chance, the authors of *Phantasms of the Living* distributed a questionnaire to 5,360 people asking if they had had a vivid dream of the death of someone known to them in the past twelve years. "Only one of every 26 persons queried had had such a dream, a fact that spoke against the chance hypothesis."[18]

Though precognition and telepathy are known to occur both waking and sleeping, the preponderance of evidence suggests that dreams account for the majority of such incidents. "In cultural surveys quoted, dreams (precognitive or telepathic) account for 64.6% of the 7119 cases reported by Rhine (1962), 63% of the 1000 cases reported by Sannwald (1959, a, b), 37% of the cases analyzed by Green (1960), 52.4% of the 900 experiences of Indian school children reported by Prasad and Stevenson (1968), and 38% of several hundred cases collected by Hanefeld (1868) and considered paranormal."[19] In the majority of cases, the authors note that *paranormal* means "precognitive." "Saltmarsh (1934) reported 281 cases of precognition, of which 116 occurred in dreams."[20]

The sheer volume of evidence accumulated over many years by many investigators, argues against the skeptical idea that the dreamers are all sociopaths or dupes. Although the majority of cases illustrate the intimacy criteria, when great catastrophes take place (the tragedy criteria) the intimacy criterion may or may not be met as well. "Stevenson reported ten cases of precognition related to the sinking of the Titanic [eight of which involved dreams]. Barker collected 35 cases of precognition of the Aberfan [UK] coal slide in 1965, 25 of which occurred in dreams."[21]

But the sheer weight of anecdotal evidence has never seemed enough to persuade those of critical or skeptical mind, so rigorous attempts to explore telepathy and dream telepathy under highly controlled circumstances have ensued. These include the REM monitoring technique using EMG and various physical recorders to measure EMG, GSR, and eye movement, for instance, as well as the EEG. Subjects slept in different rooms, and there was an attempt to transmit targets—usually pictures or drawings—from one subject to the next, as REM periods occurred. It should be noted that parapsychologists, including the famous J. B. Rhine, have not hesitated to introduce the most rigorous controls possible to:

- eliminate all possibilities of sensory cues relating to the target reaching the subject,
- arrange for an independent (blinded) outside judging of possible correspondences between target and dream, and
- work out appropriate statistical techniques to evaluate any matching processes.

Much of this work was carried out subsequent to the establishment of a dream laboratory at Maimonodes Medical Center in Brooklyn in 1962. The care that was taken to provide a controlled environment matches or exceeds controls in other social science studies. The fact that results were obtained without the criteria of intimacy or tragedy—or both—is astonishing. But like the all too carefully documented work of J. B. Rhine's laboratory at Duke University (which Stephen Larsen visited a few years ago), the scientific data mean nothing to those whose personal myth is already formed against the acceptance of such data. In other words, rejecting the null hypothesis, that the results were due to chance, means little or nothing, because they are only likely to accept such results when those results agree with their already formed hypothesis! (Anyone who disbelieves in scientific or materialistic forms of fundamentalism is directed to the later chapters of Stephen Larsen's *The Fundamentalist Mind*.)

CLAIRVOYANCE IN DREAMS

If you would like to undertake your own research, the following steps may help.

You might not be up to the stringent controls of the early parapsychology researchers, but what fun it might be to try a few clairvoyance experiments.

- Have a lover or friend read a book or poem, look at a painting, or listen to a piece of music while you are sleeping.
- Ask them to send you, with intent, while you are asleep, the

core feeling, narrative story, or melody you wish to dream about.

- Upon awakening, you can journal, hum, or write about whatever came to you, whatever works best for you, to better reflect what you have dreamed about.

- Compare notes with the person who was sending you the telepathy.

- Keep an open, symbolic mind to what might have "come across."

- Don't get easily discouraged—remember you are entering uncharted territory. Try this as many times as you wish!

- Exchange the favor and do it the other way around.

In the Words of Coauthor Stephen Larsen

Confirming Ullman and Krippner's Research

Since I have been working on this book in a serious, committed way, unanticipated phone calls or letters have come to me. They say, in one way or another, "I have to tell you this dream; I have to tell you what it meant to me, and how it came." True, these people know that I am an open and trusting psychologist of dreams, but they usually did not know that I was working on a book on dreams, nor a particular chapter on dreaming, nor a particular theme.

Below is a clinical example from Montague Ullman, that great pioneer of the past century, that leads almost seamlessly into several examples from my own practice. It demonstrates the developmental quality of the psyche undergoing a regimen of neurofeedback, and it speaks of how dreams break through the ordinary mind's concerns.

I had just found and begun to read the monograph by Dr. Montague Ullman (Stanley Krippner's collaborator at the aforementioned epochal Maimonides Medical Center Dream Research Laboratory in Brooklyn). The name of the monograph is "Dream Telepathy—Experimental and

Clinical Findings." In this published paper, Ullman reviews the literature in psychology and psychiatry, describes his own controlled experiments, and establishes the criteria for how we can judge a dream to be
truly telepathic (more on this later). He begins with one of these personal stories that is hard to explain and difficult to forget.

Dr. Ullman's Clear Case of Telepathy

The year was 1945. Dr. Ullman was not long back from having served
in World War II and was exploring clinical internships in clinical psychiatry, which included (often Freudian) training analysis. After he had
found an analyst who seemed to fit, he was moving along in his training analysis. The night before the following event, he dreamed of Nat,
another psychiatric trainee in the same clinical program who, in the
dream, was dancing onstage in a ballet. The dream seemed noteworthy
and rather whimsical to him because Nat was a heavyset man in his fif-
ties and anything but a ballet dancer.

Ullman dutifully brought the dream in to his psychoanalyst, and,
as he sat with the doctor (an M.D.), a phone call came that the analyst
took. The analyst laughed in a surprised way at what the inaudible voice
at the other end of the phone call was saying. It turned out that the call
was from Nat, who was working with the same analyst. Nat was reporting that, much to his surprise, he had auditioned for a role in a ballet at
the Metropolitan Opera House—and had been accepted, to everyone's
astonishment.

Ullman uses the incident not only to show the clear example of
telepathy but also to offer his own psychological explanation of why
it happened. Having a strong interest in the paranormal, and in fact
doing research on it, he was afraid that his therapist, an overtly "mate-
rialist Marxist," would look down on him. The incident, a rupture
of the ordinary space-time rules that occurred out of the blue, would
unequivocally demonstrate to the analyst that Ullman's interest was
something real and make him acceptable to the man, rather than
merely a weirdo.

To me, the remarkable thing about this story is its level of self-disclosure on the part of the writer, in which Ullman reveals himself as vulnerable to the analyst's approval—given his weird interests. Ullman goes on to say that, from other examples, he thinks that such instances occurring in therapy usually signify something about the transference (the relation between the patient and therapist), or some other fact of significance in either of their lives. (It is also a remarkable synchronicity in that the call came *before the end of the session,* as if to exclude any alternative explanation. *The psychiatrist has no choice but to marvel*—or open his mind in a new way!)[22]

This is the exact explanation often found in the writing of Jan van Ehrenwald, a Dutch psychiatrist who has written extensively on ESP in dreams. The evidence from psychotherapy mimics exactly the evidence from "real life." The normal boundaries that keep us from hearing the thoughts of other people and from feeling their feelings *are not ruptured except in exceptional circumstances*—a tragedy, a death, a great discovery. (Great discoveries, we know, often come to very different people in different countries at the same time. Sometimes people will come up with the same theory at the same time, or each be awarded a Nobel Prize for the same simultaneous discovery.)[23]

Common Ground: The Neurofeedback "Body Shop"

The day after I read and took in Ullman's paper, as I was researching this chapter, I went to my clinical office as usual, telling no one of my preoccupations. In the early afternoon I met with a Vietnam veteran, a man who had come to my practice as the proverbial basket case neurologically: he was an insomniac, with unremitting pain and fibromyalgia/fatigue from his many injuries and traumas. Yet after a year of treatment, the man had made remarkable progress. Instead of having to be driven the ninety miles each way to our center for his session, he was now driving himself. Instead of weakly slumping in the chair like a man without a skeleton, he sat up straight. Instead of limping across the floor, he walked in rather normally, looked me in the eye, and shook my hand. (These were the therapeutic effects of about forty sessions of neurofeedback spread over a year—see my books

The Healing Power of Neurofeedback and *The Neurofeedback Solution*.)
Occasionally I had asked him for a dream to help monitor his progress,
but we were focusing our treatment more on neurological healing than
on psychological healing.

The session was virtually over.

"Oh, by the way," he said, "you know how I've been dreaming about
that warehouse factory where I fix up old cars?"

"I remember," I said. "You often dream of it—and I've been so
happy with what you're telling me *of actually cleaning it up*—a sign that
you're making progress."

"Yup," he said, "and each time I dream—it often takes place in that
setting. The place is more and more fixed up too. Well, the one last
night really got my attention—"

*The place was really fixed up—a state-of-the-art body shop. The walls
were painted white; the tools were organized. It was great. We were
working on a Mercedes that I recall—in real life—I had done an
incredible job on. Then in came these teachers and students. I think
they were speaking German.*

I asked him how he felt on awakening. He said, "Great! I felt like
I'd really done something, accomplished something. I told my massage
therapist about the dream, and she said, 'You know—body shop?' I think
it's not only your body, but your brain that the dream is reflecting."

"She's a smart lady," I told him.

He smiled. "That's why I've been going to her for seventeen years—
and she's seen the amazing changes since I started neurofeedback, and I
can actually feel them in my body."

Now, I hadn't noticed during this exchange, but my clinical assistant
Heather—who helps me with the neurofeedback treatments—was in
the room. She was standing behind my patient and staring at us both
with wide eyes.

"Do you want to hear *my* dream?" she asked.

We both nodded in the affirmative.

Last night I dreamed of an old friend from the Pacific Northwest, Sy Mada, a Kalish Indian who often has trouble finding work. He had gotten a new job! He was in a state-of-the-art auto body shop, making a car out of a World War II plane—a German plane. It was purple and blue. I think people in the shop were speaking German. (We haven't been in touch in a year and half, and I was worried about him.)

The dream was so striking, Heather said, that she decided to look up her friend on Facebook the next morning. There it was, and she was astonished! It was all over his Facebook site: Sy had just gotten a job at a well-known body shop, Rat Custom Cars. He was delighted and bragging about it. "I wrote and congratulated him!" Heather told us. (We all laughed at the amazing coincidence. It was the end of a long, cold winter, and I think we needed some cheering up!)

On later reflection I remembered that Heather had also been badly head injured—attributing her sometimes uncanny psychic abilities in part to this—and she, as well as my Vietnam vet, needed a marker that they were well along in the healing process.

That excellent "body shop"—the neurofeedback therapy—had clearly done its work!

Shared Dreams of Waterslides and Other Simple Pleasures

My *next client the same day* was an artist, who is my near contemporary given that he was also born in 1941. His dream was very simple.

Someone has given me a tube. It is white and rolled up. When I unroll it, I realize it is a water slide. We start to play on it; it is a lot of fun!

Under ordinary circumstances, this would not have yielded a lot of content, but this gentleman and I, after some difficulty at the beginning of our relationship, had been bonding more and more—exchanging interesting extracurricular resources and books.

I must have gotten a strange smile on my face; and then I told him my own dream of the previous night.

I am at what seems like a conference center, which is very upscale. There I encounter this warm pool that goes down a waterslide to another pool. The warm water, the aesthetic environment—I can't resist. I go down the slide. Then I climb up what seems like a set of monkey bars to do it again!

The coincidence made us both laugh—we're both in our seventies playing on waterslides, on the same night, in our dreams!

My client had given me a book on Edgar Cayce's work on dreams. I had been holding off reading it because I thought it was a little unscientific. There was a section on telepathy in dreams, and he wanted me to read it, having just sent me an e-mail that pointed to the page and section. At the end of our session he looked at me intensely and said, "Read it!" He is a great fan of Cayce and had in fact known of my work on a book on dreams (but not that I was at that moment focused on precognitive and telepathic dreams). (We will be discussing Cayce further a little bit later in this book!)

In both cases, my patients had been through a successful course of therapy with me and would be leaving for a while to go traveling. I felt a connection with each one (incidentally, both of them were seventy-three years old—I had just turned seventy-four). It was as if each of them wanted to give me a gift in parting, to thank me for our work together and to demonstrate how successful it had been. I was very touched, and felt honored by these men.

Dreams of Chestnut and "Gold Stone"

The following day I visited a friend, the internationally renowned artist Carolee Schneemann (also in her seventies), who lives down the road in a beautiful 250-year-old, prerevolutionary stone house. As we sat at her writing desk, I told her about my work on the dream book.

"Oh, I wouldn't have gotten this house if it weren't for dreams," she said. "It was dreams that told me it should be mine."

Once again surprised (though by now I shouldn't be), I asked, "How was that?"

"The house was in dreadful shape," she said. "No one would want to live here. It was owned by a couple of elderly cousins of mine. It was an ugly, unappealing blocky house with linoleum floors. It had no heat and one tap of cold running water; that was about it."

"My husband, Jim, and I would come up from the city and sort of 'camp out' in it with sleeping bags, camp stoves, and the like. There is this sort of obnoxious guy who comes into my dreams and speaks in a coarse, harsh voice. He treats me as if I am very dumb and don't know anything."

One night I had a dream in which he appeared. This obnoxious guy said—speaking as if he were the house, "I am not what I seem to be, tear up the linoleum; you will find chestnut!"

"I was really nonplussed, but Jim and I did as he said: And there they were—these gorgeous sixteen-inch-wide chestnut boards [now visible on both floors of the house, as it is now]."

He came back a second time, and said, "Take a hammer and smash that cement [on the outside of the house]. You will find gold stone!"

"It looked so blocky and ugly, we never suspected it was really a classic Hudson valley stone house [in fact, it's one of the three prerevolutionary Huguenot houses that was allowed outside the New Paltz settlement]. We took the hammer and smashed the cement, and, much to our astonishment, found this beautiful stone that you see now—two-foot-thick walls. It took us years to chip most of the cement off, but the stone really was kind of 'golden!'"

He came a third time and said, "Take a hammer and smash open those ceilings—you will find chestnut!"

"It was scary to do that. I didn't how to fix a ceiling once you destroyed it, but we did it, and there they were—those beautiful beams that you see here today."

Fig. 7.2. Carolee Schneemann's prerevolutionary home near New Paltz, New York, with "buried gold"—beautiful eighteenth-century masonry— beneath the cement. Courtesy of the Artist.

*Fig. 7.3. Carolee Schneemann's chestnut floorboards
and ceiling beams revealed to her in a dream. Courtesy of the Artist.*

I was surprised and intrigued by just who this guy might be. "Does he remind you of anyone you have known?" I asked.

"Nope," she said. "I've never seen him; I just hear his voice. It always sounds the same—kind of gruff. He showed up when I was at the Gerson Clinic in Mexico getting treated for cancer. I had dreamed what I thought was a silly dream—of these young teenage girls in plaid skirts. His voice said, 'Welcome them, appreciate them, they are your lymphocytes!'" ("Allies in her healing" was how she interpreted it. In fact, she started to get better after that.)

Carolee shared more. "He even helps me in my art. I had this show honoring fourteen dead friends; it was called *Mortal Coils*. I had to design the coils. I did this and then projected videos about each of their lives. He told me to use three-quarter-inch manila rope and to have the motors that turn the coils go at exactly 6 RPM. Don't ask me why—but it worked! Lots of people have been to see that show and found it very moving!" (It was, in fact, an award-winning show, featured at major museums around the world!)

Just a couple of nights ago, I went to a retrospective at nearby Bard College where Carolee is an alumna. The show honored her, and thus

Fig. 7.4. Artwork derived from the dreams of Carolee Schneemann as featured in her show, Mortal Coils 1994–1995, at the Samuel Dorsky Museum at the State University of New York at New Paltz. This was a multimedia installation and featured four slide projector units with motorized mirror systems and seventeen motorized manila ropes. Photograph of Mortal Coils (1994) Multimedia Installation. Photo by Melissa Morton. Courtesy of the Artist.

was I able to see how major her impact—as a woman artist and as a performance artist who has changed the face of art in a male-dominated field—has been.

I Sheltered the Souls of Three Murdered People in My House

My friend Jim is a very mystical fellow. He has had more head injuries than you can count on both hands, and we've both joked that his intuitive abilities and rich dream life come, perhaps, from "cracks in the cosmic egg." He's an exhibiting artist and cultural creative from Kingston, New York. I expected a quirky story from Jim, and I got one.

According to Jim, "In 1976, I owned a shop in Sugarloaf, New York. My girlfriend and I had had an argument, and I went to sleep alone. I dreamed the following dream."

> There was a loud banging at the door. When I tried to turn the light on, I realized that I was kind of on the ceiling looking down. There were roses all over the floor. The door opened somehow, and three baby goats came running in. I guess they sheltered there for the night.

"It was strange, but I was okay with it! The next day the headlines screamed: 'Three Dead in Sugarloaf Shootout!' It involved the guy who had a shop across the alley from my shop. He had murdered his girlfriend, and then the police came. He shot one of them dead, between the eyes, and then the cops killed him. The bodies were put under blankets, lying in the street. It was an unexpected, unbelievable event!"

"I had no choice but to think that I sheltered those three people's spirits in the form of goats."

Bypassing the Boundaries of Time and Space

The above examples indicate a kind of passing-through of consciousness, where the classic Cartesian-Newtonian boundaries say it has no right to go. Why were we willing to put these three examples of nonordinary communication in a single chapter? Simply because there is a unitary reality underlying these three incidents.

Telepathy posits that our minds may communicate with each other. Famously, the sister of EEG-inventor Hans Berger did so when she dreamed of what she thought was her brother's demise—but which was in reality a very close call. It was a clearly emotional event. It is not certain whether it was only *clairvoyance*—a word that has earned its own right to currency in the French vocabulary—or *telepathy* (mind-to-mind communication). Whichever it was, Berger could not accept the coincidence explanation, and it set him off on a decade of research that ended with his invention of the EEG.

Taken together, these events—ideographic, not nomothetic—could shake modern science to its roots: Time and space are not the absolutes that certain minds among us have taken them to be! They are constructs, the absolute reality of which is as permeable as the rest of this universe in which "charmed quarks" call each other up on their (minuscule) cell phones and appear to be in contact across unfathomable gulfs of space.

Dreams reveal the metaphor—if not the truth—of this, by combining people from our ancient past with contemporaries; by predicting the future, by warnings and confirmations. Most importantly, dreams confirm that the universe itself is not dead but instead very much alive! *Dead* means that our minds could not possibly communicate with each other. *Dead* means that we are only accidental particles hurrying along through a continuum that is essentially material—particles colliding and leaving residues (the billiard table model of the universe).

We are back to the modeling of the universe with which we began. Is it alive or is it dead? Is it sentient or insensible? Are we the only intelligent beings in an unfathomable continuum, which we are just beginning to grasp? Are we the only beings who dream?

Or is the universe itself dreaming itself onward?

African Americans and Precognitive Dreams

The extraordinary and poignant story of Harriet Tubman raised questions in my mind. Was Tubman's clairvoyance and precognition merely an anomaly, or did it in some way characterize a whole (formerly captive and often socially disadvantaged) population: African Americans? The fascinating monograph by Anthony Shafton, quoted earlier as mentioning Tubman's premonitory knowledge of emancipation, helped to inform my views on this.

From my friend and mentor Vusamazulu Credo Mutwa, a Zulu Sangoma (lore master), I knew of the extraordinary place and power accorded to dreams in the African culture. (See *Song of the Stars,* republished as *Zulu Shaman*—edited and with an introduction by me.) *Song of the Stars* is full of prophecies, many of which only came true years later. For example, Baba Mutwa told me in a 1994 international phone call, "The present president of the United States could be brought down by a woman. She won't rule America, but she could cause great trouble in the year 1996. There is a shadow of a woman standing very tall over him. A woman who is frustrated, a woman who needs help. She will bring much sorrow to the people of America. I don't know why, because President Clinton strikes me as a very good young man."

I hadn't the vaguest idea what the Sangoma was talking about but decided to take a chance and put it in *Song of the Stars* anyway, given that I was doing my best to be a faithful ethnographer. The book was published in 1996, the same year as Monica Lewinsky, a complete unknown at the time, was hired to the White House staff—and the liaisons began. The accusations did not surface until 1998, during the Paula Jones trial. Another White House employee, Linda Tripp, secretly recorded phone calls with Lewinsky wherein Lewinsky gave details of the liaisons. Tripp shared the illegal recordings in exchange for immunity. President Clinton denied the allegations until they were proved later. The real trouble visited upon the president was not the affair itself but rather lying about it under oath.

Some months after the revelations and trial I thought to myself, *Holy cow! Too bad Clinton didn't read my book—or consult with the elderly Sangoma who seemed to know all about the events before Lewinsky was even hired!*

During my conversations with Baba, as I called him, he told me many more things that I chalked up to a rich imagination. "The next great war will be in the Middle East, between Christian nations and Islamic ones. It will be very bloody, and hundreds of thousands will perish!" (He said this with great sadness.) This was at least six years before the Bush presidency that launched the Iraq War. Also, "I see America at war with Afghanistan! How could it be, Sir? A great nation like America at war with a small poor nation such as Afghanistan?" We both agreed it made no sense, and he asked me to do some research on Afghanistan, because he had no access to the Internet then. (More recently, since about 2008, his young wife, who is a nurse, has been helping him.) America at war with Afghanistan?!

Baba Mutwa was full of curiosity, and he asked me for help to understand the things he couldn't wrap his mind around (in the early 1990s). "I am embarrassed to talk about this, Sir, but can one actually have sex over the computers? I cannot imagine how this could be!" (We are well into the new millennium, and a reality that would stretch the imagination of twenty years ago has come into being!)

On my visit to South Africa in 2001 to celebrate Baba's eightieth

Fig. 7.5. Sangoma (lore master) and high Sanusi, Vusamazulu Credo Mutwa, with his student and companion Salezi (Virginia), performing a ceremony in celebration of Credo's eightieth birthday at his home near Johannesburg, South Africa, in 2001 (photo credit: Stephen Larsen)

birthday, we spent the better part of a week with him at his home an hour and a half from Johannesburg. I saw person after person, usually Zulu or Ts'wana, come out of the (private) audience shaking their heads and saying things like, "I don't know how that man could know that . . . How *could* he?" (Winnie Mandela was among those who consulted him, though we did not see her on that occasion.) In our casual conversations, Baba told me always to attend to my dreams, and how doing so on more than one occasion had saved his life—by warning him away from peril.

African Americans and Psychic Abilities

The question remained: Did any of that paranormal ability survive the slave ships and the demeaning treatment that the Africans, often forbidden to even talk about their own culture, received? Certainly

Harriett Tubman is an illustration of how psychic abilities may serve people in an extremely dangerous situation.

Anthony Shafton, author and dream researcher whom we mentioned previously and whose book *Dream-Singers: The African American Way with Dreams* we have discussed, says, unequivocally yes! And he summons statistics to back this up. While belief in psychic events and precognitive dreams ranges somewhere between 25 percent and 50 percent in the general white population, it is as high as 92 percent in the 116 African Americans Shafton interviewed. At the same time he notes that captivity and the slave culture, including forcible conversion to Christianity, "bulldozed virtually all specific customs from the homelands, the beliefs among Africans and African Americans were remarkably similar."[24]

The African Description: "Dreams convey messages or warnings pertaining to one's future. In this process, ancestor spirits act as intermediaries for the Supreme Being."[25]

The African American Description: "Sometimes the Ancestors deem some information so important, that they send it to the subconscious mind without being consciously asked. Then we have prophetic dreams, rich in symbolism and unforgettable."[26]

Maisha Hamilton-Bennett, an African American deputy health commissioner says, "Many African Americans think that there's something in the dream that's going to tell you what's going to happen."[27] Shafton gives examples of even very skeptical, secularized African Americans, who feel that if you dream something it may come to pass. And Credo Mutwa says that in Africa the belief is so strong that, if you have a dream, you must try to *act it out* in some way. (This is not unlike the Iroquois belief, documented in *The Shaman's Doorway* or Moss's *Iroquois Dreaming,* that dreams represent wishes of the soul and to ignore them or neglect to act them out—even symbolically if necessary—is to provoke disaster.)

Shafton notes that although the precognitive interpretation predominates, even educated African Americans are not immune to psychological interpretations as well. He cites one poignant example where a woman dreams that a sexual rival (for her husband) has come back into town. Naturally, she is upset and jealous.

But then, in a waking dream sequence, a similar event actually happens in real life, including the exact location as in the dream (a football stadium), and, incidental, specific details that occurred. The dreamer notes that in her dream of her rival, she seizes the woman and stuffs her head in a toilet, drowning her by repeated flushings (a very graphic description of the animosity she must have felt). The dreamer was then aware enough to notice that when the prophecy was fulfilled in real life—by meeting her rival in a football stadium—her animosity apparently had been satisfied by the dream violence, and she felt quite neutral to the woman (who was a friend of a friend).

Here we see, as in Ullman's example above, that both psycho-emotional and precognitive dimensions may exist simultaneously and actually accomplish a psychological function for the dreamer. With Harriet Tubman, her dream clairvoyance and precognition was indissociable from the emotional concern she felt for her people, especially those who entrusted their lives to her. We are tempted to hypothesize that even though the trappings of their native culture had been stripped from the slaves, their DNA contained generations of conditioning, and their disempowered condition in the alien slave culture could have provoked elemental survival techniques of an extreme kind. Harriet Tubman, before escaping from her coldhearted master, a man named Brodess, prayed first (and for many years) that the Lord would "change his heart, and make him a Christian."

When that didn't work, and she had watched two of her sisters sold off for easy money to work in the Deep South, that ol' black magic—otherwise known as vodoun (voodoo), which became so famous among African Americans—surfaced: "Okay, Lord, you can't change that man's heart, kill him . . . so he won't do no more mischief." (Tubman was able to escape to Pennsylvania before the prayer-turned-curse was fulfilled—Brodess reaped what he had sown. We can hardly blame a person in her position for animosity toward a ruthless, cruel, and tyrannical overlord.)[28]

Quite interestingly, Shafton indicates that African Americans do not uncritically embrace psychic reality. And they specifically mistrust it when there is a commercial or media emphasis. The visions have to come from a person who is spiritual or close to God. One of his interviewees says, "We are using things that we don't understand, and we don't understand how precious they are . . . and maybe even sacred."[29]

Andrea Garrison's Grandfather

My friend Andrea Garrison is one of the more important African American cultural creatives of our time. She is a media personality with ongoing radio audiences of several million people, and herself has been a guest on more than a few TV talk shows. When she first approached Robin and me about the subject of relationship (after the publication of our book *The Fashioning of Angels: Partnership as Spiritual Practice*) we were just a little skeptical. Many media personalities don't do their homework, and our book required more than a superficial look-through.

But this woman had read our book, and in considerable depth, and she asked us important, leading questions about it. Afterward, she interviewed us on the subject of Emanuel Swedenborg (and our pictorial biography, which was more than five hundred pages long). At the end of the (several) interviews, I was astounded. She was not only sympathetic to the subject but had read virtually every article in the massive tome as well.

This was true as well of my book *The Fundamentalist Mind*. Not only had she read the book closely, but she also asked penetrating and intelligent questions about it. I was happy to help her get published with the Swedenborg Foundation a few years ago and worked with her rather closely on her own book. As well, I wrote an introduction to her book *The Presence of Angels: Reflections on Mattie Pearl and Emanuel Swedenborg*. Andrea told me the following story at the time; it is very congruent with what we now are learning about what is the considerable metaphysical bent of African Americans.

I will never forget the time when my mom told me the story of her dad when he was twenty-seven. He gathered the entire family to the dinner table. They prayed, and he told my grandmother and five children— two girls and three boys all under the age of eight—that he had seen his mother and father in a dream. In the dream his mom and dad were inviting him to join them on the other side. He did not want to leave my grandmother [his wife] and his five children, but he had a greater calling that required him to leave.

For the next month my grandfather made preparations for his departure by chopping extra wood for the fireplace and doing other things around the home. He wanted to do as much as he could for the family for the short remaining time that he was here.

No one believed that he was going to die, because he was a healthy twenty-seven-year-old with a full life in front of him. But I guess my grandfather knew otherwise. One month from that day when he sat with his wife and five children at the table, suddenly he left this physical Earth to be with his mom and dad on the other side.

Andrea is such a modest and nonvindictive person that it was only with difficulty that I extracted from her the reason for her grandfather's early demise: He had been severely beaten by a racist lynch mob and carried his wounds in his brain (I believe he ultimately died of a stroke). She herself was reluctant to talk about it, as were her own parents and grandparents.

I myself belong to a race that inflicts such harm, and as such, I am ashamed for my own people. I hope that this primitive form of violence—the effects of which can often be felt for generations—dies out in our time!

The Sleeping Prophet

This chapter would not be complete without mention of Edgar Cayce (1877–1945). Cayce is often called "the sleeping prophet." After humble beginnings in the South in the late nineteenth century, he became famous in his own time for dream diagnostics, even from a distance. His work is continued by the Association for Research and Enlightenment (ARE) in Virginia Beach, Virginia.

What is not well known about Cayce is that his own clairvoyance began after he'd suffered a traumatic brain injury (TBI). At about four years of age he was playing on a porch when he fell off headfirst and was impaled through the top of his head by a nail sticking through a board. No sophisticated medicine existed nearby, so he was doctored by having turpentine poured into the wound. He apparently recovered well, but a few years later he began seeing angels and talking about them.

Later on, as an adult of growing renown, Cayce used dreams to help him diagnose illness. Either he would dream his own dreams about a patient, which he would then interpret and the knowledge of which he would apply, or he would be presented with a dream by a patient, which he would interpret in spiritual terms. Without any formal education, his interpretations were often uncannily accurate, for he often saw things about patients that neither they themselves nor their family knew—such as the advance of an illness or an impending disaster. Sometimes, based on the things he saw in a dream or a vision, the patients would go to a physician and have the reading confirmed by the independent practitioner.

While not a conventionally religious churchgoing person, Cayce often used dreams to illustrate his patients' spiritual level of attainment or dilemmas. Thus would he ask the particular patient for an account of what was going on in his or her daily life, as well as their dreams—as completely as they could remember them. He emphasized, as did Christopher Whitmont, that even a fragment could sometimes be revelatory. Like the Native Americans and the Africans, he urged that dreams needed to be acted upon and that regular mining of dreams produced clearer and better dreaming. He likened the subconscious to "a woodland spring to be dipped out and kept flowing, if it is best used."30

Dream series could be useful, and like "using two stars of the Big Dipper to sight the North Star, one can line up two or more similar dreams and perhaps some waking reflections and happenings to sight clear through to important knowledge about living: how the levels of the mind interact, how love draws love, how fear and doubt cripple, how concentration quickens ESP, how tasks of demanding service draw the aid of both the living and the dead, how prayer brings consciousness to a Center not its own . . ."[31]

These latter concepts would be completely congruent with those of our ancient friend Synesius, who counseled that one could avoid the various pitfalls of narcissism and egotism by finding a center not one's own. This is also consistent with Jungian and other transpersonal psychologies, such as Assagioli's psychosynthesis.

In summary, this wounded healer Edgar Cayce, like many other souls down through the centuries—from Daniel to Synesius to Joan of Arc to Harriet Tubman to Carl Jung to Edward Whitmont—urges us that attention to our dreams is a valid spiritual path, one that is available to us all. It is a corrective for our inflation, a kindly light for our blind spots, an aid assimilating the shadow, and a beacon that not only shows us what lies ahead but also illuminates our way home!

8

Dream Incubation

Seeding the Unconscious

We go to sleep at night and, unbidden, dreams come. In a regular, rhythmic way we receive over two hours of dreams per night—the length of a major feature film. When researchers have interrupted this natural cycle and people are deprived of dreams, they become restless, disoriented, and eventually crazy—until they are allowed to dream again. Dreams are as natural and necessary to physical, mental, and spiritual health as eating and breathing. And there is no way to predict what we will dream. That's one of the great delights of dreaming—the endless surprises and unpredictable possibilities.

Although we cannot predict what we will dream about, there is a profound relationship between the waking world and the dreaming universe, a deep dialogue between our waking and dreaming selves. This dialogue, this conversation, goes on whether or not we consciously participate in it. Be that as it may, all around the world for thousands of years across cultures and spiritual traditions, people have turned to their dreams and actively asked them for guidance and healing for a particular concern, question, or illness.

This is because human beings have realized that in the dream state we are open to the possibility of connecting with a deep, sacred source of wisdom, guidance, and healing. Thus have ritual incubation practices, called "dream incubation," been created consciously to contact this sacred inner source of wisdom and healing. The dreamer, by asking a question of that mysterious source within us from which all dreams come, incubates a dream response to their question or concern. This ongoing, natural, and necessary dialogue between the known and unknown, the conscious and the unconscious, the awake and the dreaming parts of the psyche, is at the very heart of the practice of "temple sleep," another name for dream incubation.

Temple Dreamers and Their Temples

In almost all cultures there were temples, if you will, sacred places dedicated to the practice of consciously entering the dream state with the intention of receiving the gift of guidance and healing. The temple could be a grove of trees sacred to the Iroquois or a Taoist cave in the mountains of China, the grave of an ancestor or next to the body of a saint enshrined in a small chapel in a sixth-century Catholic church or in a deep cave inhabited by wild animals.

These were sacred places of all kinds, considered to be so because the veil between the worlds was believed to be thinnest in these in-between, liminal areas, which were thought of as openings to the underworld. The veil between sleeping and waking, between the animal and the human, between the dead and the living, was permeable here. In the sacred places where the veil is thinnest, that "still small voice within," that conversation between the known and the unknown, the visible and the invisible, the conscious and the unconscious, is heard a little more clearly, a little bit louder, and we are somewhat more open to the wisdom that comes to us from these areas between the worlds. Dream incubation, like watching your breath during meditation, makes an inner process—one that is usually left to function unconsciously on its own—more conscious. Humans have found, as with meditation, that a great deal may be gained by entering consciously into the process of dreaming.

Mary Oliver's poem "Sleeping in the Forest" captures this ancient experience of temple dreamers. Her poem expresses so beautifully the spirit and experience of this in-between place of temple sleep, that world between dark and light, life and death, human and animal, waking and dreaming. As she is falling asleep she is aware of the "small kingdoms" breathing around her, "the insects and the birds who do their work in the darkness." All night, she says, "I rose and fell as if in water, grappling with a luminous doom. By morning I had vanished at least a dozen times into something better."[1]

We are not talking about what has come to be called "lucid dreaming," that amazing moment when we become conscious of dreaming within the dream itself. (We explore lucid dreaming in the next chapter.) With incubation, there is still a profound trust and humility in the presence of the great mystery, which is what we imagine dreaming to be. Dream incubation involves evoking—seeding the dreaming mind with questions that allow the dream to respond with its own solutions. Dream incubation is founded on a profound trust in the dream's autonomy, freedom, and unhampered spontaneity to provide insights, wisdom, and healing to the dreamer. There is a sense that if the waking ego-dominated mind can get out of the way and submit to the wisdom of the dream, solutions and insights will emerge that are not accessible to the waking mind. As Mary Oliver says, "By morning I had vanished at least a dozen times, into something better."[2]

In the Words of Coauthor Tom Verner
Dream Incubation among the Senoi

In the mid-1970s, I was introduced to the world of the Senoi, a tribe of Malaysian people who were studied in the early 1970s by anthropologist Kilton Stewart. I learned of the Senoi and their work with dreams from a delightful psychologist named Jack Johnston. There has been much written about the Senoi, beginning with the work of Kilton Stewart. Johnston studied Stewart's work and learned Senoi dreamwork from Stewart's students. Over the years some of Stewart's claims about the Senoi have been called into question, but his work nonetheless has inspired many creative ways of working with dreams. (For a balanced discussion of the controversy surrounding Stewart's work on the

Senoi see Patricia Garfield's preface to the second edition of her book *Creative Dreaming*.)[3] The work of Kilton Stewart has been carried on and developed into an interesting and creative method of dreamwork by his widow, Clara Stewart Flagg. As well as inspiring psychologists and dreamworkers, the Senoi have inspired a number of novels, among them Ursula K. Le Guin's *The Word for World Is Forest* and Dorothy Bryant's *The Kin of Ata Are Waiting for You,* both of which portray cultures consciously inspired by incubating and working with their dreams. At the heart of the Senoi dream culture is an intimate moving back and forth between the waking world and the dream universe.

With the Senoi, dreamwork begins in early childhood. The Senoi lived in multigenerational longhouses with a central room where the generations gathered each morning for a "dream breakfast" during which they all shared and talked about their dreams.

Based on Kilton Stewart and Patricia Garfield's work, let us imagine how a Senoi family might respond to the typical childhood nightmare of finding oneself terrified while falling in a dream. Patricia Garfield cites research that states, out of a hundred children surveyed, 63 percent said they had dreams of falling.[4] If a Senoi child wakes up scared from a falling dream, the parents' response might not be the typical response of a parent today, who might attempt to comfort their child by saying, "It was just a dream, don't worry, just go back to sleep. It's okay."

Instead, based on material learned from Jack Johnston, we might imagine the Senoi mother or father sitting on the edge of the child's bed and saying to them:

You were beginning to fly, but you forgot that you were in the dream universe and you got scared and thought you were falling. You were not only starting to fly, but you were flying to a very magical place where you were going to meet someone who loves you very much and was about to give you a gift that expresses their esteem for you. So now when you go back to sleep, find yourself back there on the edge of that cliff and this time, and it will take great courage, leap off the cliff and fly to that magical place. If you get scared standing there you may want to invite someone with you, a dream ally who will give you the courage to fly. In the morning you will tell us your dream and describe the gift you received.

The parents would sit with the child until he or she fell back to sleep. The parents were following a fundamental Senoi principle (one that we frequently repeat throughout the book, because it's so powerful and important): Where the fear is, that's where the power is. The Senoi know that the dreamworld is a safe place in which to practice daring and courage, a safe place to face our fears. They know that we first do it in the dream, and then we do it in our waking life. If we can face our fears and have courage in our dreams, we will face and overcome our fears in the waking world as well.

In the morning at the dream breakfast the child would tell the dream and describe the gift he had received in it, perhaps a song or a piece of clothing, a beautiful blowpipe, or a bow and arrow. With the help of an adult the child would spend the following days actually making the gift from his dream. Regularly the Senoi had village gatherings that were dream show-and-tell, where people would present the textile designs, the songs, the recipes, the weapons, and whatever else they'd received in their dreams. The Senoi, like many ancient and indigenous people, know that the dream comes first and then waking cultural life. This is a culture that consciously integrates dream incubation into their daily life so as to create personal and collective culture and character.

HELPFUL BOOKS WHEN WORKING WITH CHILDREN'S NIGHTMARES

Below are some wonderful books—also listed in the bibliography— that could help you help your children with their dreams—and nightmares! They are written from a variety of perspectives.

The Dream Book, Patricia Garfield

Dreamcatching, Alan Siegel and Kelly Bulkeley

Nightmare Help, Ann Sayre Wiseman

Build Your Own Dream House, Paula Craig

Cookie Monster
Takes on New Meaning

Here is another fun and effective way of responding to children's dreams of monsters. Monster dreams can be powerful, scary nightmares for a child. I developed this way of working with children's monster dreams inspired in part because my first remembered dream was a very scary one of Frankenstein. In the 1970s I conducted a number of Monster Dream Playshops for children.

Six or eight children would gather for three or four hours to work/ play with their monster dreams. The playshop began with some theater, group, and trust building games, after which the children gathered in a circle to tell their monster dreams. They then drew pictures and/or created sculptures using colored Sculpey clay to make their dream monsters. Next they engaged in simple Gestalt-inspired exercises, talking to and from their monsters. They became the monsters, and acted scary and occasionally silly, as the room filled with creatures from the sometimes terrifying world of dreams.

Gradually there was a sense of increasing power and play in the room. The children were playing and having fun with monsters that in the middle of the night had the power to scare them witless. When you face the fear and embody the fear you embrace the power. That seemed to happen during the Dream Monster Playshop.

The playshop ended with all of the children gathered around a large bowl of cookie dough and bowls of colored icing, making their monsters into cookies. After the cookies were baked and decorated into monsters with claws and horns and blood dripping out of their mouths, we sat down for lunch, and, for dessert, we all ate our monsters. The children literally "in-corporated" their monsters, transforming them into their own flesh and blood.

There is something playfully primitive about this way of working with one's dragons. Somehow it has the feeling of working with a dream in a manner that is as dreamlike as possible. The parents who were present during the playshop were asked to let me know if the monster nightmares then stopped or continued. In almost all cases the monsters never showed up again.

Dream Incubation in Ancient Greece

Much has been written about the ancient practices of dream incubation, especially those rituals of ancient Greece where the practice of temple sleep was raised to the level of a sacred healing art. Around the year 500 BCE, the time of the axial age, there were hundreds of incubation temples all over Greece and the surrounding Mediterranean that were dedicated to Asclepius, the god of healing. People would make a pilgrimage to the sacred temples to seek guidance from Asclepius in their dreams. The most sacred and developed of these temple sites was the town of Epidaurus, a few hours' travel from Athens. Epidaurus was what we might call today a holistic health center, centered on the Abaton, the temple enclosure where a pilgrim would eventually sleep to receive a healing dream.

Let us imagine a pilgrim making his or her way to Epidaurus. While traveling there the pilgrim would turn his or her question over and over in their mind and heart, clarifying and deepening their intention. They would abstain from food and sex, keeping their mind on the hope of receiving a healing dream from Asclepius. As they entered the sacred town of Epidaurus they crossed under an arch on which was written "Pure must be he who enters the fragrant temple. Purity means to think nothing but holy thoughts."[5]

From the moment they arrived at Epidaurus they were awakened in body, mind, and spirit. First they would go to the mineral baths and soak in the herb-infused waters and receive massages to soothe their world-battered physical bodies. Out on the streets, they would encounter the peripatetic philosophers, perhaps Socrates himself or another philosopher of the day. The philosophers engaged the pilgrim in deeply thoughtful questions such as "What is the good life?" or "What makes a human being human?" In the process, their thinking body was awakened and nourished.

In the evening they would go to the great theater on the mountain, along with perhaps seventeen thousand other people, to have what Aristotle called catharsis—an emotionally cleansing experience. One might experience a tragedy of Aeschylus or Sophocles, or laugh with a comedy of Euripides or Aristophanes. Theater is rooted in the same etymology as the word *therapy;* both awaken and cleanse the emotional body. Over a number of days the pilgrim would be awakened in body, mind, and heart, all the while turning their question or concern over and over, which let the god know that they were serious in their belief in the healing power of dreams. All of this was in preparation for their temple sleep; the night they hoped to receive guidance and healing from Asclepius.

On the way to the temple, the pilgrim would pass testimonials of past pilgrims carved into the walls. This graffiti testified to the healing received by others before them; healing received while sleeping in the Temple of Asclepius. When they arrived they were greeted by one of the temple attendants known as the Therapeutae, from which we get our modern term *therapist.* Fully awake in mind and body, they sat and spoke with the Therapeutae, clarifying their question and deepening their intention even further.[6]

As darkness fell, the pilgrim—full of expectation and profoundly prepared—entered the Abaton (the interior sanctuary of the temple). In the Abaton were large blocks of marble covered with sheepskins from sacrificed lambs. On these the pilgrim would sleep the night on the couch, or *klinikos* (the root of our modern word "clinical"). In the dark one might hear or sense the movement of the great (nonpoisonous) snakes that slithered along the floor of the temple. The pilgrim brought offerings for the snakes, which were regarded as embodiments of the god himself. As the pilgrim drifted off to sleep, the last awareness was of the temple attendants walking softly through the temple, whispering words of encouragement. The pilgrim now moved toward the dreamworld. Carl Jung once referred to "the small secret opening in the innermost recesses of the psyche, that opened out into cosmic night. Into that world that was Psyche long before ego and would be Psyche long after ego went into eclipse."[7]

It will come as no surprise, then, with all this preparation and, surrounded by the healing history of the place, the encouragement of the temple attendant, and the deep intention and expectation of the pilgrim, that healing dreams might come—if not that night, then perhaps a following night. The pilgrim must be in a profound state of waiting, for "in your patience is your soul," the great alchemist physician Paracelsus used to say. As James Hillman wrote in *The Dream and the Underworld,* "the soul is found in the reception of its suffering, in the attendance upon it, the waiting it through."[8] From the soul's viewpoint, there is little difference between patient and therapist. Both roles are rooted in an attentive devotion, "waiting on and waiting for." So even with all the preparation, all the clarified intention, all the profound belief in the healing power of the god-in-the-dream, the pilgrim-patient-dreamer is always in a posture of submissive waiting through their suffering—*patient* means both "to suffer" and "to wait." As the medieval alchemist Paracelsus would say, "dreamwork is soul work, and soul work is slow, patient work."

Upon receiving a dream, the pilgrim would bring his or her dream to the temple attendants (Therapeutae) for further conversation and clarification. The pilgrim left the temple beginning to heal; renewed as he or she headed home ready to live the injunction given to them by Asclepius, ready to fulfill Jung's ethical demand of the dream: "What are you going to do with this dream, how are you going to live it in your life?"

So what are the essential elements of the dream incubation experience, and how can we learn from these ancient dreamers? How can we find ways of asking our dreams for help and healing? Is this ancient practice of dream incubation something we can learn to do today in our own lives? To help answer these questions, let's explore how one of the authors has used dream incubation as part of the dream retreats he's been conducting for more than forty years.

A Modern Embodiment of Dream Incubation

Inspired by his work with Dr. Henry Reed, a master of dream incubation research and practice, my artist wife, Janet Fredericks, and I have created dream retreats for groups of people since 1975. Dream incubation is a centerpiece of the retreats. Ten people gather for a week at our country home in the mountains of Vermont to work with their dreams. The days are structured in such a way that there is constant movement back and forth between the waking world and the dream universe. The schedule conspires to allow us to spend as much time as possible in the in-between worlds. Among other things, this makes dream recall and creative responses to the dream more likely. Throughout this discussion of the dream retreat, many ways of working with dreams will be described. The reader can consider this description of the retreat a small compendium of dreamwork techniques.

On the Eve of the Dream Retreat

The retreat participants arrive around four in the afternoon, find a place to nest, set up their tent or settle in one of the rooms of the house, and gradually meet the other participants over a cup of tea. We begin supper with a welcome and blessing from the Mayan tradition. We pass an offering plate around and each person takes a morsel of food from the table, breathes on it (the Mayans believe the gods recognize us from the signature scent of our breath), says a word of gratitude, and places the food on the offering plate. When all have placed their offering on the plate, two people take the plate to a small altar beyond the house where the wild and the domestic meet—one of the many liminal, in-between places that we utilize throughout the week. During the night the animals will come and eat this food, taking it to the spirit world. The rest of the group holds the silence until the two return. We then say a final blessing on our food and on the week ahead before we sit down and eat the first of many meals together.

After supper, the first evening session begins and involves setting the tone for the week's work and placing the dreamwork we will be doing in the context of our current lives. After a meditation and a few words about the nature of "re-treat" (see chapter 11 for more on this concept of "re-treat"), each person selects a haiku from a list of forty haiku that somehow expresses this time in the person's life. Each person is given a handmade haiku journal in which reflections on their cho-sen haiku will be written throughout the week. We begin each session with meditation and everyone reading their haiku aloud to the group. Each person then makes a journal entry reflection on their haiku and the connections they are seeing with their current life questions and concerns.

Part of the purpose of working with the haikus in this way is to tune up the metaphoric mind and develop the ability to mine an image for ever more possible meanings and connections. This is just one of the ways in which poetry is used during the dream retreat. We have found that reading and writing poems from our dreams and the dreams of others in the group is a wonderful way of creating and enhancing an atmosphere of image—the language of the dream—during the retreat. Both poetry and dreams have been called "the forgotten language" (by Erich Fromm and W. S. Merwin), and the retreat is a time of relearning the forgotten language of the dreamworld.

The other journal work we do the first evening to set the context for the dreamwork is inspired by Ira Progoff's Intensive Journal Method. Each person writes a Present Period Log (for details about how to write such a log, see chapter 3) by placing themselves in "this time in their lives." This is not the present moment but rather the *period* you find yourself in at this time in your life. As Progoff writes, "We stretch the present moment back as far as it needs to go in order to include as much of the past as is still an active part of the present."[9] Our lives move in periods and when we pause and reflect we are often very clear "when this time in my life" began, maybe even the exact day. We may be in a period of exhilaration or depression, a time of intense work or a pause between projects. The period may stretch back a few years since an auto accident and hospitalization and the ongoing changes the accident has brought about. We may have just begun a new job or relationship and feel that we are at the beginning of a new period in our life. We may sense that we are in the middle of a time in our life or in a period that is coming to a close. Each person's Present Period Log will be unique to them.

The reason for doing this Present Period Log is rooted deeply in our way of understanding dreamwork. Following Jung, we understand that dreams often perform a balancing, homeostatic function in response to the events of our present waking life. The dream is often but not always a response to our present life concerns, questions, and challenges. To follow our dreams is to have a rudder that continually corrects our waking course.

Along with the Present Period Log and the haiku expressing a certain time in their lives, we ask the retreatants to consider what issues they are presently working on. In this way, each person gets a clear sense of what their dreams may be working with and responding to during the dream retreat.

The opening session ends with a meditation/presentation on the dream incubation rituals at Epidaurus and writing a prayer/invocation to the dream source within, thanking it for all the many marvelous past dreams and asking it for dreams during the retreat. A few moments of meditation end with a bit of music (maybe something like Jean Redpath's "John O'Dreams") before heading off to our feathered beds to receive the first night of dreams.

Day One of the Dream Retreat

At 4:45 in the morning the dreamers are gently awakened with flute music and allowed to lay in bed for five minutes or so in the twilight state between sleeping and waking. The flute music comes around again, encouraging the dreamers to write down their dreams. We all then wend our way through the half-light to the meditation room, where we do half an hour of guided meditation. Mark Thurston, at the Edgar Cayce Foundation, has conducted research on the ways in which meditation enhances dream recall. The meditation is taking place in that in-between time of night and day, in the dreaming and waking, conscious and unconscious, states. This twilight time, the dawn, the crack between the worlds, is regarded as a powerful time among many indigenous peoples (as are the "times-between" during the solar year: the solstices and equinoxes).

After the half-hour meditation, the dreamers head back to sleep. They will be awakened again in an hour and a half, one ninety-minute dream cycle (as we talked about in "The Dreaming Brain" chapter). Again the flute music awakens them, often with a dream. From 7:00 a.m. to 9:00 a.m. the retreat participants are free to write in their dream journals, take walks along our canopied country road, go for a swim in one of the nearby river's many swimming holes, eat breakfast, and slowly awaken, preparing for a day of working with their dreams.

We gather for our first session, beginning with another meditation, often a "between breaths" meditation from the Tibetan Buddhist tradition. This practice invites the meditator to find that place after exhalation, before the next breath, waiting, open, in that powerful place between breaths, between what is conscious and what is unconscious. Again we are in between, in a state of waiting, submission, and trust. Each person then reads their haiku aloud and makes an entry in their haiku journal. In this way the participants are brought back to this time in their lives and making an entry in response to the haiku, any new connections they are making between the images of the haiku and their present lives.

Everyone tells a dream, if not recalled from the night before, then one from the recent past. Next, we all give our dreams three or four titles and write two or three haiku summarizing the dream. The first two lines, the first twelve syllables of the haiku, summarize the dream, and the last five syllables make an "interpretive response" to the dream—a first sense of what the dream might be saying to the dreamer about his or her life situation. This is a technique* dreamwork master Henry Reed and Tom developed in a research project they conducted at the Association for Research and Enlightenment at the Edgar Cayce Foundation in Virginia Beach, Virginia. (There are more ideas of how to use the haiku with dreamwork in chapter 11, "Dreams and the Poetic Imagination.")

In chapter 11 we will talk about and give some examples of how powerful poetry may be when we are working with our dreams, but for now a quote from the Jungian analyst and scholar Marion Woodman expresses one of the many reasons why poetry and dreams work so well together.

---

*For a detailed account of this practice of using haiku to enter and move toward the meaning of a dream, see Henry Reed's book *Dream Medicine: Learning How to Get Help from Our Dreams.*

To make prose sense of a dream subjects the dream to a grammatical logic that may be alien to the symbolic logic of the dreaming state. The dream is closer to poetry than to prose. . . . Dreams live in a world free of the restrictions of time and space. Only the fluidity of the arts—movement, poetry, myth, and art—truly carry their messages well to waking awareness. If we limit the dream to verbal analysis and reductive definitions, the dream dries up. However, if we feed our dreams with our creativity and curiosity, they will nourish our understanding for days, even years.[10]

After a break of half an hour, we gather on the grass outside Janet's studio for fifteen minutes of movement to music. The movement is done with the dream, the titles, the haikus in the back of our minds. The dream begins to move through our bodies as we embody the dream awakening within us. Getting out of our minds and into our bodies in this way brings the dream alive. This prepares the dreamers for what we will now do with Janet in her studio.

With the dreams moving in our bodies and the haikus and titles in mind, we take Japanese brush and ink and make a number of *haiga*— "visual haiku" brush paintings. The haiga are not meant to illustrate, but rather to express and hopefully illuminate the dream. These calligraphic, sweeping brushstrokes express the sense of the dream beginning to slowly arise within the dreamer. This is a sense of the dream that's not exactly the same as the meaning of the dream. We sniff the dream as an animal dream body might move around and slowly toward a dream, sensing what it might be. We hope to keep the dream strange and mysterious as we slowly begin to puzzle out what it might be saying to us. Each person creates about half a dozen haiga.

We end the morning in a circle wherein each person speaks and begins to sense the connections between the dream, the titles, the haiku, and the haiga.

After lunch and a break of a couple of hours, during which folks can nap, walk, write in their journal, and/or go for a swim, the retreatants gather again in Janet's studio and begin work on an art dream book.

This dream book is a project that folks work on all week. The accordion folded book with pockets, called a gypsy wagon, is usually about eight inches by eight inches. Throughout the week it is collaged and painted in by the participants—with images from their dreams and journal work. It becomes filled with dreams, haiku, haiga, and reflections on what seems to be moving in their inner and outer lives. The book is a spirit trap to capture the many moments and images of the retreat and the person's life as a whole.

People have written to us regarding how important these books have become for them—reminding them of the profound work they did during the dream retreat, work that often continues throughout their lives. These dream books can become totemic touchstones capable of reminding and reconnecting the dreamer to his or her creative source within and teaching them how to continue working on their dreams and allowing their dreams to work on them.

The Finishing Touches of the Dream Retreat

The final night of the retreat we dress up in imaginative and fun ways for an opening. The studio is decorated, delicious finger foods are prepared, and each person's book is on display. We all move around the gallery and admire the often startlingly creative work each dreamer has done. Many folks who do not think of themselves as visual artists are amazed by the depth of creativity that working with their dream images has awakened in them. Guy Jean, an acclaimed Quebec poet who has attended the dream retreat a number of times, talked about this. He said, "I am not a visual artist, I am a poet, and yet during the dream retreat because we dwell in 'the space of dreaming' when not asleep, a space of being neither awake nor asleep, a liminal space of creativity, I was able to create visually in ways I never thought possible."

The great twentieth-century Spanish poet Antonio Machado expresses this thought of Guy Jean's in his poem "Is My Soul Asleep." As the poem ends, the poet states that the soul "neither sleeps nor dreams, but watches, / its eyes wide open / far-off things, and listens / at the shores of the great silence."[11]

Dream Incubation During the Dream Retreat

Each day while the group is working on their dream books, one of the retreatants has been spending the day in the dream incubation house, a small house on the property devoted to dream incubation. There he or she works all day in preparation for sleeping in the dream incubation house that night. The dreamer has been doing journal exercises designed over the years by Tom to help focus the dream incubation question. The individual has perhaps gone for solitary walks, he or she may have spent the day fasting and/or may have spent a couple of hours talking with Tom refining the incubation question they will bring to their dreams that night.

☺ Dream Muse Exercise

In the evening after supper, the individual will join the group, and, using a variety of techniques, we further help prepare the person for sleeping in the incubation house. The individual describes the question or concern in as much detail as he or she feels comfortable sharing. We might do a dream muse exercise wherein we listen to one of the individual's dreams and each of us writes a poem in response to the dream and reads it back to the dreamer. The dreamer is then given the poems—a dozen poems inspired by one of his or her dreams.

Or we might use a method developed by dream researchers Montegue Ullman and Nan Zimmerman, described in their book *Working with Dreams,* which has been titled, "If This Were My Dream."

☺ If This Were My Dream

The dreamer tells a dream and each member of the group writes it down in as much detail as possible, exactly as the dreamer tells it. The group may ask the dreamer to clarify an image or a detail but not ask for any interpretation or associations. The dreamer then sits back and listens while each member of the circle simply tells how they felt when they heard the dream. "The point of this is to make you sensitive to the fact that dreams originate in feelings and express feelings. We are not asking for objective comments on the dream or on the dreamer. We are asking how the dream affects you."[12] Later we check out these feelings with the dreamer. Then we go off for twenty to thirty minutes and look at our own lives through the images of the dream, as if it were our own dream. We then come back together as a group and share our thoughts about our own lives using the images of the dream.

In the process, as Ullman and Zimmerman say, "we create a reservoir of possible meanings for the dream."[13] In some ways this is an enactment of a statement that has been attributed to many people. I first read it in the work of the Russian philosopher Nikolai Berdyaev—"That which is most personal, is most universal."[14] If we each go to the deepest places in ourselves in working with the dreamer's images, we often connect with a place in us that is deeply personal and deeply universal—often saying something meaningful for the dreamer about their dream. This technique is a very powerful method for working with dreams in a group. Each member of the group, more often than not, gains some valuable insight for themselves from looking at their own lives through the images of someone else's dream. And for sure, the dreamer gains a great deal.

When the time feels right, and no more preparation seems necessary, the group—with the dreamer in the center—slowly moves in a procession, with torches and chants, through the dark out to the dream incubation house. The group gathers around the dreamer, chanting softly, and one by one each participant moves into the center of the circle and whispers wishes to the dream pilgrim for a night of healing dreams. When everyone has wished the dreamer well, one of the group chosen by the dreamer leads him or her into the incubation house and tucks them in for the night. Outside the dream house the group continues to chant and, when the time is right, slowly processes back to the main house. Inside the house there's a closing circle during which we connect with the dreamer, sending him or her final blessings. We then head off to our separate beds, feeling like, as the poet Robert Bly says, "sleepers joining hands."

All this preparation and attention to the dream pilgrim, as well as the structure of the ritual, places the dreamer in an open and receptive state. As Mary Watkins writes of the incubation rituals at Epidaurus, "The outer symbolic actions of the ritual were able to create a state of awareness and certain inner attitudes that allowed the incubant to gradually separate himself from the usual frame of consciousness in order to be able to participate in the visionary realm with the god."[15]

The next morning the dream pilgrim is the last dreamer to tell their dream to the group. We have been waiting anxiously to hear of the experience in the dream house. Here are a few examples from folks who have slept in the dream incubation house over the years.

Kevin, the Marine Sniper

Kevin was a marine sniper in his early thirties who'd made six deployments to Iraq and Afghanistan and other combat areas. Kevin trained snipers for the Marine Corps and was a highly decorated veteran. He came home from the war a shattered human being, having seen the faces of almost every person he killed up close in the scope of his rifle. And now that he was home he saw those faces, and those of his dead platoon buddies, almost every night in his dreams.

Sleep terrified him. It was not a source of rest but of nightmares and terror. He had not slept in a bed for six years when I first met him. He slept by the door of his house on the floor, protecting the premises and his girlfriend from any possible intruder or harm. Kevin was a haunted human being, with a profound sense of emptiness. There was a hole in the center of him where his soul used to be.

Kevin showed up at the dream retreat, having been dropped off by his girlfriend. He was two hours late racing to the retreat from a tour with his high octane rock 'n' roll band. Playing music was one of the few sources of pleasure, relief, and release he had in his life. Kevin, a charming, delightful young man, immediately found a place in the hearts of the other retreatants.

After a couple of nights witnessing the work people did sleeping in the dream incubation house, Kevin expressed a tentative interest in trying it, even though the idea really scared him. But being the brave soldier he was, he had decided to confront the horror of his dreams head-on, even though the prospect terrified him for many reasons. For one thing, it would be the first time he would be sleeping in a bed after many years. He would also be facing the very thing that he had come to be most frightened of—his dreams.

As with the other retreatants who had slept in the dream house, Kevin spent all day fasting, working in his journal in the dream house clarifying his question and deepening his intention, and taking solitary walks and talking with Tom for two hours.

We gathered after supper for the final session of preparation before Kevin processed by torchlight and chanting to the incubation house. Beth, one of the participants, had a small camper that she parked not far from the dream incubation house. From its window she could see the dream house and someone in the house could see the light in her camper. In a brilliantly insightful moment, Beth had said to Kevin, "I will stay awake and keep vigil all night guarding the property, and you'll be able to see my light from the dream house." This was an essential piece of his preparation for the incubation experience. He could now let go and open himself up as much as he was able to, knowing that someone else was keeping guard through the night.

There was something particularly powerful and moving in the procession with Kevin out to the incubation house. It seemed as if he had been walking toward this night for many years. He was entering the dream house not just to have a healing dream, but to retrieve his lost soul. Outside the house Kevin stood in the center of the singing circle for a long time. A beautiful full moon illuminated our faces, and in that light Kevin's face seemed to glow with some strange mix of hope and fear and gratitude. Kevin asked Tom to accompany him into the house. Once inside, he seemed like a little boy heading off on his own into the wilderness, perhaps a young Sioux boy heading off alone on a vision quest. Trembling with fear and excitement, Kevin hugged Tom and thanked him for making the experience possible, and then he said, trying to be a good boy, "I'll do the best I can to have the dream that I need."

Like a soldier and a little boy all in one, he then climbed into bed to confront that which scared him the most. Tom said good-night and kissed him on the forehead like he would a son. He then left the dream house and rejoined the circle. The group chanted for a while and slowly processed back to the main house. As they did so, the line from William Butler Yeats kept running through Tom's mind, "It takes more courage to examine the dark corners of your own soul than it does for a soldier to fight on a battlefield."

That night, Kevin had one of the most powerful experiences that anyone had ever had in the many years that dreamers have been going to the dream incubation house. The next morning, as Kevin told the dreams he'd had the night before, it seemed as if we were hearing a voice coming from the great depths of psyche, as if something profound was being witnessed. Here is Kevin's first dream.

> *I am strapped with leather constraints to a bed in what feels like a VA hospital. I can't move. I look up and see my grandmother who raised me and was my true mother. She's standing in the door of my hospital room, and I can see in her hand my kbar bayonet that I carried with me during all of my deployments as a marine in Iraq and Afghanistan. She walks toward the bed and raises the knife. I know that I am about to die, and I am terrified. As she gets next to the bed she brings the knife down and cuts the four leather restraints with my knife. And she looks at me and says, "Get up, you're free."*

Here is Kevin's second dream.

> *I arrive at the main building of the college I attend, and there's a large crowd on the lawn looking up at the building. Someone in the crowd tells me the building is on fire and that there is a Tibetan lama, a holy man, trapped inside. I rush into the building and down the burning corridor to the chapel where the Tibetan lama is sitting with his leg badly burned.*
> *The lama looks at me and says, "Why have you come?"*
> *I say, "I have come to save you."*
> *The lama looks at me and says, "Then I can't go with you."*
> *I am shocked and confused, but I know I must leave. I head back*

down the burning corridor and after about twenty steps I stop and turn
around and head back to the chapel. Again I enter the chapel. The
Tibetan lama is still sitting on the floor.

He looks up at me and says, "Why have you come?"

I look at him and say, "I have come to save myself."

The lama looks at me and says, "Alright then, I can come with you."

I pick up the badly burned lama and carry him through the burning
building to the outside and lay him down on the lawn. Instantly, the
lama's leg and the other parts of his burned body are healed.

Kevin worked with these dreams the next morning in the group. He told us that both of the dreams really felt like one dream. His grandmother sets him free, in a sense saying he must die in some way, and he walks out of the sick place he has been living in. He now finds himself free but in a burning structure; maybe his old life is burning down around him. He runs into this burning structure and finds a profound spiritual teacher.

Kevin said, "This inner work, this dreamwork, is really scary, really hard." At this point in the group, Tom shared the thought he'd had while walking slowly back from the dream house when Kevin was falling asleep: "It takes more courage to examine the dark corners of your own soul than it does for a soldier to fight on a battlefield."

Over the next year, this inner spiritual teacher (as symbolized by his grandmother and the lama) helped Kevin "examine the dark corners of his soul" and helped him slowly heal the profound wounds and soul loss that had plagued him for years. When Kevin went home after the dream retreat, his girlfriend, Mary, kept saying how profoundly he had changed. Kevin told me she kept saying, "You feel freer, more available."

Months later, Kevin said, "Everything is now different. I can't exactly say how, but some part of me that was locked up is now available for me and for others. There is more space inside." This echoes what G.M. said about his profound dream experience in "What Makes for a Big Dream" (chapter 4). "To explain how I was changed is difficult for a few reasons. The effect was so ethereal that, like air or water, it seeped into everything. In a way I can say it changed nothing, but everything, because my eyes were changed. . . ."

This sense of being changed on a profound level, as a result of sleeping in the dream incubation house, has been a common experience. Sometimes very specific problems are solved, specific guidance is given, and/or solutions to questions are found. These are wonderful gifts the dreamworld has to give. But on some deeper level a more profound shift happens. John Weir Perry, a Jungian analyst who studied at the Jung Institute in Zürich and was in analysis with Jung, once said, "When I would walk out of the session with Jung, I may not have exact answers, specific solutions to problems, but I always felt more open and more spacious. There was more space between the parts of myself, more of me was available."[16] Variations of Perry's sense of spaciousness and being more open and present have been voiced by dreamers after sleeping in the dream house, as we have very clearly seen in Kevin's case.

Diane and the Owl Queen

Diane came to the dream retreat when she was at a crossroads in her life, a time of demanding choices and change in both love and work. On the day of preparation for her night of temple sleep, Diane allowed her life questions and challenges to get clearer and clearer. She took long walks in the woods, spending time sitting by the stream running through the property. She had a startling encounter with a mother grouse who flew directly at her, protecting her young babies. She felt the terrible beauty of this fierce mother bird. She wrote and painted many hours in her journal, clarifying where she was in her life and the choices she was facing. She talked with Tom about the overwhelming fear surrounding the choices she felt she was being called to make. As she sat in the dream house she formulated a question to present to her dreams. Her question was simple and yet, as she said, "It felt like the distillation of where I was and what I needed to ask: 'What must I do at this time in my life and what qualities do I need to do it?'"

The next morning, before she relayed the dream that had come to her the night before in the dream house, Diane said to the group, "During the procession through the dark out to the dream house, I felt in front of me the thousands of others who have gone before me, who have slept in dream temples through the ages. I felt the love and support of the other dream retreatants, and the fear and excitement coursing through my body. After I was tucked in by one of my fellow dreamers, and the procession moved back to the main house, I lay there in the dark, and, as I was falling asleep, I felt a strange sense of peace, like it was going to be okay. I woke with one of the most spectacular dreams of my life—more like a shamanic journey almost."

I am flying through the air holding on to the talons of a huge owl.

I know and trust her. We are flying over a deep pit filled with fire—like a volcano. The owl tells me to let go. I am too afraid. The fire is spouting out of the pit. She says to me, "Let go. Trust." I let go and am falling into the fire. I'm so frightened I think my heart will burst. Everything becomes a blur.

I am now in water, very muddy water, and I am crawling out onto a rocky beach. My skin is burned and black. My hair is gone. I am naked. My blackened flesh is hanging from my arms in several places, and thick mud is stuck all over me.

The beach is not sandy, but covered with small white pebbles—not heavy like normal rock, but more like pumice—light and full of holes. I can see green grass and light beyond the rocky beach, but it seems a long way off. As I crawl across the beach, small, dark, crablike things are biting at my flesh, but I feel no pain. By the time I reach the grass the mud is gone and I am standing whole again.

I cross the grass to where I see a doorway in a thick forest. The doorway is made of three logs—two upright and one across the top, an entranceway. The owl is perched on top of this entranceway. She says, "Enter."

I do.

There is a clearing in the woods that I couldn't see before I entered through the gateway. It is beautiful—breathtaking. The brightness is unearthly, yet not glaring—almost surreal. There is lush green grass and foliage, wildflowers, animals of all species and sizes—all peacefully milling around together. It's an enchanted forest. I can walk upright now. I touch and talk to the animals. I understand them and they understand me.

I see a woman sitting on a crystal chair—almost like a throne— near a small pond below a waterfall. She has reddish-blond hair and blue eyes. She's wearing a bright red dress and has a crystal band around her forehead that flashes rainbow colors—like a prism. She is barefoot but has gold anklets shaped like serpents around her ankles. There is a hawk on her shoulder. I have never felt such tranquillity and peace as I do in her presence. I look into the woman's eyes and recognize her—she is the owl.

I wake up.

Diane wrote a haiku from the dream. In the dream she said she felt like she deeply connected to all the elements of life, to the Mother of Life. "I felt like I almost became each of the elements. I felt the healing, renewing presence of Mother Earth. I fell through the air into the fire, found myself in water, and crawled out covered with mud." She felt like the dream immersed her in all of life, each element doing its unique healing. She summed it up in a haiku.

> *Letting go to fall*
> *thru Air, Fire, Water, Earth-Life*
> *Blessed be the Mother.*

Diane worked with the group on her dream the next morning, but we mostly sat in awe at the power and beauty of her dream experience. She kept saying in various ways, "The dream felt like it was really happening. I was there where I dreamed I was. The dream means what I experienced." She struggled to find words to express her dream. Tom kept thinking of the Talmud saying "The dream is its own interpretation." At some point Tom said to Diane something he had heard Ira Progoff once say in response to a particularly powerful journal entry someone had read out in the journal group: "I feel something has just been added to the scriptures of the world."

Diane had worked diligently on her incubation question and allowed herself to feel and face all the hopes and fears of that time in her life. Her work was richly rewarded with a powerful, transformative experience. She stayed in touch over the following months and years. She left her job in the corporate world and started down a road that led to her new life as a college professor, work she still does and loves. She also had the courage to let go of a relationship that was destructive and needed to change. In the dream she had died and been reborn. The great mother goddess owl became a totemic guide and source of strength. She honored the dream by building an altar for the owl and making regular offerings to it. The dream let her know that she had a source of courage, vision, and power within her that would guide her. This enabled her to realize, with Thoreau, that "if you advance confidently in the direction of your dreams and live the life you imagined, you will meet with success unexpected in the common hours."[17]

The dream retreats and the dream incubation rituals are a heightened version of the work we can do with our dreams all the time. Ultimately it is about developing and nourishing a relationship with our soul, the imaginative dreaming part of who we are. One of the Tasaday peoples, a Stone Age tribe living in the Philippines, when asked what the soul was, replied, "The soul is the part of us that sees the dream."[18] Dreamwork connects us with our soul. This is the real work of our lives, the work of psyche, the work of that deep imagining part of who we are, both awake and asleep. This is the slow, patient work of a lifetime.

Dreamwork invites us to pause in the rush of our lives. It invites us to go inside and listen to the still small voice in the innermost recesses of the psyche, where Jung said the dream resides. To question the dream, to learn to question and listen to the psyche's slow, deep response, is the essence of dreamwork, the quest ("quest-ion") of our lives. But as Heidegger says, "To know how to question means to know how to wait, even a whole lifetime. But an age which regards as real only what goes fast and can be clutched with both hands looks on questioning as 'remote from reality' and as something that does not pay, whose benefit cannot be numbered. But essential is not number, the essential is the right time, i.e., the right moment, and the right perseverance. 'For,' as Holderlin said, 'the mindful God abhors untimely growth.'"[19]

The religious alchemical maxim "In my patience is my soul" expresses a great deal of wisdom and guidance for working with our dreams. The rewards of dreamwork are immense, but they often come, as with most spiritual work, at the end, after hours of quiet, attentive, creative work. This often hard, slow work is beautifully expressed in the powerful poem "Night Work," by Thomas McGrath, where the dreamer, upon awakening, finds the world "hardly changed at all."

The psyche changes slowly, but it "hardly" changes. The soul grows and deepens through patient, hard, creative work. One of the marvels of dream work is that it not only gives us transformative images and experiences but also gives us the energy to live these transformative images in our waking lives. Dreamwork is natural change. As Marie Louise von Franz says, "Dreams are the voice of nature within us."[20] We change in response to the "all night chipping on the stones of sleep . . . on the old, known statue of solitude." We hardly change, but we change in deep, transformed ways.

9

The Cauldron
of Inexhaustible Gifts

In the Words of Coauthor Stephen Larsen

Listen: there was once a king sitting on his throne. Around Him stood great and wonderfully beautiful columns ornamented with ivory, bearing the banners of the king with great honor. Then it pleased the king to raise a small feather from the ground, and he commanded it to fly. The feather flew, not because of anything in itself but because the air bore it along. Thus am I, a feather on the breath of God.

HILDEGARD OF BINGEN

Let us learn to dream, gentlemen, then perhaps we shall find the truth. But let us beware of publishing our dreams till they have been tested by waking understanding.

FRIEDRICH AUGUST KEKULÉ

It is called Ceridwen's cauldron in Celtic mythology, the grail, in Arthurian lore, the Tsampo in the Finnish Kalevala. This magic vessel from which all good things come is often sought, feverishly fought over, and is one of our perennial representations of what depth psychologists call the creative unconscious. This chapter is to underline how, through the portal of dreams, a ceaseless flow of good things comes into our lives. In the inventory of things described in this chapter we will find inspirational music and poetry, great books, and also many inventions and scientific discoveries that have helped our world become what it is today.

The inventory is so incredibly vast, however, that to list everything it includes is well beyond the scope of this chapter. Thus our intention is just to illustrate the principle—so that you may become reluctant to devalue the oneiric world or use the silly expression "just a dream" ever again!

A few principles should be discussed at this point. They are as follows:

- First, the expectation that some good things can come from your own dreaming should be entertained—this chapter may, in fact, help with that.
- Second, the field of dreams should be seeded in the same manner as described in the chapter on dream incubation. (That is, a seed idea—something you would like to dream about—should be held in mind or meditated upon. But then you must also be attentive to what comes!)
- You will see in the examples below, that inspiration or the dream breakthrough favors, as Pasteur said, "the prepared mind." Powerful creative breakthroughs tend to come to people hard at work on a project; or there is an urgent need to help someone—even a whole culture—and the dreamer is working on it. As psychologist Jerome Bruner put the sequence: perspiration—inspiration—more perspiration . . . (and so on in a never-ending sequence for those who aspire—or perspire—to be cultural creatives).[1]

Even when a discovery of undeniable value is made through dreaming, there are skeptical minds who mock or disbelieve anyway. Thus our contention, as authors, is that unless you have tried the process yourself, really tried it, keep your disbelief and mockery to yourself, please—so as not to discourage other creative dreamers, especially children!

Famous Visionary Dreamers of Europe

Hildegard of Bingen (1098–1179)

> *These visions which I saw were not in sleep nor in dreams, nor in my imagination nor by bodily eyes or outward ears nor in a hidden place; but in watching, aware with the pure eyes of the mind and inner ear of the heart.*
>
> HILDEGARD OF BINGEN

You were promised a walk with Hildegard in chapter 7. In that chapter we looked at the clairvoyant and precognitive dimensions of dreaming, with a special look at three creative women (Joan of Arc, Lucrecia de Leon, and Harriet Tubman). In Hildegard's story, although paranormal features are present, they recede into the background in the face of her immense access to the visionary and creative dimensions. The vision of humanity embedded in nature, interrelated with all life-forms, but also expressing God, within and without, is absolutely extraordinary for a woman of the twelfth century. Her music and art are immortal. Her dreams and visions, as well as her sermons (she had an active circuit around Europe as a lecturer), are as extraordinary in the world of her time as are the exploits of Joan of Arc two centuries later.

Hildegard was born in 1098, in Mainz, Germany, the tenth and last child of her devout, well-to-do parents (her father was a knight). Her visionary gift was obvious from age three, when, it is reported, there came to her a "brightness so great that her soul trembled." (We will return to her "trembling" in just a little bit.) Her visionary gift seems to have begun then, along with recurrent illnesses, probably migraine headaches. After this first flooding with the inner light, so prevalent in her later visions and so familiar to shamanism, her clairvoyance was accurate enough to enable her to ascertain the colors of a calf that was still in its mother's womb, later to be verified as correct.

With her clairvoyance and precocious spiritual instincts, it is little wonder that Hildegard's parents decided that she would be their tithe (though this normally means giving a tenth of one's income to the church, in this case the couple gave their tenth child to the church!). Hildegard was eight when she was sent to the monastery of Mt. St. Disibode. The order was a little unusual for a German monastery/convent—it was a Benedictine Celtic order, founded by St. Disibode, who, although trained in the Irish tradition of St. Columba, wearied of the contention of the Irish monks, and set off on a pilgrimage, ending up in Germany. It was probably at Mt. St. Disibode that Hildigarde learned the beautiful illustrative calligraphy that characterized her writing and her art. (You may have wondered, as the authors did, why Hildegard's illustrations resemble those in the Book of Kells.) See plate 7 in the color insert.

At the age of eighteen, Hildegard would take vows and commit to the religious life. Under her tutor, Jutta von Sponheim, an anchoress from a noble family, she learned to read and write Latin, although imperfectly, later to be refined. Hildegard would continue her education with Volmer of St. Disibode—a monk not much older than she. Volmer would become her secretary and lifelong friend.

The biographies of Hildegard complain that she had almost forty years of illness, again, probably including migraines. Oliver Sacks, professor of clinical neurology at the Albert Einstein College of Medicine in the Bronx and popular writer on neurological subjects, looking at her art, said, "The style of the pictures is a clear indication that the seer suffered regularly from migraine attacks. Migraine sufferers tend to see things in this manner."[2] Migraines are related to seizure activity, hence the early "trembling" that Hildegard reports may correlate with this assessment. The migraines probably were not grand mal seizures—she is not known to have evinced headaches of this type—but something closer to temporal lobe epilepsy, which is known to be attended by visionary activity, and which, not uncommonly, provokes elaborate theological constructs.

The migraines dwindled as Hildegard approached the age of forty, and when her tutor Jutta died in 1136, Hildegard was appointed interim abbess in her stead. At this time, free from the authority of her mentor, Hildegard's visions increased mightily. She began composing her early music in 1140, and in 1141 she had a blinding vision accompanied by what she felt was a divine call to bear witness to what she had seen, by writing about it. When she neglected to do so, matters didn't go well for her—her illness returned.

Thus began one of the most extraordinary creative journeys of the late Middle Ages. During the subsequent years of her lifetime, until she died in 1179, Hildegard wrote, painted, composed, preached, and did everything women of the time never got to do. She corresponded with popes, archbishops, and contemporary kindred spirits of all kinds.

According to James E. Kiefer, "Hildegard wrote and spoke extensively about social justice, about freeing the downtrodden, about the duty of seeing to it that every human being, made in the image of God, has the opportunity to develop and use the talents that God has given him [or her], and to realize his God-given potential. This strikes a chord today. . . . And she wrote explicitly about the natural world as God's creation, charged through and through with His beauty and His energy; entrusted to our care, to be used by us for our benefit, but not to be mangled or destroyed."[3] Following are some examples of the most famous quotes attributed to Hildegard.

> *We cannot live in a world that is not our own, in a world that is interpreted for us by others. An interpreted Humanity, take a good look at yourself. Inside, you've got heaven and earth, and all of creation. You're a world—everything is hidden in you. An interpreted world is not a home. Part of the terror is to take back our own listening, to use our own voice, to see our own light.*

—

> *Glance at the sun. See the moon and the stars.*
> *Gaze at the beauty of earth's greenings.*
> *Now, think.*
> *What delight God gives to humankind*
> *with all these things.*

All nature is at the disposal of humankind.
We are to work with it. For
without we cannot survive.

〰

Humanity, take a good look at yourself. Inside, you've got
heaven and earth, and all of creation. You're a world—
everything is hidden in you."

〰

There is the music of Heaven in all things.

Argentinian composer Alejandro Viñao imagines that in the midst of her visions, Hildegard dreams a dream that is "too awesome, too frightening, to beautiful to be recorded or even to be acknowleged to anybody, perhaps not even to herself."

It was a musical dream: the armies of the Islam are overrunning Europe. Hildegard is attending a performance of one of her vocal compositions which the Lord had "revealed" to her in one of her visions. The piece is being sung by 80 nuns of her own convent. Half way through the performance the nuns start singing long notes which unfold micro tonal intervals and motives which no longer speak of God, but suggest the forbidden modes of the infidel. The original melismatic rhythms had now turned into figurations with no clear meter, the text, still in Latin, features both the names of Christ and Allah in it. The dream would be an intolerable nightmare if the music were not so overwhelmingly beautiful. Hildegard is suddenly woken up by her own singing.[4]

"Too awesome, too frightening, too beautiful," are clearly words that characterize a big dream. Viñao used the inspiration from this imagined big dream to compose a score that attempted to capture these elements.

An earlier section of our book introduces the visionary's relationship to the vision: "I will not let you go unless you bless me!" Here is the answering response from the creative unconscious to the human recipient: "I will not let you go unless you respect me, unless you manifest, write, sing, perform my children!" (Here we mean "my children" to be the songs, poems, plays, and works of art described in this chapter.) Hildegard writes that, after 1140 (her forty-second year), the spirit left her no option. If she did not write, paint, sing, preach, or otherwise perform her visions, things would not go well for her. This could be one reason for the prodigious creative output that caused some to label her one of "the most important woman figures in the history of the Middle Ages."[5]

Hildegard left us approximately seventy poems and nine books. Two of them are books of medical and pharmaceutical advice, dealing with the workings of the human body and the properties of various herbs. She wrote seventy-two songs, including a play set to music. As well, she left literally hundreds of drawings and illuminations including mandalas, mandorlas (oval shaped mandalas), and paintings of devotional subjects scattered in collections around Europe and the Americas. She preached sermons all over Europe, in places where a woman had never been heard before.

To return to the theme of this chapter—the cauldron of inexhaustible gifts—it is quite clear that this one outstanding twelfth-century cultural creative left a legacy that continues to inspire humanity into the present time. Included in her original thought is the concept of *viriditas,* the "greening" element in things; a profound respect for the world in which we are embedded, an anticipation of what Matthew Fox has called "creation spirituality," and perhaps a warning that should echo and resonate down through the twenty-first century: "All of creation God gives to humankind to use. If this privilege is misused, God's justice permits creation to punish humanity."[6]

Hildegard's genius is perennially inspirational, as is her music, art, and poetry, now beloved of New Age followers. There is something reminiscent of Synesius's universal humanity, so evident in his book *On Dreams.* We should remember that in her time, the Middle Ages was morphing into what we now call the Renaissance. It would be marked by illustrious figures such as Eleanor of Aquitaine, Bernard of Clairvaux, Abelard (and Heloise), and by construction of the great cathedral of Chartres. What we now call Western Civilization was beginning its most creative formative years; and dreams often guided the process!*

Researching dreaming in the centuries immediately after Hildegard leads us into the vision-dream that permeates European letters for the next several centuries and through the time of Shakespeare. In this tradition, the poet mingles dreams and visions together in a creative work. Thus begins a curious era in which the very existence of dreams becomes a literary device, in which the poet often starts his vision, usually allegorical in nature, with a dream. The reason is simple: not only philosophical tracts and "scientific works" but any creative act, any public statement whatsoever, was subject to an excruciating scrutiny by the church. Dreaming became (perhaps) a permissible excursion, which everyone, including members of the Inquisition, had to acknowledge as being beyond human control.

Christian ecclesiastical history and Greek and Roman mythology were the zones from which the creative imagination might draw its narratives. We find this in the literature, art, and music that begin to emerge in the thirteenth century. The metaphor of encountering all this via dream allowed the poetic imagination a kind of freedom to move fluidly between these realms. Gods, daemons, saints, and angelic visitations were all permissible, because they were understood to be the common experience and cultural birthright.

Italy's Dante Alighieri

Surely Dante Alighieri (1265–1321) is the outstanding progenitor of the dream-vision tradition. In his early work titled *La Vita Nuova,* Dante dreams of the death of Beatrice, a beautiful young creature whom he met when she was eight years of age (he was nine). The fact

---

*Shortly after Dante, Petrarch (1304–1374) and Boccaccio (1313–1375) celebrate dream-like ladies of poetic inspiration and celebrate love as a neglected sacrament that leads to the Divine. Boccaccio, shortly before his death, would write a biography of Dante.

that he never really knew her establishes her as an immortal inspiratrix, a Jungian anima indeed. Dante's Divine Comedy is now recognized not only as the greatest opus of Italian but also European literature in general; and it rocked the world of its day. (T. S. Eliot would say that for several centuries, the literate world of Europe was divided between these two: Dante and Shakespeare! "There is no third."[7]) Though the dreamlike sequence is set in the Christian afterlife, Virgil, Greek author of the *Aeneid,* is Dante's guide. The work has been called visionary, and it certainly is, in its textured and sweeping descriptions of the afterlife spaces. However, it is essentially a moral allegory in which Dante gets to pillory the narcissistic and entitled gentry of his time—and even put the pope in torment for his personal shortcomings.

The Divine Comedy has set the tone for the Western intellectual and visionary imagination. Spatially, it moves through worlds depicted as underworld, through places of penance and atonement, to unity with paradise and the Divine. Our imaginations now include the visions that Dante saw in his own poetic imagination and wrote about. (It is worthwhile for us to read the classics, for this if for no other reason.) Dante enlarged our mythic and dreaming imaginations immeasurably; his hell became our hell, his heaven our own—but because he was a poet, not a pope, we were free to respond to the spirituality he presented in our own way!

England's Dante Gabriel Rossetti

Dante's dreams of Beatrice have ignited the Western artistic imagination, among the most salient, the artist named for him: Dante Gabriel Rossetti. Rossetti's 1871 painting, *Dante's Dream at the Time of the Death of Beatrice,* is not only world famous but also influenced an entire generation after him with its theme. The painting shows Dante, among others, gathered at the dying Beatrice's bedside on June 9, 1290. In the painting, an angel kisses the dying girl. See plate 9 in the color insert.

At the same time as we fed our mythic and dreaming imagination, we were fed universal human morals and ethics. These, in fact, are the deep structure of the visionary imagination as Dante presents it, because, just as in the Eastern concept of karma, in effect, more grandly than had ever been done before—either in the Greek, or for that matter the Christian culture zones—the afterlife was mapped out for us as an inflection of our own attitudes and choices in this life.

It has been mentioned that dreams that permeate our lives—our lives, our times, our culture, and our ethics—also shape what we know of the afterlife. Dante gave us an image far more vivid than the tenebrous underworld of Hellenic mythology and less dichotomously reward-and-punishment based than the traditional Christian one. It is an imagining that came out of the twelfth century but haunts the mythic and dreaming imagination of today.

There is one more little embellishment that the reader who has savored chapter 7 might appreciate. If The Divine Comedy is one of the great dream/vision epics of Western Civilization (and it clearly is), it is even more enchanting to see the big dream itself clairvoyantly making sure it is not lost or mutilated. When Dante passed away in 1321, a portion of the manuscript was lost, perhaps never to be found . . . until, as Alighieri's son attests, his father appeared to him in a dream and took him to where the missing piece was located. The dream—or visitation—was striking enough so that forthwith, Dante's son went to the place his father had indicated and found the missing portion.[8]

England's Geoffrey Chaucer and William Shakespeare

Geoffrey Chaucer was profoundly influenced by The Divine Comedy, and with a mind perhaps as wild as Dante's, changed the culture of his time, profoundly mingling dream and literature. "Chaucer's dream visions have idiosyncratic features that are not always found in other dream visions: The dreamer's inexperience in love is emphasized; dream lore is usually treated respectfully; the dream grows out of the narrative contained in a book the dreamer reads before he falls asleep; the dream, in turn, inspires the dreamer to write something after he wakes."[9]

The important point in Chaucer's dream visions is that Chaucer saw "new poetic and artistic possibilities in the use of dream." He linked the dream with both reality and the proceeding action; he intentionally used the illusion inherent in the dream, and in addition to that, he portrays his own second self within this dream-world. "Artistic problems of specific nature thus arose, which Chaucer solved in his own way: the transition into the dream state, the relation between dream and reality, and the rendering of dream psychology."[10]

A new genre was being formed, which is the departure, in literature, from narrative description to dream to poetry and back to dream again. This device will become salient in Western literature from this epoch onward. We can see it as an historic literary convention and an affirmation that dream is pivotal and indispensible to creativity (the theme of this chapter).

Perhaps no writer more than William Shakespeare has mentioned "dream" as frequently in his work. He used it as a metaphor for waking life, interchanging dream, drama, and waking states of consciousness—thus affirming their commonality.

A Midsummer Night's Dream has enchanted audiences for centuries and moves so freely between dream, folktale, mythology, drama, and back into dream that it must stand as the acme of the dream-vision genre. Shakespeare has given us some of the most memorable quotes in the English language concerning dreams. We use an example from *Hamlet* for an excursion into one of our recurring themes of this book: "To die, to sleep. / To sleep, perchance to dream—ay, there's the rub, / For in that sleep of death what dreams may come / When we have shuffled off this mortal coil, / Must give us pause."

In this most famous of all soliloquys, Shakespeare has taken us back to the identity of death, sleep, and dreaming; and waking life as well.

What Dreams May Come, titled from Shakespeare's phrase, is also a book by Richard Matheson. Matheson was previously a writer of horror stories who changed his genre for this important story, based on some recent philosophical readings, including Emanuel Swedenborg's accounts of the soul's state in the afterlife. Matheson stated in an interview, "I think *What Dreams May Come* is the most important (read effective) book I've written. It has caused a number of readers to lose their fear of death—the finest tribute any writer could receive."[11]

The book was made into an Academy Award–winning movie starring Robin Williams, and with strong associations both to Dante and the mythic story of Orpheus and Euridice. In the story, Chris Nielson (Robin Williams) is killed in an auto accident. His wife then commits suicide over the tragedy. To rescue her he has to go into a lower region of the "world of spirits" (Swedenborg's term for the "vestibule realm," of the afterlife). The lower region, which also looks like a nightmare version of their—almost, but not quite, hell—is reserved for suicides. Nielson is thus also in the mythological role of Orpheus, the musician-hero rescuing his beloved Eurydice from the realm of shades.

This story, reaffirming the consanguinity of Thanatos, Somnus, Morpheus, and Phoebetor, illustrates the profundity of Shakespeare's quote from *Hamlet*. If waking life can be dreamlike (or nightmarish, as depicted in many of his plays) what dreams, indeed, may come when we are in the spirit world after Thanatos has done his work? It is a trenchant question, because we are free from the body, its desires and appetites, as well as its grounding presence. Shakespeare, in a single phrase, against the profound backdrop of the play, has shown us the interpenetration of these worlds.

The way that Shakespeare frames and executes his dramas shows us that they occur in a consciousness that moves from the social, historical world, to dream, to myth, to allegory and metaphor. In his last play, *The Tempest*, enacted on a more mythical than geographical island, and in a more mythical than historical time, he concludes the play with Prospero's great soliloquy: "These our actors, / As I foretold you, were all spirits and / Are melted into air, into thin air / . . . We are such stuff / As dreams are made on, and our little life / Is rounded with a sleep."

Emanuel Swedenborg's Journal of Dreams

Emanuel Swedenborg, the Swedish nobleman and natural scientist turned mystic whose work Richard Matheson researched for *What Dreams May Come,* began his postscientific, previsionary phase (at about the age of fifty-five) with one of the first thorough dream journals ever recorded in the West. In it, he not only records much of a year of dreams but also endeavors modern interpretations of them, not too alien to psychoanalysis or Jung's analytical psychology, for that matter. In that journal, written in about 1744 (but not published until much later, after his death), Swedenborg details his spiritual conversion experience from scientist to mystic, in a face-to-face confrontation with a figure of "Holy Mein," in whose face he trembled. This, clearly a big dream, or a cross between a vision and a dream, converted the career natural scientist to an interpreter of biblical texts, on which he spent his next thirty-plus years.

Swedenborg affirms in his dry prose what Shakespeare the poet says more concisely and elegantly. With the exactitude of a natural scientist, he examines what happens when people bring their characters and characterology to a bodiless existence. Unlike the traditional crime-and-punishment model of "God the Judge," Swedenborg offers a model psychospiritually similar to Dante, or Buddhism, for that matter. People carry their spiritual freight with them into the afterlife. If we awaken a little before death, or attend to our dreams, the proclivities of our energy field, our "ruling love," as Swedenborg calls it, will inexorably take us to inferno, purgatorio, or paradiso.

The reader has detected by now that in this chapter we are moving forward in historical time, but with repeated attention to dreams and creativity. It would be curious and interesting to explore the ambivalent relationship of Swedenborg and William Blake. There can be no doubt that dreams are important to Blake's visionary and artistic productions, but we will first pause in Blake's own time (curious that Blake was born in the year, 1755, that Swedenborg says his "spiritual eyes were opened") to discuss two of his contemporaries, perhaps closer to our theme of this chapter.

England's William Wordsworth, Samuel Taylor Coleridge, and William Blake

"Ode: Intimations of Immortality From Recollections of Early Childhood"

Our birth is but a sleep and a forgetting:
The Soul that rises with us, our life's Star,
Hath had elsewhere its setting,
And cometh from afar.
Not in entire forgetfulness,
And not in utter nakedness,
But trailing clouds of glory do we come
From God, who is our home . . .

WILLIAM WORDSWORTH

The era of the dream-vision or vision-dream culminated in the eighteenth century in the work of Wordsworth, Coleridge, and Blake. Wordsworth says it clearly: Our origin is divine, this life is delusional; "forgetting" supervenes more and more as we age, becoming immersed in the world of time and space and things social and economic. As children we still knew glory. We may recover it when we shuffle off this mortal coil and come face-to-face with it again. In between, as no one shows better than Shakespeare, we are dreaming, dramatizing; acting as if we were really awake.

In regard to Blake, it is evident in his whole corpus that the dream-like visionary quality emerges throughout his poetry and visual art. He does not recount dreams verbatim, rather his entire corpus of myth, drawing, and poetry is suffused with dream (see color insert, plate 10).

Wordsworth and Blake, though contemporaries, were not exactly on good terms. Perhaps their best mutual friend was Samuel Taylor Coleridge, who was willing to travel back and forth and talk to each of his creative peers. One afternoon, having ingested a posset of laudanum (a mixture of opium and alcohol), and having earlier read of Kubla Khan's creations in Xanadu, Coleridge experienced in a vision, and then wrote out as if verbatim, one of the most famous dream poems in the English language (though he himself said he regarded it as a "curiosity").

What we would like to underscore here is that, to the prepared mind, dreams may speak in an intact, metrical, incantatory voice. Coleridge clearly possessed a highly educated and exercised poetic mind. His mythic imagination followed suit, eventuating in the poem. Curiosity or not, the poem itself bristles with archetypal fullness! It is a world that Gaston Bachelard would have understood, the landscape and architecture of dream: a sacred river, an ancient forest, a garden bright with sinuous rills, a deep romantic chasm, caverns measureless to man, a sunless sea—and of course, "a pleasure dome."

In regard to *Kubla Khan*, Bachelard is right: the poetic landscape and geometry contains its deepest layer of meaning—in fact, those things embody the message and the deep structure of the poem. There are few dramatis personae, except for Kubla Khan himself, or the "Abyssinian maid" in the latter part. Otherwise the poem summons a mythic landscape so compelling that all the centuries since Coleridge regard the poem as incantatory and evocative.

England's Mary Shelley and Her Monster

When I was a young lad of about ten, I was allowed to see the original movie *Frankenstein*. It scared me beyond belief. The idea that a monster could be galvanized to life, and that it would then, mindlessly, stalk the landscape, wreaking terror and havoc, was very, very frightening—as it has been to many a child. I had many nightmares—involving the implacable visitations of the monster, and this recurring dream formed what I would call the "terror" region of my childhood imagination.

Tom has shared with me an additional similarity between us: his own earliest nightmare was of the *Frankenstein* monster.

Therefore, it should be no surprise that the monster himself was conceived in the middle of the night by Mary Shelley—in a visionary moment, not separable from a dream (dream monster stalks children's dreams!).

"It proved a wet, ungenial summer," Mary remembered in 1831, "and incessant rain often confined us for days to the house." Sitting around a log fire at Byron's villa, the company amused themselves with German ghost stories, which prompted Byron to propose that they "each write a ghost story."[12]

Unable to think of one, young Mary Godwin became anxious: "'Have you thought of a story?' I was asked each morning, and each morning I was forced to reply with a mortifying negative."

During one mid-June evening, the discussions turned to the nature of the principle of life. "Perhaps a corpse would be re-animated," Mary noted. "Galvanism had given token of such things." It was after midnight before they retired, and, unable to sleep, she became possessed by her imagination as she beheld the grim terrors of her "waking dream," her ghost story: "I saw the pale student of unhallowed arts kneeling beside the thing he had put together. I saw the hideous phantasm of a man stretched out, and then, on the working of some powerful engine, show signs of life, and stir with an uneasy, half vital motion. Frightful must it be; for supremely frightful would be the effect of any human endeavour to mock the stupendous mechanism of the Creator of the World."[13]

Thus, the demand that a bright, creative woman must keep up with the creative men in her life (Percy Shelley, Lord Byron) "galvanized," if you will, a dream—or a dreamlike vision that has since galvanized the nightmares (scary dreams) of many generations of children.

We live in a "Frankenstein" world where our creature, intended to be beautiful and wise, is anything but—it is mechanical and destructive. Are not technology, bureaucracy, and the corporations the monster?

Mary Shelley's was clearly a big dream, a collective dream about our mutual themes: Why young people are so obsessed with "zombies," the interface of that "which ought to be dead" with life. We are here in an existential "liminal zone" in which neither life itself nor death itself, but the relationship between them, is what counts.

GIFTS FROM THE CAULDRON

- The filmmakers Federico Fellini and Ingmar Bergman often used dreams as inspiration for their films.

Fig. 9.1. Frontispiece to the 1831 edition of Frankenstein—*the first science-fiction novel. The work was derived from Mary Shelley's dream.*

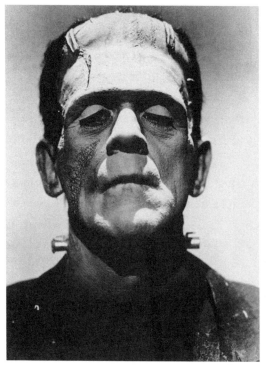

Fig. 9.2. Boris Karloff as Frankenstein's monster (from the 1935 film Bride of Frankenstein)

- Ingmar Bergman claims his film *The Virgin Spring* is taken almost verbatim from one of his dreams.
- Robert Louis Stevenson dreamed the characters and plot for *Dr. Jekyll and Mr. Hyde.*
- *Sophie's Choice,* the novel by William Styron, later made into a powerful, award-winning film, was inspired by a dream.
- Poe's "The Raven," Voltaire's *Candide,* Dostoyevsky's *Crime and Punishment* were all inspired by dreams.
- The great writer Graham Greene said, "A major character has to come somehow out of the unconscious. I catalogue my dreams, searching for tracks of a fresh character. . . . I have always been interested in dreams and the unconscious."[14]
- Jack Kerouac kept a detailed dream journal.
- Not surprisingly, many of Salvatore Dali's paintings were first seen by him in a dream.
- Many of Stephen King's novels were inspired by dreams; for example, *Misery* and *Dreamcatcher.* As King might say, "Perhaps in dreams we are all novelists."
- Jack Nicklaus discovered a new golf swing in a dream; it brought him out of a slump.
- Elias Howe's invention of the sewing machine was inspired by a dream.
- Wagner's *Tristan and Isolde* derived from a dream.
- Guiseppi Tartini's "Devil's Sonata" was also inspired by a dream. The nineteenth-century composer dreamed that he handed the devil the score, then proceeded to play a sonata of great beauty. Although he said it was the best sonata he had ever composed, its quality, apparently, did not match the one he'd heard in his dream. See plate 8 in the color insert.

Music and Dream

Much modern (as well as classical) music owes its genesis to a dream. Founder of the award-winning African choral group Ladysmith Black

Mambazo, Joseph Shabalala, said he heard singing in a recurring series of dreams prior to assembling the (young male) singers who went on to make the group famous.

"Yesterday," one of the most popular and widely recorded songs in the world, had a complicated birth that illustrates some of the themes of this chapter. According to biographers, Paul McCartney composed the entire melody in a dream one night in his room at the Wimpole Street home of his girlfriend at the time, Jane Asher.[15] All that came was the melody; no words. But he acted, upon waking up, as any musically entuned dreamer should: to avoid forgetting it; he went to a piano and played the tune—the equivalent of writing a narrative or a poem or doing a drawing in your dream journal.

The tune had a haunting, immortal quality that McCartney couldn't forget. He became obsessed by the idea that he had heard it somewhere and couldn't remember where (a phenomenon psychologists call cryptomnesia). Evidently McCartney, who shows us his sense of ethics along with his obsession with the tune, tried to find its origin, looking all over the musical world for it. He couldn't find it; it had emerged, all newborn, from the cauldron of inexhaustible gifts.

His interviewees said, "No, it's lovely, and I'm sure it's all yours." According to McCartney, "It took me a little while to allow myself to claim it, but then like a prospector I finally staked my claim; stuck a little sign on it and said, 'Okay, it's mine!' It had no words. I used to call it 'Scrambled Eggs—oh my darling how I love your legs!'"[16]

The other Beatles didn't feel the tune really fit in with their style and weren't sure they liked it. George Harrison said, "Blimey, he's always talking about that song. You'd think he was Beethoven or somebody!" It became a kind of joke among them, and they continued to call it "scrambled eggs."[17]

McCartney said the breakthrough with the lyrics came during a trip to Portugal in May 1965. "I remember mulling over the tune 'Yesterday' and suddenly getting these little one-word openings to the verse. I started to develop the idea . . . da-da da, yes-ter-day, sud-den-ly, fun-il-ly, mer-il-ly and yes-ter-day, that's good. All my troubles seemed so far away. It's easy to rhyme those a's: say, nay, today, away, play, stay, there's a lot of rhymes and those fall in quite easily, so I gradually pieced it together from that journey. Sud-den-ly, and 'b' again, another easy rhyme: e, me, tree, flea, we, and I had the basis of it."[18]

Musical geniuses have sometimes gotten unforgettable lyrics and had to go hunting for a tune. In this case it went the other way around—an immortal tune in search of lyrics. (We see the formula: inspiration—perspiration—inspiration.) In this case, McCartney was the only one who believed in it—that there were "intimations of immortality" in a song not quite fledged. It missed two Beatles' albums while it lay in its incubator before, on its release, rising to ascendancy and becoming one of the most popular songs of all time.

Science and Dreams

Alfred Nobel should have won a Nobel Prize! Only there wasn't one yet—he had to endow it himself—and mostly the world does not know that the inspiration for the explosives that made Nobel wealthy emerged from sleep, and in the middle of the night.[19] And we will see that many of the great scientific, humanitarian, and creative inventions for which the innovators received Nobel's prizes came through the dream portal.

Our first example chronologically preceded the institution of the Nobel Prize, and in fact August von Kekulé, who, as the founder of modern organic chemistry, and received many honors equivalent to the prize, lived in exactly the same era as Nobel. (However, early in the 1900s, Kekulé's chemistry students Jacobus van t'Hoff (1901), Emil Fischer (1902), and Adolf von Baeyer (1905) did each win the Nobel Prize.)

During the early part of the nineteenth century chemistry had come to a halt—a seemingly insuperable enigma blocked the way. The periodic table of the elements, itself a gift from the dream cauldron to scientist Dmitri Mendeleev, had been largely articulated. As a result of his dream, Mendeleev organized the table to show the relationship between those basic elements—hydrogen, carbon, oxygen, and so on, based on

*Fig. 9.3. Dmitri Mendeleev dreamed a scientific discovery:
the periodic table to the elements. While asleep, he saw the table with all the
elements correctly placed; he woke and immediately wrote it down.*

their valencies (their tendency to bond, due to positive or negative charge, based on electrons and protons). But there lay a great unknown beyond—organic compounds: the stuff of living matter, the missing link between chemistry and biology—that still lay shrouded in mystery. For example, the compounds urea and ammonium cyanate each contained equal amounts of carbon, hydrogen, oxygen, and nitrogen atoms (in the ratio: 1:4:1:2) but had extremely different chemical properties. Why?

Chemists, around this time "were working in the dark," suggests science writer Royston Roberts.[20] There was no structural theory of organic compounds, nor how the elements that formed them, held together.

Kekulé, who first wanted to be an architect, was inspired by the chemical pioneer Justus von Liebig. After his graduation from university he gained a position, first at the University of Heidelberg, Germany, then at Ghent, in Belgium. But it was while he was residing in Clapham, England, that the first great vision happened—in some ways more like a daydream than a dream. He was riding on the upper level of a bus, heading toward his residence, when

> I fell into a reverie, and lo, the atoms were gamboling before my eyes. Whenever, hitherto, these diminutive beings had appeared to me, they had always been in motion, but, up till that time I had never been able to discern the nature of their motion. Now, however, I saw how the larger ones formed a chain, dragging the smaller ones after them but only at the ends of a chain.[21]

Then the conductor shouted out "Clapham Road!" and awakened Kekulé from dreaming. That was, he said, the beginning of the structural theory for which he became justly famous.

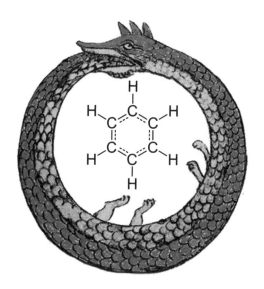

Fig. 9.4. Kekulé's dream: A snake swallows its tail, helping him visualize the structure of the chemical compound benzene.

It was when he was in residence in Ghent, Belgium, in an "elegant bachelor's quarters," that the sequel occurred: benzene was a volatile aromatic from whale oil, used in lamps and public lighting all over Europe, and which contained carbon and oxygen in equal proportions.[22] (The same aromatic compound was also found in the tar distilled from coal.) It was tremendously useful and very important—but no one could suggest a structural pattern for the molecule, which contained an equal amount of carbon and oxygen atoms (six of each). Both of the quoted passages herein are from Kekulé's own lips, in the speech given, at an occasion to honor him and his discovery, in Berlin's City Hall, in 1890.

> I was writing on my own textbook, but the work did not progress, my thoughts were elsewhere. I turned my chair to the fire and dozed.
>
> Again the atoms were gamboling before my eyes. This time the smaller groups kept modestly in the background. My mental eye, rendered more acute by repeated visions of this kind, could now distinguish larger structures of manifold conformation: Long rows sometimes more closely fitted together all twining and twisting in snake-like motion. But look! What was that? One of the snakes had seized hold of its own tail, and the form whirled mockingly before my eyes. As if by a flash of lightning, I awoke; and this time also I spent the rest of the night in working out the consequences of the hypothesis.[23]

Though some scientists have since disputed that there could be anything like a dream at the basis of Kekulé's profound discovery,[24] the forgoing are his own words. Kekulé's dreams enabled modern organic chemistry to find its way into such discoveries as plastics, synthetic fabrics and rubber, many medicines, and dyes.

Nobel, who died the same year as Kekulé (1896), decided his prize should be awarded to persons who have "conferred the greatest benefit on mankind," in the fields of physics, chemistry, literature, and an "idealistic" contribution to peace between nations and all mankind.

☙

A dedicated researcher like August Kekulé, Professor Otto Loewi was working on a known problem in neuroscience in 1920. How does the electrical activity propagated by one neuron get to another neuron across the space called a synapse (the micro-space between neurons, which do not directly touch each other)? A neurochemical basis for the transmission had been proposed as early as 1877 but never was experimentally proved. (Santiago Ramon y Cajal had discovered the contiguity theory of neurons, including the synapse—for which he was awarded the Nobel Prize in 1906—but no one had yet discovered the medium of transmission across the synapse.)

Loewi, a graduate of the University of Strasbourg, had been first given a position at the University of Marburg in Germany, then an appointment as professor of pharmacology at the University of Graz, Austria.

The solution first came to him in 1920, in a dream that he wrote on a thin slip of paper, but felt he didn't really "have it." It then recurred, and this time he awakened and wrote it down in great detail. He then designed the experiment that proved the theory, an experiment involving the acceleration and deceleration of frog hearts, which proved the neurochemical basis of neuronal stimulation.[25] He called the "calming" substance he had discovered *vagustoff* (acetylcholine), while the stimulating substance was called *acceleranstoff* (epinephrine).

Now remember, reader, that we have discussed in chapter 2 how these two neurotransmitters are alternatively dominant during waking consciousness and sleeping—the biochemistry of consciousness. When the brain is awash in the adrenaline—epinephrine-style neurotransmitters—it is awake. When it is awash in the acetylcholine, it is usually asleep and dreaming.

The Nobel Prize (shared with H. H. Dale) was awarded to Loewi in 1936.

The fact that Loewi made public the source of his discovery in a dream affected and enabled another researcher to win the Nobel Prize. Australian born John Eccles traveled to England on a Rhodes scholarship and came to work with renowned physiologist Sir Charles

Sherrington, and published with him on the subject of reflexes of the cat spinal cord.

D. Todman writes of how Eccles

> recalled in his memoirs, "Then in 1947 I developed an electrical theory of synaptic inhibitory action which conformed with all the available experimental evidence. Incidentally this theory came to me in a dream. On awakening I remembered the near-tragic loss of Loewi's dream, so I kept myself awake for an hour or so going over every aspect of the dream, and found it fitted all experimental evidence." The details were diagrammed and published in *Nature* in 1947 and became known as the "Golgi-cell theory of inhibition." It was an ingenious model which used the current flow of an excited interneurone to generate electronic foci on neurones upon which the synapses were placed."[26]

Eccles would write more on his speculations about dreams and psychological creativity in his dialogues with Karl Popper in *The Self and the Brain*.

Einstein Dreams Relativity

We can have very few doubts that Albert Einstein was a dreamer. He credits his discovery of the relativity theory to a dream: In his dream, Albert was sledding. "He was hurtling down a mountainside. He speeds faster and faster upon which he looked to the sky and saw the stars were altered in appearance as he approached the speed of light."[27]

Einstein was a visionary—that is, he saw ideas as images, and then made further deductions about the ideas. In his autobiography, he records

> a paradox upon which I had already hit at the age of sixteen: If I pursue a beam of light with the velocity c (velocity of light in a vacuum), I should observe such a beam of light as an electromag-

netic field at rest though spatially oscillating. There seems to be no such thing, however, neither on the basis of experience nor according to Maxwell's equations. From the very beginning it appeared to me intuitively clear that, judged from the standpoint of such an observer, everything would have to happen according to the same laws as for an observer who, relative to the earth, was at rest. For how should the first observer know or be able to determine, that he is in a state of fast uniform motion? One sees in this paradox the germ of the special relativity theory is already contained.[28]

Einstein riding on a rainbow has inspired a whole generation of dramatists, novelists, and new scientists to imagine how inspiration came to the great wooly-haired genius. What we do know is that dreams and visionary experiences were very influential for Albert Einstein. An evidently fine amateur pianist and violinist, Einstein wrote, "All great achievements of science must start from intuitive knowledge. I believe in intuition and inspiration. . . . At times I feel certain I am right while not knowing the reason."[29] Thus his famous statement that, for creative work in science, "imagination is more important than knowledge."[30] He told Max Wertheimer that he never thought in logical symbols or mathematical equations, but rather in images, feelings, and even musical architectures. Einstein's autobiographical notes reflect the same thought: "I have no doubt that our thinking goes on for the most part without the use of symbols, and, furthermore, largely unconsciously."[31] Elsewhere he wrote even more baldly that "[n]o scientist thinks in equations."[32]

Einstein preferred to think creatively in music rather than equations.

His son Hans amplified what Einstein meant by recounting that "[w]henever he felt that he had come to the end of the road or into a difficult situation in his work, he would take refuge in music, and that would usually resolve all his difficulties." After playing piano, his sister Maja said, he would get up saying, "There, now I've got it." Something in the music would guide his thoughts in new and creative directions.[33]

An Example of Problem Solving with a Dream

An intriguing example of engineering problem solving occurred in my practice and has never been elsewhere recorded. A retired electrical engineer who was bringing in a relative for treatment heard that I was writing this book on dreams and dreaming. A very modest and conservative-seeming man, he became exited hearing me talk—remembering how a dream had helped him solve an engineering problem more than forty years before. Here is his story.

During my early years [circa 1972] as a new hardware-design engineer at a large computer company, I worked with a small team that designed and tested an adapter that provided an interface between large mainframe input/output [I/O] channels and a smaller microprocessor-based controller in development at the time. For testing purposes, we built hardware models of the design using transistor-transistor [TTL] bipolar logic gates. We used an asynchronous rather than a synchronous design approach.

In a synchronous design an electronic oscillator generates a repeating series of equally spaced pulses called a clock signal. This clock signal is applied to all the memory elements in the circuit, called latches or flip-flops. The output of the flip-flops only change when triggered by the edge of the clock pulse. Changes to the logic signals throughout the design begin at the same time, at regular intervals synchronized by the clock. The outputs of all the flip-flop memory elements provide the overall state of the design. The state of a synchronous design changes only on the clock pulse. In contrast, an asynchronous design has no clock. The state of the circuit changes as soon as the input changes. Since they don't have to wait for a clock pulse to begin processing inputs, asynchronous designs can be faster than synchronous designs, and their speed is theoretically limited only by the propagation delays of the logic gates. Because of the speed advantage and lower power consumption, we decided to go with an asynchronous design.

However, asynchronous circuits are more difficult to design and subject to problems not found in synchronous circuits. This is because the resulting state of an asynchronous circuit can be sensitive to the relative arrival times of inputs at the gates. If transitions on two inputs arrive at almost the same time, the circuit can go into the wrong state depending on slight differences in the propagation delays of the gates. This is called a race condition.

Due to the difficulty of asynchronous designs, we encountered several timing/race condition issues during our testing. I remember one such problem, which was particularly difficult to diagnose. The design would work flawlessly for hours, even days. Then suddenly the hardware would go to an incorrect state and fail. Our design team struggled for days trying to determine the cause of the problem so that a solution could be developed. Our design and testing tools at the time were not nearly as advanced as they are today using software simulation. I would think about this problem day and night with visions of pulses setting and resetting flip-flops dancing around in my head constantly. Then one night, I woke up from a dream about the problem. A clear cause and solution to the problem came to me during this dream. I immediately got up, pulled out a paper copy of the logic design, and went straight to the flip-flop that the dream indicated was getting into an incorrect state. Due to the arrival times of certain inputs, a small pulse, or glitch, was being generated that would periodically reset the flip-flop to the wrong state and cause the failure that had us stumped for days.

The next day we designed a solution by adjusting the delays of certain circuits to get rid of the reset pulse. Of course, we encountered other problems during the testing of this design, and we worked through them one at a time. Dreams did not come to the rescue again. However, I still remember this one incident more than forty years ago and how amazed I was that a solution to a problem could come to me through a dream!

Postscript

After citing Einstein and Kekulé, why should we finish with such an ordinary-seeming story? The answer, the reader will find, is embedded in our question. Many of the more famous examples have been published elsewhere and perhaps become familiar to some readers.

The cauldron does not distribute gifts only to the already gifted, nor the rich and famous. The process goes on daily in our lives. We wanted to combine this unique collection of dream-creativity, because each and every story contains a gem of some kind—brilliant and diamondlike, leading to prizes and valued works or solving problems that we might call small and quotidian.

The formula remains the same whether for Einstein or for the ordinary person: perspiration—inspiration—perspiration. Or as we have seen time and again, our deep and purposeful preoccupations become interwoven with our creative unconscious. The answers it comes up with can be breathtaking and brilliant, but they mirror the integrity and tenacity of the individual human quest.

10

Dreaming While Awake,
Waking in the Dream

We know there is such a thing as a daydream because most of us do it. We do it, however, mostly without awareness—although every now and then we catch ourselves red-handed—triggered by an exotically beautiful person or a critical situation in which we behaved suboptimally and now are correcting our ineptitude. We tell off the critical employer or relative; we give the bully what he or she deserves; we approach the person we found attractive. It is satisfying and vindicating to do so—at least for a little while—while the daydream lasts.

The prototype of this wish-fulfilling or compensatory daydream is found in *The Secret Life of Walter Mitty,* wherein James Thurber shows how an ineffectual Walter Mitty compensates his wimpy character in real life by grandiose episodes of adventure and conquest. Our daydreams may enact this kind of compensation for real-life failures, or more practically, rehearse us with the ideal putdown or clever strategy that defeats the bully next time. It is a truism that the more bland the outer environment, or the more ineffectual our capabilities, the richer the daydream— or the more introverted or passive the character, the more brilliant the imagined solution. But sometimes such creative daydreaming is the response to an unasked question, as when Einstein gratuitously rides a rainbow and looks at the speed and flow of light. It is clear that all of us, even the most creative, may benefit (or suffer) by dreaming while awake.

Less well known but also explored in this chapter is the idea that waking consciousness may penetrate the dream, as in the lucid dreaming taught by the Senoi dream teachers or Stanford's Stephen LaBerge. Can we wake up in the dream without rupturing the fabric of the dreaming? Can we inhabit this other world that visits us at night with something like our daytime consciousness? It is not hard to find immediate uses for such mingling of the different forms of consciousness. If dreams are creative, can we question them on the spot, as it were?

Think of Elias Howe's invention of the modern sewing machine, where the dream put him in a situation in which he was about to be parboiled and eaten by dream cannibals unless he discovered the riddle (of how to make a working sewing machine). He became lucid enough to notice the king's guard's spears, with a perforated tip, and realized that contained the right answer for his dilemma—put the "eye" at the tip of the needle. He had to wake up a little to realize that the richness and creativity of the dream put the answer right before his (dreaming—but potentially awake) eyes. If he had stayed lost in the dream, he would have drowned in the fear of the cannibal-king's pot and not noticed that the answer he sought in the waking world was twinkling right in front of his dreaming gaze.

And yet, as we shall see, there are dangers that the ever-egocentric waking mind, or ego, will misuse or endanger the natural wildness of the dream unfoldment by intervening or destroying its pregnant-with-meaning quality, or *polyvalence,* with conscious fundamentalism, or self-centered, well, egocentricity.

By considering both species of these minglings of waking and dreams, we are suggesting that they are complementary and available to all of us who wish to surf the Internet of consciousness—that is, the wave forms of waking-dream, dreaming-wakefully, or both. Our goal is to raise the reader's own consciousness to make the choice of what seems healthy and productive, or conversely, maybe escapist, self-serving, or grandiose! The reader who has followed us attentively so far has probably formed the idea that we subscribe to a continuity of consciousness into the realm customarily called the unconscious and back out again; from waking into dream to waking again—a never-ending story.

Revisiting the Seething Sea of Brain Waves

The idea that there is no false dreaming is first introduced in chapter 1, "Ancient Dreaming," particularly in the work of Synesius; however, the states that accompany dreaming vary in the quality of attention we bring to them. Moving through the yogic theory of Patanjali, and our second chapter, we show how modern brain science echoes the ancient wisdom of yoga in pointing out that all of the brain wave ranges—delta, theta, alpha, beta, and gamma—are visible in a sequence of EEG at any one time; *thus they interpenetrate anyway!* We also mentioned that the proportions vary with the age of the maturing child, so that infants have predominantly slow delta (0.5–4 Hz) waves of sleeping; the young, frequently daydreaming child shows the next range, theta (4–8 Hz); finally around ten years of age, the beginning of teenage years (and Piaget's "fully operational," or logical, thinking), alpha (8–12 Hz) predominates; with bursts of beta (12–22 Hz) corresponding to concentration or mental effort. Hi-beta (22–28 Hz) corresponds to all the well-known anxieties of adulthood, sleeplessness, and hypervigilance. Above that, there is even some idea that gamma (28–50 Hz) accompanies highly intensified consciousness as in spiritual masters and makes "time slow down" (because the brain is moving so fast!).

We add to this the idea that deep sleep (delta) is interrupted by REM states, often overlapping with the experience of dream sequences in which waking consciousness is seemingly present in the dream, as people imagine themselves solving problems or carrying their waking concerns into the dream. The mirror image is of course the daydreaming child or adult, who, even with eyes open and seeming wakefulness, is preoccupied with inner realities. We also mentioned how the yogi—or the iatromantic initiate—can move freely between the states, on the turiya thread of continuing consciousness.

Alpha-Theta Training

When I first began to study neurofeedback as the key to consciousness, alpha training was all the rage. It bestowed something similar to spiritual disciplines and long-term meditation. There was even the idea that alpha training could bestow happiness. So neurofeedback manufacturers made pocket-size alpha devices that could help put people (not just Californians) in a permanent state of well-being.

Not long after the alpha-craze, Elmer Green and others at the Menninger Foundation discovered that theta, the range below alpha, was associated with the recovery of deep emotional memories, early traumas, even spiritual experiences. The only problem with pure theta training was that while the wave form seemed to be the key to deep emotional states, it also could provoke a literal reliving of the trauma, or re-traumatization. This was exactly what Freud and his followers had postulated as the key to emotional relief from pains of the past—the reliving, or emotional catharsis, of past experiences.

It was while working with Vietnam veterans—a highly resistant population—that Eugene Peniston seemed to discover the magic bullet. It was called alpha-theta training. The theta training would allow the veterans to relive their PTSD or combat-related traumas. The alpha, simultaneously cultivated, would "pour oil on the water" of emotional trauma. That meant that traumatized people—from military or domestic violence—could relive their traumas more safely. It has been known by psychologists of trauma for a long time that reliving a trauma itself is traumatizing. But if the soothing alpha is simultaneously brought in, the trauma is, well, less traumatizing. It can be relived more safely.

Thus a mingling of brain wave states—as when an analyzed patient brings the dream to discussion on the couch, or we bring a waking consciousness into the dream state, can be seen as not only tolerable or acceptable but also as a route to understanding our own deep and perilous depths. The logic of waking and the deep archetypal logic of the dream state are somehow brought into consciousness together, and an alchemy ensues. What Peniston found was that alpha-theta training was the most effective cure to wartime trauma that had been discovered until that time (1980s and on). Vets who had been alcoholic or drug addicted turned themselves around and became more functional—or embraced socially contributive causes. Vets estranged from their families were able to return home—without scaring others and themselves silly with their pent-up wrath and violence.[1]

Whether brought to consciousness in a psychotherapeutic session or relived in a group setting (see Tom's beneficial work with a war veteran in chapter 8), a vet is put into a safe and supportive space to relive and reprocess his savage wartime experience. When our traumas show up in our dreams, there is an excellent chance to confront them—to introduce healing into a ravaged psyche. The problem, as stated above, is that revisiting trauma is itself traumatic. Again, however, what the alpha-theta protocol seems to afford is a kind of calm detachment (alpha, 4–8 Hz) to be present while the pain-filled trauma itself is relived in theta (4–8 Hz). It's a kind of elegant theory, but what Eugene Peniston demonstrated was that it worked in actual psyches that were drug addicted, alcoholic, or violently explosive. It seemed too good to be true. Freud's model of reliving trauma had been "recall with affect." Here, thanks to neurofeedback, we had recall with the *affect muted or neutralized*—and it seemed to work (see case histories presented in my books *The Healing Power of Neurofeedback* and *The Neurofeedback Solution*).

Without going into the complex world of neurofeedback therapy, the point we wish to make is that therapy lies in the crossings-over from one state to another, the subject of this chapter. Bringing dreams to consciousness and consciousness to dreams; living in the liminal space back and forth between the dimensions; is this not what life is about? And is life not richer, more creative, more open to healing when this happens?

The purpose of this chapter, then, is to clarify the relationship between waking consciousness and the dream state. We also invoke the ethics of each practice, asking the following questions.

I. IN REGARD TO LUCID DREAMING

- Under what conditions is it okay or even helpful for the conscious perspective, equated with the ego, to interfere with the spontaneous movements of the mind substance—dreaming, in its pure form—allowing our lucidity to utilize or change the dream state?
- Or does lucid dreaming open the mind to a radical area of consciousness best left alone, as it has been since time immemorial? (Let the dream unfold naturally—or even do its million-year-old work without interference.)

II. IN REGARD TO ACTIVATED IMAGINATION

- Are reverie, daydreaming, imagination while awake to be trusted at all? Isn't it just wish fulfillment, avoidance of hard work by fantasy activity?
- Can daydreams be (phenomenologically) used to continue or complete night dreams? How do we keep the ego from enacting its wishes while ignoring the truly pristine, gifting quality of the unconscious?

Waking Dreams

We have deliberately borrowed, for this section, the felicitous title of Mary Watkins's groundbreaking book (of about forty years ago!), *Waking Dreams*. And we have also allowed her research, as well as that of Jerome Singer, whose work Stephen studied intensively at that same long-ago time (the 1970s), to guide us here. These two thinkers have explored the texture and phenomenology of the daydream so that it doesn't just languish on the junk heap of popular opinion, and be known as an activity mainly for ADHD children, or distracted and childish adults.[2]

When Watkins and Singer were writing, the goal was to use the daydream to extend the insights of depth psychology into creative visualization. In the intervening time, brain research has emerged that shows not only the usefulness of the daydream but also its omnipresence throughout our waking life. I am referring to the EEG-based research quoted in the second chapter, mentioned above, that shows how our brain states interpenetrate each other. Particularly, there is evidence that some very important aspects of memory utilize theta as the main frequency for encoding long-term memory in a little organ (consisting of millions of neurons) called the hippocampus (the term means "sea horse," because the organ, spanning the limbic system and the cerebral cortex, looks a bit like a sea horse).

There is also the work on state-dependent learning, which says that memories are best accessed in the state or condition of consciousness in which they were laid down. This is no small discovery, for the implications are vast! We know that all new learning requires old learning; that is, that novel experience doesn't just land in our brain like an electronic tracing on a CD or DVD. Rather, it stimulates and enlists vast networks of association, so that what we seem to learn de novo actually is *a part of who we are at a very deep neurological level.* Learning builds on learning and carries an emotional (limbic) stamp as well. This is why our daydreaming almost always steps off from an affective (emotional) state. (This important aspect of consciousness will also be touched on in chapter 11, our chapter on dreaming and the mythopoetic imagination.) Dream and poetry have common origin in our states of feeling—or if you prefer mythopoetic language, *in our climate and condition of soul!*

Quite frankly, what appears to be a condition of logically moving from one thought or idea to the next has a hidden, moving power based on our feelings (affect). It is why making dream associations is so powerful—when we explore the hidden labyrinth of our feeling lives we discover that we aren't such rational creatures, after all!

Watkins does a wonderful job of showing how, while the extroverted Americans during the twentieth century were focusing on behavioral psychology (see Tom's story of the death and restoration of Jung in chapter 6), not only the Freudian psychoanalysts of Europe but also the French school of Eugene Caslant and his student Robert Desoille in the 1940s were exploring the "directed daydream." (It was known as *réve éveilé,* in which patients or subjects were directed to explore a deep cave or take an ocean journey that would bring up emotionally charged symbols.) In Germany, Hanscarl Leuner was exposing patients to archetypal themes such as, for instance, the ascent of a mountain, exploring a house with many stories, or being a motorist on a deserted road. In some of these methods there were positive symbolic props: a magic sword or ring or a helping spirit or animal.³ The general intent, whichever method was involved, was to use mythic situations or symbols to evoke the psychodynamic issues of the patient—a very far cry from the (extroverted) American behaviorism.

Indwelling the Dream Figure or Image

One way of bringing the dreamworld and waking (dream) world together is to take a figure, or even an image from a dream, and meditate on it until it begins to move by itself, takes on a new life, or even begins to talk. By doing so, we enter the symbolic level almost automatically and leave behind the literalism or fundamentalism that bedevils most of our waking thought. If the human figure or animal or even tree or grotto is made of mind-stuff, it is alive in its essence and can be counted on to communicate or metamorphose (due to its protean, morphic nature).

One of the most interesting forms this can take is "unpacking" the symbol ("I will not let you go unless you bless me!"). Jung, Whitmont, and two authors who we will now introduce the reader to, do this. This lineage points out that because the dream symbol is made of living matter, it contains energy or a kind of primordial power. In their provocative and well-written book *Dream Symbol Work,* Dr. Patricia Berne and Louis Savary have taken a single big dream, an undernourished frightened child trapped in a golden mask, and turned it into a revelatory book. They do this in an instructive manner that includes the reader in their process.⁴

1. **Identify the symbols as a dream report:** Make a list of the most important symbols in one particular dream.
2. **Choose a symbol** on which to focus: Pick the one that has the most potency for you.

3. **Get immersed in the symbol:** Indwell or be the symbol, and see if it does anything.

4. **Amplify the symbol:** What does it feel like; what are its uses?

5. **Carry the symbol forward in time:** See if the symbol points to something to come.

6. **Bring the symbol backward in time:** What is the symbol's history?

7. **Associate to the symbol:** Bring in your personal memories and feelings.

You can try this with every significant-seeming symbol in any dream. In other words, allow each and every element of the dream to come alive. You can use elements from these metamorphoses or indwellings to form lines of poems. Patricia Berne does a beautiful job with showing how the mask represents both beauty and danger; it is clearly valuable—but at what price? She will not allow the mask to be removed from the child in an easy or facile manner—a goldsmith is needed. The interested reader can reference *Dream Symbol Work* to feel the care and the detail that can be put into this process.[5] One big dream and the work the author did on it not only fills a 150-page book, but—she says—it occupied her more than a decade with its intriguing insights into her character and its development. Stephen Larsen and his wife, Robin, have developed a powerful mask-working method, which they describe in *The Mythic Imagination* and in an article for *Parabola Magazine* in 1980.[6] Indwelling a mask can lead to very powerful insights into the nature of the self.

One of the most powerful dimensions pertaining to this process is pointed out by Mary Watkins in her *Waking Dreams*.[7] By "place-taking" you learn things from a different perspective than the perennial waking ego. Suppose a disagreeable dwarf has beleaguered your dreams. What might such a creature have to say? (This is a made-up example, using Watkins's method.)

DREAMER: Why are you bothering me?

DWARF: Because your world is so limited, and you're stuck there.

DREAMER: Why are you so disagreeable?

DWARF: Because you consistently ignore me.

DWARF: Why are you so small and ugly?

DWARF: I am what you think of as an insignificant part of you; I may be ugly, but not insignificant!

(And so on and so forth.)

As we have found over and over in our dream groups, and as Jung, Whitmont, and Hillman have alerted us, as well as Watkins, Berne, and Savary, out of such a dialogue can come both new energy and new perspective. A "personality," as we observed in chapter 5, is a collection of masks: potential aspects. This type of oneiric exercise, called place-taking, expands our perspective past—our claustrophobic (or egocentric) perspective. The ugly dwarf tells us off; the animal takes us to an earth-centered lair or habitat and expands our world; the peregrine falcon takes us soaring above our pedestrian landscape; the wise snake tells us to do yoga (particularly the cobra postures)—"you're so awfully stiff!"[8]

Stephen's friend and colleague Stephen Gallegos has developed an imaginal method in which (from one of his own visions, while running in the mountains) he saw that the chakras of his own body had what appeared to be spirit-animals living in them—as it were, a "personal totem pole" (the title of Gallegos's first book). Dialogue with the animals as he invites them to talk with him is immensely powerful, and he often culminates with a "parliament of the animals" in which the animals instruct the shaman in techniques for "feeding and caring for your chakras—expressing power, security, relationship, etc."[9]

Place-taking is known to be a cognitive stage of development related to socialization (and especially emotional intelligence). It is critical to our maturation to be able to put ourselves in another's place; in fact the failure to do this could leave us stuck in an autistic or sociopathic persona. Imagine, rather, a world in which children were taught to do indwelling or place-taking as part of their cognitive development—starting, perhaps, with dreams. (This is not infrequently a part of Waldorf school education—or other traditions that include the imaginal in their development models for children. Imagine if the adults who advocate war instead of diplomacy or say carpet bombing your enemies—who nonetheless dwell among civilian populations who are not enemies—had practiced indwelling or place-taking.)

Daniel Goleman has written in *Emotional Intelligence* that "EQ" (or emotional quotient, which is synonymous with emotional intelligence) is a far better predictor of success in life (including social and economic dimensions) than simple IQ.[10] If the dream itself by definition offers to broaden and deepen our EQ, why not include imaginative dreamwork into curricula? If Kilton Stewart has found that regular dreamwork makes societies both more peaceful and cooperative, this is a paradigm from societies we mistakenly designate more primitive than our own. We can always grow past our progenitors—but only if we really learn from them!

Lucid Dream Technique: Its Value and Its Limitation

My own modest contribution to the use of social and public enactment in dreamwork was in *The Shaman's Doorway,* published 1975. I relied on two areas of traditional dreamwork: The first was Iroquoian lore on dreams and wishes of the soul. This area has since been explored in great depth by Robert Moss. It is based on his own unique experience of meeting a wonderful instructive dream personage he called "Island Woman," who instructed him in the Iroquoian dream lore, in danger of disappearing entirely from the stage of history.[11]

Even before Moss, I relied on the series of volumes called *Jesuit Relations,* collected in the sixteenth century by French Jesuit priests (especially one diligent Father Ragueneau). These priests were the only literate white people to encounter the Iroquois First Nation folk in that day and age! What emerged, as I wrote in 1975, was an amazingly sophisticated dream psychology far beyond that of any of the settlers, steeped in their illusion that their own (primitive) Christianity was superior to anything embraced by "savages."[12]

☻ The Dream-Guessing Game

You may remember the terrible task Nebuchadnezzar laid on the soothsayers of Babylon: Guess my dream and interpret it on pain of death! We have a much nicer one for a liberal society. It's based on a Native American guessing game we learned from Ron Evans, a Native American scholar of Iroquoian dream lore: I (or you) have a dream and I can't remember it. Would you help me? Could I help you? (The only penalty is "Not quite but thank you so much for trying!" The reward—if successful—is a delighted giggle and a warm hug, and oh, by the way, if you guess someone's dream or they guess yours, a special friendship springs up between you; you belong to the same tribe!)

To give you a little help, use the four elements and the architectural grid first.

Is there a landscape? Are there mountains, caves?

Is there water in your dream? Fresh or salty, big or small?

Is there air, big space, quiet breezes, big storms?

Does anything ignite or blaze? Do you sit in front of a candle or a comforting fire?

Are there animals? Are they wild or tame? Real or mythical?

Is there a house? If so what room are you in?

Are there other people; how many? Are they known or unknown to you?

Are there people who have already passed? Long passed?

Are there mythical or supernatural persons?

Did you wake up feeling happy, sad, nostalgic, or frightened?

Dream guesser: If you suddenly get a hit, you might try it: Are you at that summer place you used to go to? Is old Uncle Albert there? I see you on a canoe paddle; it takes longer than you thought, and a storm comes up, but you get home safe! There are friendly people and a big feast waiting for you. It reminds you of old times on Lake George.

Whether or not you are close, or deadly accurate, don't forget these questions: What activity, what thing, have you always wanted to do but never have done? What does this dream inspire you to do? Is there a problem it could help solve? Someone you need to talk to?

Managing the Dream

The Iroquois wisdom tradition said that dreams contained wishes of the soul and were only ignored at our peril. They had sophisticated (and funny) dream-guessing societies who wore false faces and came to people in the longhouse or around the fire to help them work with their dreams. In *The Shaman's Doorway,* I identified this as a "mythologically instructed community" and opined that we could learn from them.

When the material collected by Kilton Stewart from the Malaysian Ple-Temiar Senoi became available, it seemed to me to seal the case that, at least in terms of dream psychology (and understanding of the mythic imagination), these societies had much to teach us. Although Stewart's work has since been disputed, the principle is almost the same. In essence, as the Iroquois have it, we live better lives when we learn from our dreams! The Senoi used dreams to find game as well as to head off interpersonal problems in a very isolated community in the mountains of Malaysia. The most wonderful Senoi lore brought me full circle to one of my own earliest psychological experiences involving how our own interventions can work in the dream universe.

When I was quite young, my cousin Peter lived with us for a time. I was probably about seven when he and I had a *folie a deux*—a mutual nightmare (possibly fueled by Disney films with wicked witches and perhaps by our own Norwegian ancestry). It was a recurring dream that both of us had, as follows:

> *I am standing alone in a snowy landscape—an open space, maybe a field or a snow-covered lake. I hear a swish swish swish kind of sound, and out of the woods comes a most horrible witch—on skis. As she comes toward me, I try to run, but I am stuck in place, or my feet slip in a futile fashion. I try to call for help, but my voice is paralyzed*

*and comes out like a croak. I wake up screaming in earnest—now out
loud—or in a sweat.*

Amazingly, my cousin Peter's dream was almost identical—the swish
swish sound included. It was a few years after World War II. Peter had
lost his father two weeks before his own birth, and my father, his uncle,
kind of adopted him. His theory was that the swish swish sound was
the steam rising in the radiators of the room we were sleeping in, which
somehow became incorporated into our dreams.

While we knew the basics of Norse mythology—Odin, Thor,
Bifrost, the rainbow bridge—neither knew of Skadi, the dark goddess
from the Jotun (giants) associated with shadow, fear, and the underworld. Since Christianity, she had been kind of out of a job! No wonder
she liked to frighten little Norwegian American boys.

My mother, known for her practical wisdom, overheard us talking
about our shared nightmare. She gathered us close to her and said, "I
don't know why the poor 'Ski' needs to stay up all night frightening
little boys. The next time she comes, why don't you just ask her why she
doesn't drink Sanka coffee?" (We're talking about the decaf beverage of
the 1950s.) I didn't really understand what she meant, but that night,
I will confess I went to sleep with a secret little talisman in my mind.

> *Sure enough, the swish swish began and the Ski came—but I didn't
> try to run or scream. I just stood there in the snowy field. She came
> closer and closer, perhaps amazed that I was no longer trying to run
> or scream. The evil creature grabbed me by the scruff of the neck and
> lifted me up to look in my eyes.*
>
> *"Why . . . why don't you drink Sanka coffee?" I stammered. She
> screamed and threw me down—and I awakened with a startle. It was
> the last time I dreamed of the Ski, and after I told my cousin the story,
> I believe it was his last time as well.*

This is, in fact, the wisdom of the Senoi dream approach to lucid
dreaming. We all have the right to intervene when our own mythic

imaginations frighten us. It is especially important for children to be able to feel that they have a little bit of power, especially when a symbolic figure—Frankenstein monster, evil dwarf, zombie—arises to pursue them implacably. If you have falling dreams, the Senoi say, sprout wings and fly. If a monster or a threatening animal appears—notice if it has teeth or a big mouth and find something to feed it. If that doesn't work, ask for a magic defender or a light-sword or weapon and fight it off. A last ploy is to let the monster eat you—but, carry a penknife and cut your way out of its belly. Another strategy is to face the monster squarely (the Sanka coffee approach) and say, "You are in my dream; I own this place, what do you want? This is my dream! Speak your piece; I'm not running anymore!"

Lucid Dream Interventions for Adults

Now I am going to take the opposite approach for adults, especially those with some sophistication in dreamwork. I will start the discussion with another story!

I was at a humanistic psychology conference in the 1980s. Clara Stewart Flagg already had gained a following for the Senoi approach, and Stephen LaBerge of Stanford had already published provocative and interesting research on how we can become lucid in dreaming. There had even been something published called the *Jungian-Senoi Dreamwork Manual* by Strephon Kaplan Williams (ignoring that these approaches might actually be opposites, as you will see). A lecturer was addressing a group in a large ballroom space on his method; there was a crowd of maybe three or four hundred people. The lecturer asked the audience for a dream. A man raised his hand and said:

There's this really amazing dream that has come to me repeatedly over my life. Whenever I am in the midst of turmoil or trouble, I dream of this man in a loincloth. He sits there as if meditating. Then he gets up and does an amazing dance; it's kind of wild, but strangely, when he's done, I feel better. Then he meditates again.

The Senoi teacher who was leading the discussion took an unexpected tack. "That is your infant self, having a tantrum!" he said. "It's very clear; that loincloth is a diaper. Here's what I suggest: Put your little man in a box and keep him in there, until he gets smaller and smaller and finally disappears. You have to abandon your infant self and grow up!"

It's hard to confront the authority of a speaker in front of a large audience. But I was shaken to my roots by the audacity of the analysis and the recommendation. I waved my hand around vigorously from the back of the room.

"Excuse me," I said, "with all due respect, your approach might have missed something. There is an ancient Hindu tradition that the Lord Shiva, often shown in a loincloth as a yogi, meditates most of the time. In fact the goal is for him to be kept meditating, because his dance is kind of terrible—even including the destruction of the world. In this case, the dance of the man in a loincloth makes the dreamer feel better—the message is that destruction and chaos is an indispensable part of living. But it needn't go on forever. He goes back into meditation."

"Aha!" said the presenter to the audience with a certain charismatic glee, *"We have a Jungian in the room! I knew we'd get one of those!"* The audience laughed, a little uneasily. He got the last word. "I think my advice is the right one," he said. "In lucid dreaming we all have a right to determine the outcome of our dreams!"

It was a paradigm clash, and we both knew it, as did the psychologically sophisticated audience. But my vindication came as we were leaving the room. The dreamer sought me out and said with some feeling, "You're absolutely right! That's what the dream felt like to me—I had to accept and integrate the strife and the conflict in my life, and then I could find my own way to peace. It was like a blessing from the meditating god. Thank you so much for standing up for my dream to speak its own truth!"

His response was enough for me to feel kind of warm and happy the rest of the day. I was reminded of dream teacher Jeremy Taylor's dictum "Only the dreamer has the right to say whether an interpretation rings true or false."

In Mary Watkins's felicitous language from *Waking Dreams:*

When awareness is identified with the ego, it is the ego's eyes through which awareness perceives. In this state the ego acts as if it is at the center of all that is to be perceived. It appears distinct from the circle of images around it, because it itself is unable to be perceived by awareness. . . . However when the ego is seen as an image among images, it takes its place on the circumference of the circle . . . awareness would travel among images and would recognize them as such. *The change in perspective could be likened to the one which occurred when people realized the earth was not the center of the universe, or that humans were not the first, and thereby most important creation.*[13] [italics added by Stephen Larsen]

Using Waking and Lucid Dream Approaches with a Recurring Dream
In the Words of Coauthor Tom Verner

A recurrent dream is a dream that appears on a fairly frequent basis for an individual dreamer. Studies have shown that most recurring dreams are disturbing and generally are first experienced in childhood or early adolescence. According to Robert Van de Castle, "Approximately two-thirds of adults experience some form of repetitive dream and most are associated with stressful events."[14]

Carole was in her early twenties. She came from a traditional Catholic family. As a teenager she could not wait to leave home and be out on her own and out from under the oppressive thumb of her family. With only a high school education she was having a difficult time getting a job that would enable her to save enough to move out on her own. She met a young man her own age and fell in love. Quickly they got a place together, and she was free at last. Life was going along fine until she became pregnant. The baby arrived, and very soon her boyfriend was overwhelmed and abandoned her and the baby. Now with the full responsibility of the rent, the baby, and everything else, she had no choice but to move back home with her parents, who were very unhappy with her situation but felt obliged to take her in, albeit with an attitude of "I told you so."

Carole felt trapped, became very depressed, took an overdose of pills, and ended up in therapy with me after a brief stay in the psych ward of the local hospital. She began having a dream that recurred a few times a week. The dream is terrifyingly real because it takes place in her bedroom. She is in bed; the door opens and it "awakens" her. A dark figure comes toward her. The figure gets closer and closer and, terrified, she wakes up in a cold sweat. She had had the dream a few times the previous week before she brought it to therapy.

I asked Carole to close her eyes and relax as much as possible. I asked her to imagine herself in her bed sleeping and the dream begins. She was able to stay with the dream as the figure gets closer to her bed. She was sure the figure wanted to kill her.

We talked about the dream and how terrible she felt being back in her parents' home with the baby, how trapped and alone she felt. I encouraged her to try something. I asked her if she had the dream again to try and become conscious in the dream and ask the figure, "What do you want from me?"—to face the fear in her dream, as terrifying as it was. I said this would take great courage, but I thought she could do it. She said she would try to do it.

I had been studying the Senoi people of Malaysia and their ways of working with dreams. They encourage this kind of lucid dreaming in which a dreamer stops in the dream and faces the fear, asking, "What do you want from me?" I was having success with this method in my own dreams and with other patients. This notion is captured in the Senoi proverb we have already mentioned, "Where the fear is, that's where the power is." This is a simple, profound psychological truth based on the principle of projection, which Jung described as "turning the world into a replica of your unknown face."

Carole came to the next session reporting that she had continued to have the dream almost every night. The dream was becoming more and more intense and terrifying. She had managed to become conscious in the dream but was unable to get the words "What do you want from me?" out of her paralyzed body. But a new detail had emerged: the intruder had a large knife and the sense that he wanted to kill her became frighteningly clear.

We did another dream enactment, and she got closer to saying "What do you want from me?" but was still unable to speak to the intruder. The dream continued to haunt her sleep, and new details continued to emerge. One of the most interesting to appear was the detail that the intruder was wearing one of her favorite high school jackets.

The final terrifying detail to emerge as we got closer to the naked reality of the dream was based on something she had failed to mention during our sessions: her baby daughter slept in the room with her, and it slowly emerged that the intruder was heading in the direction of her baby and not her! She began painfully to touch on her feelings of resentment toward her daughter. She felt her daughter had ruined her life, had destroyed her relationship, and had forced her to move back into her parents' home. She wept bitterly as she talked about these feelings. Her shame was as strong as her resentment. She loved her daughter but found a powerful part of herself wishing she had never been born. She was caught between these powerful poles.

Finally she had the dream for the last time. The intruder came into her room, and she found the courage to say out loud, "What do you want from me?" The intruder was headed toward her daughter's crib. Again Carole screamed, "What do you want from me?" The intruder now came toward her bed and stood over her with knife raised. The intruder brought the knife down, as if to plunge it into her heart. But as the knife got to eye level it transformed into a brilliantly lit torch. The torch revealed the intruder as the most startlingly beautiful version of herself she had ever seen, wearing a white dress and standing illuminated in the light.

I was overwhelmed with awe when she told me the dream at the next session. What a testimony to the power and creativity of the dream source within us. Facing her fear, facing the truth of her murderous feelings toward her daughter, had revealed, in a most wonderful way, her own beauty and power. It had taken months to work toward the truth and the terrifying beauty of this dream.

Things then began to shift for Carole. Within a few months she was able to apply for a program at a local community college that supported single moms wanting to continue their education. It took time, but her life gradually reflected the illuminated, powerful person she saw in her dream.

The recurring dream lets us know that real change, deep transformative change, may involve facing unacceptable parts of ourselves. The purposeful part of the creative psyche is revealed when it won't give up. Here the dream itself says, "I will not let you go until you face your fear and accept the blessing I have brought to you!" The poet William Blake asked, "What is the price of wisdom? Shall it be bought for a song, or a dance in the street?" And then he answers his own question, "Nay, it takes all that a man [or woman] hath."[15]

This recurring dream of Carole's gives us a truly masterful example of a therapist's trust in the integrity that lies in his own client's core, and in the wisdom of the dream (though in the beginning it seemed like a nightmare!). Most importantly, he was able to provide a safe space in which she could face her own deepest fear of her ambivalence toward her own baby—unacceptable in the conventional world from which she came but not in the wiser world of her own eventual wholeness.

Imagination Is the Star in Man

Carl Jung discovered, or called attention to, the waking imaginative faculty in people, because nighttime dreams often would finish abruptly, or in an unsatisfactory but provocative state. In these circumstances, a third thing between sleep and waking modes would be invoked. It was called active imagination. In effect you could finish a dream in an *imaginal* state (originally derived from the Persian ideas of Henri Corbin). *Imaginal* here does not mean the "imaginary," which often carries a pejorative connotation in Western culture, but something else. It is not the same as our dreams, as in the lively events that occur to us all five to eight times per night. Nor is it the so-called fully awake conscious state (also equated with beta, or reality-engagement and problem solving) but a third thing—related to the theta as limned above and utilized by Peniston and others to bridge the gulf between the two.

For grown-ups, an incomprehensible or even disagreeable symbol in the dream may be precisely the difficult thing they need to face. The dreamer's ego may be, in fact, the part that needs fixing. For this part to exert its hegemony still further alienates the sometimes subtle, wise architect of the dream. To put it even more simply, we may do an injustice to our wisdom body when we exert the ego's prerogatives in the dream.

It might be legitimate for a child, however, victimized by his own dreams (usually coming out of uncontrollable events in his or her life: abuse, parental conflict, playground bullies) to stand up to the symbolic terror presented by the dream, thus growing the ego into an organ fit to cope with the challenges of life. It seems a wiser course for the adult, especially in the second half of life, to try to *understand* the dream, rather than manipulate it, thereby helping to make it a center of one's own potential developmental wholeness.

11

Dreams and the Poetic Imagination

For years Tom thought he had two great loves, poetry and dreams. As the years have gone by he realized that they are really only one love, "the poetic basis of mind,"[1] as James Hillman calls it. Jung said it as succinctly as he could have, "Psyche is image." At the heart of the dream and the poem, at the root of psyche, is a sense of the symbolic, poetic, mythic, imaginative nature of the human being. As Harvey Cox writes, "However unreligious or 'secularized' someone may claim to be, he instantly relapses into being a mythic and symbolic creature as soon as he falls asleep and begins to dream."[2] As we have seen throughout this book, there is a refreshing spring, a source within each of us from which both the dream and the poem, as well as great scientific theories and works of art, emerge. This source has been called the soul, the imagination, the diamond body, the atman, the still point within, or, as we call it in chapter 9, the cauldron of inexhaustible gifts.

As we mentioned earlier, Freud also expressed this notion when he said, "Wherever I go in search of the psyche, I find a poet has been there before me." The psyche's primary function is to imagine (to create images), whether awake or asleep. We see through the imagination. All the time, it seems, we are dreaming up what we see and experience. For those of us who have been trained to think of the imagination as unreal or imaginary, this is an unfamiliar notion. That our perception and experience of the world and ourselves is deeply imaginative is not so apparent to most of us while we are awake, but when we fall asleep and begin to dream it is clear that we are all startlingly imaginative and poetic creatures. In a culture that values the *rational* above all else, we seem trained to think of the spontaneous imagination as irrational or crazy. In our dreams, our friend is a raccoon, or our hands are bird claws. Often when people recount a dream they preface it with, "I had a weird dream," or "My dream was really crazy," or the like. But as we saw in chapter 9, great works of art as well as revolutionary scientific discoveries have often come through the weird and crazy dreaming imagination.

When we look at the scriptures of the world, we also see that the dream has been acknowledged as the place where the Divine may communicate with the human. When Joan of Arc was on trial for her heretical claims that God spoke to her, one of the Inquisitors said to her, "You say God speaks to you, but it is only your imagination," to which Joan responded, "How else would God speak to me, if not through my imagination?"[3] Dreams and imaginative visions appear throughout the scriptures of the world, as described in wonderful detail in Morton Kelsey's book *God, Dreams, and Revelation.*

The highest sources of wisdom available to us seem to speak through the dreaming, poetic imagination. Following Jung, we have referred to these experiences as big dreams, those dreams that express the wishes of the soul and speak to the destiny and direction, the meaning and purpose of a person's life, on the most profound levels. The truths that come to us in these big dreams are an affirmation of the religious truth that the kingdom of God is within. The symbolic nature of psyche is reflected in most dreams, big and small.

Even a fragment of a dream, a single dream image, may be layered with poetic power, wisdom, and insight if we stick with it and mine it for its meaning. As Hillman writes, "The depth of even the simplest image is truly fathomless. This unending, embracing depth is one way the dreams show their love."[4] To illustrate, we will use an example from the poet Denise Levertov of a simple dream image that unfolded into a poem with searching personal questions.

Often a dream presents a ring from which to hang the latent questions of that moment in one's life. "The Broken Sandal" was such a one. As it states, I "dreamed the thong of my sandal broke." The questions that follow—from the most literal practical ones about how I am going to walk on without it, over sharp dirty stones, to the more abstract ones:

Where was I going?

Where was I going I can't go to now, unless hurting?

Where am I standing if I'm to stand still now?

The dream demanded of the dreamer that some basic life questions be asked. That was its function. In becoming a poem, the organic process begun in the dream continued in the statement and questions that gave the poem its necessarily terse form, and the mode of the questions was provided by the dream's sandal-thong metaphor. . . .[5]

The Poetic, Multiple, Metaphoric Meanings of the Dream Image

In the realm of the poetic imagination from which the dreams emerge, says French philosopher Gaston Bachelard, "there is no value without polyvalence." And as Hillman writes in *Dream and the Underworld,* "The ambiguity of dreams lies in their multiplicity of meanings, their inner polytheism, the fact that they have in each scene, figure, image, a 'tension of opposites,' as Jung puts it. And it is more than just opposites," Hillman insists, "it is a polyvalent, multiplicity of possibilities."[6]

Not just opposites, but many possible meanings are woven into each image. As Heraclitus tells us, the essential nature of the imagination, is "like flowing water, and it must move." When we make a dream image *stand* for something; when we make it mean one thing only, we stop the flow of imagination, and the standing water will quickly become stagnant and lose its living power to nourish and heal body and soul. "The Dream," a poem by Felix Pollak, points with insightful humor and intelligence to the multiplicity of possible meanings for the dreamer's simple image of an open window. According to people in the dreamer's life, these meanings include a vagina, the dreamer's divorce, or suicide; the dreamer can't even bear to recount to his wife "such a dangerous dream"!

Remember the dream in chapter 6 of the woman who exited the highway and her brakes failed and she was speeding out of control into a busy intersection? The dream image brought up, first, that her brakes needed to be fixed. Since the exit was the one she took to go to her boyfriend's house, it suggested that the relationship was going too fast and was out of control. On a deeper level, what was brought up was that this was a lifelong pattern in her love relationships. The dream weaver wove at least three meanings into that one image of failed brakes and going too fast. The dream points to the way in which a dream image can speak to us on multiple levels all at once. The creativity of the dreaming, poetic imagination is stunning in its elegance, ingenuity, and healing creativity.

There is an even more profound multiplicity of meanings at the very heart of many dreams. As in fairy tales and myths, the character who causes the protagonist difficulty and continually puts obstacles in his or her way often turns out to be the source of salvation. All those obstacles are ultimately seen to initiate moments of growth and grace and a deepening of character for the protagonist. This is often true in the dream where the villain turns out to be a source of revelation or even an inflection, a transformation of the dreamer's own self.

In the dream of the young mother sleeping in the same room with her new baby and the knife-wielding intruder, the intruder turned out not only to reveal a murderous part of the dreamer but also ultimately led her to a transformed, deeper, and more loving version of herself. It seems that in any great poem, fairy tale, or dream, the poetic imagination is at work, weaving opposites and even multiple meanings in a single image.

In the Words of Coauthor Stephen Larsen

Using Poetry to Work with a Dream

As a way of acknowledging and honoring this poetic nature of the psyche, we often use poetry and poetic techniques in working with dreams. As we have seen in chapter 8, the dream retreat hosted and guided by Tom and his wife, Janet, is woven throughout with poems and poetic methods of working with dreams.

My wife, Robin, and I begin *our* dream groups (usually three hours every other Saturday) by reading a few dreams from the previous group—especially if one of the members has gone on to write a poem, a story, or create a painting based on their own dream—or a response to an especially striking one from another member. The poems may be free verse or use a structured (originally Malaysian, later Persian) meter that I learned from Robert Bly.

☾ How to Write a Pantoum

The Western pantoum is an adaptation of centuries-old oral Malayan poetry that first entered written literature in the fifteenth century.[7] As Edward Hirsch describes in *A Poet's Glossary,* "The Malayan *pantun berkait* is what we know as a pantoum. It is a highly repetitive form of indefinite length that inscribes something of its oral quality. It unfolds in interweaving quatrains (ABAB) and often rhymes. Lines two and four of each stanza repeat as lines one and three of the following stanza. The reader always takes four steps forward and two back. A pantoum typically begins:

STANZA I

Line 1 A

Line 2 B

Line 3 C

Line 4 D

STANZA II

Line 5 B

Line 6 E

Line 7 D

Line 8 F

STANZA III

Line 9 E

Line 10 G

Line 11 F

Line 12 H

STANZA IV

Line 10 G

Line 1 A

Line 12 H

Line 3 C

"It is customary for the second and fourth lines in the last stanza of the poem to repeat the first and third lines of the initial stanza, so that the whole poem circles back to the beginning, like a snake eating its tail."[8]

Example (written from the dream that persuaded Stephen to write this book with Tom):

"The Old Cathedral with the Warm Heart"

Oh friends, where can we meet in this hilly town?
There is a drenching rain on everything.
Rivulets run down the arches, and over the cobblestones.
Let us meet in that old cathedral.

There is a drenching rain on everything,
but these holy old halls seem dry and cozy.
Let us meet in that old cathedral,
Where generations have brought warm bread.

These holy old halls seem dry and cozy,
A gentle fragrance of laughter and food,
Where generations have brought warm bread
And told their stories of living and dying.

A gentle fragrance of laughter and food.
Oh friends, where will we meet in this hilly town?
Let us tell our stories of living and dying.
Rivulets run down the arches, over the cobblestones.

Without going into greater detail, this dream had an otherwise indefinable quality of warmth and comfort. There was music (Gregorian chants), nourishment in the form of baking bread, and support. I met Tom at the very end, walking up a circular staircase.

Hold Three Coins for the Old Wise Man

Holly, the dreamer whose dream we examine below, is a talented woman artist in her early sixties. A much beloved and long-term member of our dream group, often her dreams would be translated into beautiful and intricate paintings. Then they began to lead her through the most difficult times in her life. The one before the big dream we are about to relate here had evoked her greatest trauma. This example shows how an emotionally powerful dream (and its background) makes it into the pantoum.

In her twenties, Holly, an avid skier, was looking forward to a day of skiing on the sunny slopes. The fast-moving lift scooped her up, but she had not yet had time to pull the safety bar down. Suddenly, an unexpected gust of wind blew her off the lift, and she fell forty feet to the hard-packed snow. The ski resort called it "an act of God," to avoid liability.

But Holly wondered, "Does God not like me?" She had been shattered by the fall, breaking legs, pelvis, and spine, and began years of painful recovery. Nonetheless, she went on to a successful career as a painter, a forty-year marriage, and gave birth to two beautiful and accomplished children who are now adults.

This momentous dream came to her in September 2011, nine days after the anniversary of her mother's death—the year after 9/11—to the day.

I am in a dark theater by myself. At intermission, I walk outside into the
golden light, very bright. As I go back into the theater I meet an elderly

Buddhist monk. We have to find the footholds to climb a wall to get to the entrance stairs. (It seems harder than leaving!) When the monk gets up to the theater entrance level, he asks me to take three coins and tape them to the old-style pay phone. (The monk is elderly, with white hair and a long beard.) As he hands the coins to me, I notice two small thin, worn dimes and one heavy gold coin. I say to him—"I will hold them for you, because otherwise they will not be there for you when you return."

I drop them in my pocket, and they mix with my coins. We walk into the workshop in the theater and sit down for a moment of time. Then the workshop ends, and I invite the others around me to take a walk with me on a special path. There is a lovely Indian woman with a jewel in her pierced nose and silky black hair. She has a beautiful smile, white silk clothes, and walks with me. She goes over and over, giving me the elder's name. She touches me three times on my forehead with her little finger. Trees have been severed, but I see new growth. It is beautiful, inspirational, outside; fresh, fragrant air, clear running water in a stream, and I am inspired to see tall mountains in the background of the landscape.

Then my cat wakes me up, crying to get out.

The dream is potent enough so that the whole group feels that we are in a sacred initiation together. We see, feel, and experience what the dreamer relates—we are on her walk together, as in the dream. Holly's associations led us on a journey of both personal (for her) and transpersonal meaning. Looking at the date of the dream, it suddenly comes to her that its date was nine days after her mother's death—a year after 9/11 to the day! Then we all get the same *frisson* as she also remembers that the day of the dream sharing in the group, in December, is ten days after her mother's birthday on December 7.

Emotions are strong as the memories come. Her mother had been diagnosed with a fatal brain tumor, a glioma. Holly had flown across the country to be with her during her last days. But after several weeks, Holly had had to come back to her family and obligations in New York. Then (not an uncommon thing)—her mother died.

"So many unspoken things between us, and yet she knew I was

there for her." (Tears accompany the memories.) Her associations to the dream led her further—to a prior visit to Buddhist lending library and a magazine she found, seemingly by chance. On its cover was a woman with a beautiful, wise face. She recalls, "That was the woman in the dream! Now I recognize it. I picked up the magazine and read the article—couldn't put it down. The woman's name was Pema Chödrun; she is a much-beloved Buddhist teacher. The message in the article was 'Embrace all of life! You must go as deeply into the pain and suffering, even the depression, as you go into the joy.'"

She remembered, with deep emotion, that her mother was Norwegian and always sent holiday cookies to the entire family at Christmas. They would arrive in time for everyone to share them. Regarding the coins (two silver, one gold), she remembered that her mother had typically worn a lot of heavy silver jewelry including a Navajo belt with turquoise that her husband had just taken out on her birthday. "I have two silver earrings—made by this old Navajo man. One of the two pairs I wear. Silver and gold."

It should be mentioned that as the dreamer recounted her dream and made associations with its symbolism, a certain atmosphere crept over the dream group. We were with her in the dark, mysterious theater—and went out with her into the blinding light. Then the Lao-tzu figure asks the dreamer to hold magical coins—like those used in the I Ching, she said (an oracle she really values, using three coins).

In the dream Holly mixes the coins with her own—she takes on the same karma as the lama. (She later talked of the amazing coin collections of her own mother, and her husband's father—both now passed—and values that transcend the generations.) To the atmosphere of the workshop she associates spiritual and psychological growth. The participants of her group in the dream were the dream-group participants sitting right in the room with her, who support each other in creative, mature, and caring ways. To Pema Chödrun she associates the ethic of "embracing the dark times as fully as the light," as the dream itself dramatically mingles introverted darkness and bright illumination. The message, as Holly transmitted it to us, is "Learn to laugh and cry with a gentle heart!"

In the imaginal body of the dream group experience, we all walked with Holly, with the seraphically smiling woman, the wise old man, and Holly herself, everyman, everywoman, walking through the sun-dappled, fragrant forest, with mountains resplendent on the horizon. The amazing thing about working on such a mysterious but living dream is that it became the dream of all of us. At the end of the dreamwork, we settled down to write our poems, somehow to capture the mystery in which we had all participated. Here is Stephen's poem.

"Hold Three Coins for the Old Wise Man"

In a dark theater all my myself
Blinding golden light outside,
Hold three coins for the old wise man,
Walk with the woman with beautiful eyes.

Blinding golden light outside,
Remember the holy name
Walk with the woman with beautiful eyes,
In the workshop of the mind.

Remember the holy name,
Walk with me on my special path,
In the workshop of the mind.
Mountains, flowing water, clear air.

Walk with me on my special path,
In a dark theater all by myself,
Mountains, flowing water, clear air,
Hold three coins for the old wise man.

In a recent contact with Holly (five years after the group encounter), I read her the poem, and as she remembered the dream, and the group, she found herself weeping. She told us that she had been through a recent bout of breast cancer but that the presence of the tumor—caught early, at Stage 2—had been brought to her attention by a dream: *A huge boulder that landed in front of her on a mountain path, blocking her way.* She immediately knew something big was looming. She took appropriate medical steps and is now well along in recovery. Holly sent me a picture of herself, beautifully bald from the chemotherapy.

Robin and I looked at it. "You look like Pema Chödrun!" we said.

"Well, maybe," she replied, laughing. "I will tell you that her advice has stood me in very good stead since that dream and processing it in group five years ago! Learn to laugh and cry with a gentle heart."

From the Dream, Metaphors Emerge

Out of the dream—carefully and respectfully opened—come metaphors. Sometimes we can assign key metaphors a line or a stanza in a pantoum. Poetry tunes the metaphoric mind. It keeps images in the air even when we're not talking about dreams. It continually shows the similarity between poetic images and dreams, or where a poem might be used to crystallize the sense of a dream beginning to emerge. Then an image or a vignette in a dream might bring up a poem in a way that illustrates multiple meanings. The art of metaphor is always to say more than what you mean—through an image. That is invariably what the dream does, and that is, almost always, what makes for good poetry. Following is an example of a way of responding to a dream with poetry from an esteemed member of our dream group.

Kerttu is now approaching ninety years old and was clearly the "wise old woman" of our group when she was able to attend. She was a native Finn who had left her home in Karelia in 1943, never to return, because "the Russians were coming," and nobody, least of all a woman, could be expected to survive their pent-up wrath. The Germans had already invaded Russia in a bloody suicide mission, and now the Russians were beginning to vent their wrath on disputed territories, and they had never much believed in independent Baltic States.

Her brother was killed in a fighter plane strafing attack, and now, at seventeen, she was told that she must carry everything that she valued on her person (it was winter) across a frozen lake to a dubious safety. She lived through the rest of the war in Helsinki, Finland's beleaguered capitol, and then in Europe as an exile, and never again really returned to Finland. She did make it to China just after Japan had ravaged that great country.

Her dream was simple enough and probably hearkened back to that period.

> I'm in a dark city, walking through the streets alone. There is danger and a sense of violence. I come upon someone lying on the sidewalk by the street. I kneel down and find it is a young man, bleeding, perhaps from multiple wounds. I think he's been beaten. I don't remember if he begs me to stay with him, but I do. I hold his hand and do what I can to give him comfort. I know that I need to leave him to get help but that I dare not do that. So I kneel beside him, comforting him as he dies in my arms.

In her associations, Kerttu told us that she had worked with dying young men in Helsinki, where she had been a nurse's aide during the war; this was her experience over and over. As teenagers, she and her brother had found a dead young Russian soldier, about the brother's age, in the woods. They could not bury him but covered him tenderly with branches even though he belonged to the army of the enemy.

The following is Robin's poem for Kerttu's dream.

"Holding in Tenderness"

Innocent, we set forth;
everything living companions us:
the small, the lame, the fearful, the clever—
Trouping fools, we wander gaily from the garden.

Wandering, we lose
ourselves, our friends, our every thing,
in those bleak, dim and violent streets
Where hungry ghosts devour lost souls.

When the door opens,
and the call comes, who steps boldly forward?
Whose hands are prepared to hold
the precious burden?

Who clings, trembling,
to the bloodied post?
What is that secret power that pushes us
at last, again, outward into the unknown?

In the end,
we all must find our own way
home. What matters is the moment of holding
in infinite tenderness.

Whenever a member of Stephen and Robin's dream group captures the essence of a dream through their poem, there is a moment of silence. Tears may run down faces; the room is hushed. We understand what has just happened: one human being has entered the deep spaces of another. At best the whole group, through both the dreamer's narrative and the poem, have come to an existential moment of truth: of what it means to live, to die, and so to grow. And although in dreamwork the goal is not to create a great work of art, that might happen.

Because of the depth of Kerttu's experience and her dream, everyone in the group wrote deep and meaningful poems. The dream group inhabited emotionally Robin's poem above, which allowed them to move toward the heart of the dream in a profound and deeply touching way. Poetry, at its best, is about finding our way to the core of what really matters. Poems can often do this with a dream; we have found this time and time again in our dreamwork.

Using poetry honors the dream by working with the dream in a dreamlike way. As mentioned earlier in this book, Freud famously said, "Dreams are the royal road to the unconscious."[9] We feel the poem is the royal road to the dream. The poem might single out a particularly powerful image for the dreamer and unpack it from a variety of perspectives, as in the example from Denise Levertov's broken sandal dream. This is especially true with the way we use haiku.

☻ Use Haiku to Work with a Dream
(From Tom and Janet's Dream Retreat)

The Japanese seventeen-syllable poetic form, the haiku, can be a wonderful way of working with a dream. With its strict structure, the haiku invites us to move toward the essence of the dream, the honed down, seed-sense of possible meanings the dream may be suggesting. After a meditative reading of our dream, we write three or four haiku using the images from the dream.

The basic structure of the haiku is three lines of five syllables, seven syllables, five syllables. We summarize the dream in the first two lines, the first twelve syllables. In the third five-syllable line, we make an *interpretive response* to the dream—what we are sensing the meaning of the dream might be. (See examples in chapter 11 of how we use haiku when working with a dream.) We often suggest writing three or four haiku to give voice to the different meanings and perspectives we begin to see in the dream. You may write one haiku from the perspective of one dream character and another from the perspective of a second or third character or image (perhaps from the perspective of the weather in the dream or the setting of the dream; for a more detailed description of how to use haiku to work with dream images see Henry Reed's book, *Getting Help from Your Dreams*).

Here is an example from a dream of Tom's.

Dream: *I am looking for a school for my daughter. The issue/question is: too many rules, too few rules.*

> *Wondering about the rules*
> *Too much too little.*
> *Looking for balance*

> *The right school for the*
> *Risk-taking part of myself.*
> *To stay safe and grow.*

A school with windows and walls
Doors that open and lock.
A nest to fly from.

The Intolerable Wrestle with Words: Trying to Express the Dream Experience

The dream is, above all, *an experience*—an experience that expresses the felt, living truth of our current life situation. It often connects this present situation with the higher purpose and meaning of our life as a whole. As Jung liked to say, "If an acorn had a dream, it would be of an oak tree." The dream experience often invites us to consider "What is the purpose and direction of my life?" And what at this moment might be getting in the way of following and living that purpose? How can you move, as Thoreau challenges us in *Walden,* "confidently in the direction of your dreams. Live the life you've imagined." And equally demanding, Mary Oliver asks in her poem "Summer Day," "Tell me, what is it you plan to do / with your one wild and precious life?" The dream experience expresses our life purpose and direction using the language of symbolic, emotion-laden images. This is the imaginative, natural way the dream experience is composed and expressed in often ambiguous, emotionally charged, terrifying, or beautiful images.

How do we express this experience on paper when we sit down to record our dream in words? When we sit down to transcribe the experience of the dream, we become aware of the difficulty of translating the complex, multilayered experience of the dream into the language of the waking world. If we are faithful to the experience of the dream we find ourselves in the creative struggle of poetry, what T. S. Eliot called the "intolerable wrestle with words and meanings." If we struggle to remain faithful to the experience of the dream, we will struggle to find language that is, if not precise, at least as faithful as possible to the often ambiguous and simultaneous meanings of the dream experience. We end up with a dream record in our journal. This is the first movement in honoring and working with the dream experience.

How can we work with this dream *memory* in our journal to help enter and open up the dream to the many possible meanings it may be suggesting? Then, how can we work with the dream *record* in a way that is as faithful as possible to the experience of the dream?

What follows is a way of working with your dreams, on your own, in your journal. This exercise was first developed by Tom and Henry Reed when they were doing a dream research project for the Association for Research and Enlightenment (ARE) at the Edgar Cayce Foundation in Virginia Beach, Virginia. This journal writing exercise works playfully and poetically with the words of your dream record. The example that we illustrate, to give you a sense of how to do the exercise, is from Tom's dream journal and has been shortened for the sake of brevity.

This particular journal dreamwork exercise is a wonderful way to respond to a dream that feels like it is touching an ongoing, perhaps even a lifelong, issue that keeps coming up in one's life. This often seems to be the case—there are issues, or traits, or tendencies that we work with all our lives, hopefully getting clearer about the issue and increasingly conscious of what it is and how and why we continue to get caught by it. Some say we come into this life with particular life issues or questions connected to our destiny or fate; from our family history and ancestors; or some suggest, from past lives. That was the sense for Tom in the example we use here; the dream touched on an issue he has worked with all his life. When we find ourselves with a dream that is touching on one of these big life questions, we might commit ourselves to focusing on the question/issue for a week or two. We might create a retreat for ourselves in the midst of our lives. The following journal work is designed to do just that if the dreamer chooses—or it can simply be a onetime exercise.

Create a Dream Retreat in the Midst of Your Life

If you have a dream, perhaps a big dream, that seems to be touching on a life issue of yours, you might create a little retreat for yourself. Take an hour at the beginning or end of your day and focus on the dream and the dreams that follow from it for a week or two. You don't have to head off to a monastery or a cave. You can create the experience of "re-treat" within your ongoing life.

Retreat is a many layered, polyvalent word. In the military sense it might suggest the experience of withdrawing intentionally, retreating from what might be feeling like a battle, and reconsidering our way of going at something by thinking of new strategies. This could involve "treating" ourselves to some much needed attention as a healer might "treat" us; and/or giving ourselves a "treat," something sweet in the midst of a difficult time perhaps. Create a time to consider the "treaty" we may have come into the world with, what Caroline Myss calls our sacred contract, the destiny and purpose of our life. This is what James Hillman calls our soul's code and what the ancient Greeks called our *daimon*—our calling that we may be straying from in the rush of our life. A dream retreat is a wonderful way to get back on track when we feel we have gotten distracted from our life purpose. As part of the experience of it, you may want to reference some of the books listed a little later in this chapter. They are designed to help you use your dream journal in a creative way.

☻ Journal Exercise:
Working with Key Words/Images in the Dream

You have identified a big dream that you would like to work with, and you have previously journaled about it in your dream journal. Open your journal to that page and then, as with any dreamwork you do on our own, begin by taking a moment to invite inner calm and focus. You may want to close your eyes, finding and following your breath and allowing it to quiet the chatter of your mind and bring you into a deep silence that is open to the dream there on the page of your journal. When you work with a dream in a meditative way you are being receptive, playful, patient, and open to surprise.

Reread your dream entry, and as you do so, be sensitive to the words you originally used to describe the images, feelings, and actions in your dream.

Step One: Underline those words that evoke a special response in you, which seem to touch on a sensitive nerve, or which seem very germane to the dream.

Here is an example.

Judith and I are riding on a _train_. I look out the window and I see that we are coming into _Tibet_. The Himalayas are stretched out across the horizon; we are traveling high in them, but they are _still higher_. Brass domes of temples and little villages cling to the mountainside. I realize I have been there only a few seconds, and I am going to be there for _six weeks_. Six seconds seems like it would have been enough of a _blessing_.

Step Two: List these underlined words in your journal. If you have more than fifteen words listed, you should probably edit your list down to the fifteen most evocative words, but wait until you complete this second step before eliminating any words. Read over the list slowly, keeping in mind that these words will serve as seeds from which you will grow into a fuller awareness of the truth of your current situation. Allow yourself to experience the variety of subtle inner promptings that are evoked by each word.

Step Three: Take each word and allow it to develop into a statement of significant truth about yourself and how you are currently living your present life. For each word, compose and write in your journal several sentences about yourself, each sentence using the word in mind. Permit yourself to be playful, to be attentive to the puns and double meanings of some words. Experiment by letting your pen do the writing. Ignore rules of grammar and avoid judging what is being written. Be permissive with your pen and don't push but rather be patient and undemanding. If a particular word doesn't yield a sentence about yourself, jot down a few associations and make up any sort of sentence with the word. Continue on and come back to that word later.

Here are the sentences that came from the words I underlined.

Example: _Train_ train track. Trains feel old fashion, homey. If I were a train I'd be on a track. I need to train myself to stay on the track. I'm on a training track. I have been trying to train myself to stay on the track. I have been trying to train myself to be more single-minded lately. Judith and I are together on the train. I like to be with Judith, looking through the window at the world with Judith. Being with Judith trains me to be less self-centered. I feel at home with Judith. Judith, at home, on the track, in training. Tibet or not Tibet. Tibet is the place I would most like to go. I think Tibet is a spiritual place. Would I be at home in Tibet? Am I at home? Tibet, at home with Judith. Tibet or not Tibet. I must live here and now and not get off the track. . . .

As I continued the exercise I worked with the other words . . . still higher and six weeks and blessing, making up sentences for each of those words as well. I then wrote a few final sentences using as many of the words as possible.

The final sentences ended up being: Six weeks, sick, weak, slow down and live. I feel like my life is in such a hurry, not enough time, rushing from one thing to another. If I stay on the training track, at home as I am with Judith, I'll naturally still get higher in plenty of time. Tibet, to be at home in my spiritual home all I have to do is stay on the training track with the feeling of being at home with Judith, naturally getting still higher all the time, slowly, no rush, this would be a blessing to be on top of the world in Tibet. Tibet I hear as "To be," simply to be patient, live slowly in each moment, would be a blessing.

Step Four: Read over the sentences you have written and try to be sensitive to the moods evoked in you and to the themes that are emerging in your writing. Make some additional notes in your journal concerning the moods, meanings, and truths that seem to be coming through in these sentences. Reflect on your current life and how you have been living it, and note in your journal what has been concerning or troubling you recently, today, this past week, during "this time in your life." (Maybe, if you did a Present Period Log, described in chapter 8, you will see connections arising from doing this journal exercise.) Try to express these concerns using the words from your dream, or phrases from the sentences you wrote inspired by the key words from your dream.

Example: As I read over my sentences I am struck by the *trains of thoughts* about my understanding of time, how I use time, my perception of time, and my feeling about how time perceives me. There is the theme of being "on the track," sticking to the task at hand, not being distracted, "dis-track-ted," and the feeling of being dissatisfied, wanting to be "still higher," versus "feeling at home."

The journal entry went on further and ended with:

I feel in a hurry, not at home. This work is suggesting to me that I slow down, stay on the track, train myself to be still, to be at home, with the sense that I have enough time, enough of all that I need. Here, now, at home would be a blessing.

Step Five: Write a paragraph in your journal describing how your concern may be approached this coming week. What might you do to live the message and the meaning that seems to be coming through in the dream journal work?

Example: I have been feeling overcommitted, pulled in all directions at once, like a train trying to run on many tracks going in all directions. I try to do too much at once, and my concentration has lacked sustained focus, and I fail to stay on the track. I end up feeling scattered and not at home. This week, I will become mindful of doing one thing at a time; staying focused and on track. I will become aware of when I say "Yes" and when I say "No." I will practice saying "No" when I need to and I will become conscious of how I am spending my time. At the end of each day I will sit down with my journal and review my day in light of these goals and review how I did with my resolve that day and how I may have sabotaged or undermined my resolve. I will reaffirm my resolve for the next day.

This journal review at the end of the day will also begin to refine and deepen the expression we give to our question or concern. This naturally invites us to ask our dream source for additional guidance. As we fall asleep we ask for a dream to further guide and support our work to accomplish our resolve. As we can see, this way of working with a life concern using our dreams has a strong incubation element, deepening the dialogue between our waking and dreaming lives.

This journal exercise of working with key words from our dream record is a small sample of how to work with a dream in a poetic way in your dream journal. There are numerous books that contain other ways of working with dreams in your journal; some of them are listed below.

BOOKS TO INSPIRE YOU TO
USE YOUR DREAM JOURNAL CREATIVELY

At a Journal Workshop, Ira Progoff

Getting Help from Your Dreams, Henry Reed

Your Mythic Journey, Sam Keen and Anne Valley-Fox

The Mythic Imagination, Stephen Larsen

Creating From the Spirit, Dan Wakefield

The Mythic Path, David Feinstein and Stanley Krippner

Poetic Medicine, John Fox

Life's Companion, Christina Baldwin

There are also fine compendiums of symbols that can awaken and nourish the poetic imagination (but please don't take them literally— use them creatively!).

The Book of Symbols, Ami Ronnberg and Kathleen Martin

A Dictionary of Symbols, J. E. Cirlot and Herbert Read

The Secret Language of Symbols, David Fontana

The Secret Language of the Soul, Jane Hope

We say many times throughout this book that *dreamwork is soul work,* because the primary activity of soul is creating images. Soul is the "imaginative possibility in our natures, the experiencing through reflective speculation, dream, image and fantasy; that mode which recognizes all realities as primarily symbolic and metaphorical."[10] In this way our dreamwork and our understanding of psychology itself is rooted not in science but in aesthetics and imagination, in what Hillman calls a poetic basis of mind.

Working with the poetic imagery of our dreams invites us to stop and reflect, imagine and create, and deepen the event of the dream into a soulful experience of growth and transformation. When we bring soulful reflection to our dreams, we are nourishing our souls and enabling them to move deeper and deeper into the world, the inner and outer world—that space between where the inner and outer worlds commingle and world becomes dream and dream becomes world.

Jung felt we are suffering from what indigenous peoples call soul loss, that loss of connection to family, ancestor, totem, nature, and ultimately our own inner sense of self. He characterized Western culture in his famous phrase "modern man in search of a soul," which is also the title of one of his books.

James Hillman writes:

One day at the *Burgholzli,* the famous psychiatric clinic in Zurich, I watched a woman being interviewed. She sat in a wheelchair, because she was elderly and feeble. She said she was dead, because she had lost her heart. The psychiatrist asked her to place her hand over her breast to feel her heart beating: it must still be there if she could feel its beat. "That," she said, "is not my real heart."

She and the psychiatrist looked at each other. There was nothing more to say. Like the primitive who has lost his soul, she had lost the loving, courageous connection to life—and that is the real heart, not the ticker that can as well pulsate isolated in a glass bottle.[11]

Keeping a dream journal and working with our dreams is an ancient way of connecting with our soul. Dreams are often elegant works of artistic beauty and deserve to be approached with reverence and on their own terms. The dream is an imaginative creation and needs to be worked with in imaginative and poetic ways. We do not go *at the dream directly* but rather listen to the dream, as James Hillman suggests, with "a cocked ear," with that sense of "slant" that Emily Dickinson says is related to truth.

Approach a dream like an animal, sniffing and circling around the dream, slowly taking in its scent. Allow it to work on you as much as you work on it. Be in the presence of the dream as you would be in the presence of a work of art, a poem, a painting, a play, with an open sense of wonder and a not knowing. Don't be in a hurry; dreamwork is an art, and there are no rigid rules, except perhaps to move slowly and be patient. Allow your intuition to guide you, make connections and associations, and be alert to the multiple meanings and possibilities. The dream is not a riddle to be solved, but a mysterious work of art to be savored and enjoyed and ultimately lived. In this way, its many meanings will slowly, surprisingly, reveal themselves to you.

Your dreams will inspire you, amaze you, delight you, and maybe even disgust and terrify you. But slowly allow yourself to get to know them, to befriend them, to play with them, entertain them, to respect them (re-spect: "to look again and again and again," not just once). Don't let them go until they bless you, for invariably they will make you a more imaginative, creative, wild, and interesting person. As you begin to move from this deep dreaming place within, may you find the courage and creativity to be your best possible self as you live "your one wild and precious life."

What Dreams May Come . . .

We shall not cease from exploration / And the end of all our exploring / Will be to arrive where we started / And know the place for the first time.

T. S. ELIOT, "LITTLE GIDDING"

We are lived by powers we pretend to understand.

W. H. AUDEN

And now we come to the end of our reflections on dreams and dreaming, but the mystery of the dream goes on. When a session of dreamwork comes to a close because of time—when the dream group needs to end, when the individual dream session needs to stop, the dream source continues to live. The multiple possible meanings that did not get touched on, did not get articulated or explored, all the possible ways in which we might have worked on the dream or allowed the dream to work on us, all these possibilities remain alive in the source of the living dream.

James Hillman says, "Befriend the dream, . . . Participate in it, enter into its imagery and mood, want to know more about it, to understand, play with, live with, carry, and become familiar with— as one would do with a friend."[1] Like a good friend, the dream will give us more and more if we nourish the relationship. "This is the way the dream loves us, by giving us ever more possibilities."[2] Our dreamwork is but one bucket dropped down into the great flowing stream of images and brought up for us to be refreshed by . . . . but the great stream flows on. As Edward Whitmont put it, "The dream as a whole may have many human 'uses.' Like the water in a stream dipped up in cups and used for cooking and for quenching thirst, channeled in sluices and pipes and used for turning water mills or filling swimming pools or flushing toilets. It can be left alone in its streambed and looked at quietly, thereby 'used' for rest or boating, for contemplation, or for stimulating the reflective streams of art. So the energy flowing into dream images can have many uses."[3]

There is so much more to say, so much more that dreams and dreaming have to give us. We hope what you have read has informed and inspired you to work with your dreams—to drink from that stream, to sit by it and have your creativity awakened and be refreshed and nourished.

In the quote on the chapter head, "what dreams may come . . ." Shakespeare alludes to Hamlet's thoughts of what dreams may come to any of us when we have "shuffled off that mortal coil" (Hamlet considers suicide as one of his options). Dreams may be beautiful, creative or provocative, as we have seen, or ominous and contentious. When we no longer have our dreams grounded in the physical body and its vicissitudes, what might they be like? When we no longer have an earthly body to awaken into, and move around the world in, what then?

The House of Thanatos

We have introduced the Oneiroi—Somnus, Morpheus, Hypnos, Phantastos, and Phoebetor—intermittently throughout this book, but have we *avoided* the most terrifying brother, or conversely, left the best for last? For most humans, Thanatos offers to end everything we know, everything we hold dear . . . simply EVERYTHING!

And yet, there is more; hopefully this book has shown us that everything about the Oneiroi that we thought was true is actually a little different than we thought. Though as children falling asleep may have seemed like death itself, we know that we cannot live without sleep, Somnus. The

dreams "that blister sleep" (Joseph Campbell's words) are no less important than sleep. Deprived of dreams, we lose our ability to pay attention
in the waking world, and ultimately enter a realm of madness, like schizophrenia, in which dream and waking seem all tangled up . . . this is one
of the scariest things that can happen to a human, in which Phantastos
comes as a tormenting veil between ourselves and our lives. But we have
found in earlier chapters that even the dreaded Phoebetor (nightmare)
may give us secret treasures, or call our attention to something that needs
urgent attention. (Search for the power indwelling the terror!)

In shamanic lore, death or its simulation is the ultimate initiator,
the ultimate catalyst of growth, and almost all initiations involve some
kind of confrontation with, some kind of imitation of death. In both
Tom's and Stephen's psychotherapeutic practice, people who have passed
through a health crisis, an accident, a heart attack or stroke, often seem
twice born. It has become a truism that our life is better lived with death
looking over our left shoulder (as Castaneda has it). The near-death
experience has shown itself able to transform self-serving, shallow, or
addicted people into more mature people bestowing kindness and service upon humanity. On a simplistic level, it is often said that by almost
dying, one learns to value the gift of life. But we think there might be
even more to it than that! Is it not possible that Thanatos is the kindest,
and maybe wisest, of all the brothers? Is he the angel of death, the one
whose keen sword brings ultimate relief and returns us to our source?

As he entered the second half of his life, Sigmund Freud abandoned his sole apprenticeship to the god Eros, of life and lust, as he
announced the complementary principle, Thanatos, or the "death
instinct" in his 1923 book *Beyond the Pleasure Principle.** The social
philosopher Herbert Marcuse made understanding the death instinct
the centerpiece of his thought (*Eros and Civilization*). Womb and tomb
are not so far apart, it seems, and we all seek to return to that oceanic

---

*Freud borrowed from a brilliant essay by Sabina Spielrein on the Thanatos principle. If
Jung acted improperly from a sexual viewpoint (as retold in *A Dangerous Method,* the
feature film starring Keira Knightley as Sabina), Freud ripped her off for her intellectual
property, without a nod or a credit, publishing the idea of the death instinct as his own!

bliss from whence we came into this world of struggle, reality with its hard edges, the irreversibility of time, and the regrets of personal and social history. The desire to return to the womb is present in all addictions, from heroin to alcohol. It is certainly there for those who seek suicide, or whole societies that cultivate the ritualization of suicide: the Japanese hara-kari or the terrible mass suicides—or were they charismatically provoked mass murders?—of Jonestown.[4]

In literature and in art, death often appears two-faced. Certainly when it comes to us or a loved one prematurely or unexpectedly, its face is horrific. But when it can promise an end to suffering or offer the only way out of torture or captivity, the story is different, and death may wear the face of a beloved, or a bride. The Jungian analyst M. L. von Franz has catalogued dreams of death and marriage as, in some ways, psychologically equivalent. One can dream of death as marriage approaches, or dream of marriage with a beautiful woman (anima), or a romantic man (animus), as an announcement of death. In this ritualized symbol (or symbolic ritual) we are wedded (*hieros gamos*) to our own soul.[5]

We know that we may dream of our own death or the deaths of people we love, without the actual event coming to pass. Dreams thus, clearly metaphoric, play symbolically with what we think is simply literal, and tragically ultimate. Conversely, Carl Jung was to say that in the dreams of his patients approaching death, the dreams did not seem to take much notice of that ultimate transition we feel is so momentous.[6] Both sources are perhaps slightly reassuring; dreams can play with death as a symbol. And the dreamworld seems to focus on the tasks of psychological and spiritual growth, treating death as being of secondary importance to *individuation*. But recently there is another stream of information that seems to be coming to us at a significant time, from the field known as palliative medicine—the care of those who are aware of their approaching death.

As people approach physical death, unfinished business frequently comes up as old grievances are summoned and closure is invited. Not infrequently, early life trauma or wartime trauma make their appearances in dreams, as if asking for resolution. Relatives and friends, long dead, make surprising dream visits, as if to welcome us to the other side. Here we quote a very recent *New York Times* article, "A New Vision for Dreams of the Dying" by Jan Hoffman (February 2, 2016). (This article is also very unexpected—considering the denial of death in our society.) "For thousands of years, the dreams and visions of the dying have captivated cultures, which imbued them with sacred import. . . . They appear in medieval writings and Renaissance paintings, in Shakespearean works and set pieces from nineteenth-century American and British novels. . . ." But, the article goes on, "doctors tend to give them a wide berth because 'we don't know what the hell they are,' said Dr. Timothy E. Quill, an expert in palliative care. . . ."

Dr. Quill's language is interesting, because he summons one of the afterlife destinations (hell) but not the other. There is a distinction between these and near-death experiences (NDE), says a Dr. Grant, because "these are people on a journey toward death, not people who just missed it."[7] The distinction is important because there is a robust literature on NDEs perhaps culminating in Dr. Eban Alexander's *Proof of Heaven.* We will consider Dr. Alexander's book in this chapter also (even though his NDE was not really a dream, more like a transpersonal vision).

The study quotes a study conducted at Hospice Buffalo of fifty-nine terminally ill patients, "nearly all of which reported having dreams or visions."

"The dreams and visions sorted into categories: opportunities to engage with the deceased; loved ones 'waiting' unfinished business. Themes of love, given or withheld, coursed through the dreams, as did the need for resolution and even forgiveness. In their dreams, patients were reassured that they had been good parents, children and workers. They packed boxes, preparing for journeys, often traveled with dear companions as guides. Although many patients said they rarely remembered their dreams, these they could not forget."[8]

Dr. Tore Nielsen, director of the Dream and Nightmare Laboratory at the University of Montreal, surmised that at the end of life, such a need becomes more insistent. "Troubled dreams erupt with excessive energy. But positive dreams can serve a similar purpose."[9]

The article brings up a topic we have touched on, but probably insufficiently, throughout our text: the concept of "felt presence," something experientially different from a hallucination or delusion. Nielsen and his colleagues Elizaveta Solomonova and Elena Frantova have written about this in their abstract "Felt Presence: The Uncanny Encounters with the Numinous Other."[10] William James also had written about this in *The Varieties of Religious Experience* and other publications around the turn of the twentieth century. He coined the term *noetic* to describe the "felt reality" of a visionary experience, or the presence of another that could not be dismissed as different in any way than the most veridical of our daily experiences with real situations and real people.

Among other things, it was the noetic (ontologically real) sensation of meeting his sister in his near-death experience that persuaded Dr. Eban Alexander, a neurosurgeon, that his experiences during his own mysterious brain death and coma were not delusions. It took him awhile to realize that the magical and affectionate guide who took him through the otherworldly landscapes and realities during his extensive sojourn was his long-dead sister, whom he had never met.

Though Dr. Alexander assures us that "his experience was not a dream" (and hence, perhaps not a suitable subject for this book), his experience does resemble the visionary and real-seeming excursions to another world recorded by Hildegard, Emanuel Swedenborg, and, more recently, that famous pioneer of human consciousness Robert Monroe.*

Are the visions bestowed by Thanatos really to be regarded as *inferior* to those of his brothers?

Love Transcends Death

In the Words of Coauthor Stephen Larsen

In this epilogue we wish to share a love story so extraordinary, all interwoven with dreams, that we hope will be as moving to the reader as it is for all who knew the remarkable couple we discuss. I have written of

---

*Robert Monroe of the Monroe Institute, www.monroeinstitute.org.

Michael and Barbara Schacker elsewhere (*The Neurofeedback Solution*) and published the story of Michael's amazing recovery from stroke on our website: stonemountaincenter.com. It is also touched upon in the website strokefamily.org.

It would be a second marriage for both Michael and Barbara. Their meeting was prefigured by a big dream. As Barbara recounts:

I was pregnant with my first daughter and had a very lucid dream late in my pregnancy—it seemed unrelated to my life. I was in a room in a house; there was no color except for brown. I felt very trapped. The walls were covered with pictures of my ancestors. But there was a window: outside was this beautiful garden, with everything in color. It came to me that I was looking for somebody. I wandered around, feeling very free, and came upon group of people. There was a wooden platform. I walked up and there was a wooden bowl full of cherries. They offered me wonderful Bing cherries. My consciousness started to change. "What do you have in these cherries?" I wanted to know.

I saw this beautiful mansion with a party going on, and I went in. People were having the best time of their lives. At the top of a long stairway was this man looking down at me with an expression of love. He had dark curly hair; I fell in love. Everyone in that place had been affected by this man. He had changed my life for the better. It was a special place!

I woke up. I was back in Nebraska, in bed with my husband.

After a difficult pregnancy, we had a baby, but the marriage was not working out—we broke up; I left Nebraska and went to California.

I lived in Montezuma Ridge, outside San Juan. It was a whole new world! My husband and I tried to get together again, but after a few months I left him and went to live on a game refuge.

On Buddha's birthday, also an eclipse, I took a tiny bit of acid. On the porch of the house where the party was held was a man with dark curly hair, playing his fiddle. I thought the music was amazing; I had never heard anyone play like that! It was Michael. His sister was sitting on the back of a truck. I saw him put his arm around her and wished his arm was around me. I started having dreams about Michael. I couldn't get him out of my mind.

My friend Annie asked, "If you could meet someone, who would it be?"

I said, "Michael Schacker."

She said, "Not a chance; he has a girlfriend!"

I heard later that Michael had asked who I was, and someone said, "Not a chance; she's married!"

But I decided I wanted to meet him. I had other suitors, but I couldn't stop thinking about him. And then I realized that he was the person in my dream in Nebraska.

I dreamed about him a lot, and then learned, just after Christmas, that he'd been on tour in Idaho. I went to hear him when he came back. He was playing his amazing music again. I felt a beam of light between us. We started talking and went outside to look at the stars, and that was it. We moved in together, and were never apart. We lived twenty years in California, had many adventures, and then moved to Willow, outside Woodstock, New York.

Michael and Barbara (and their beautiful daughter, Melissa) lived happily for many years in Willow. To visit their home and attend one of their soirées was magical. After good food and drink, the music and dancing would start; it felt like we were in the home of Dionysus. We would go on until the wee hours of the morning.

All during this time, Michael was hard at work on a variety of projects: political, environmental, ecological. Barbara, already a talented visual artist, taught herself to play the violin, and the group would perform. Somewhere during this time, Michael told me that he had just finished an opera on William Blake—and it was brilliant, and stunning! (I hadn't realized it, but in the background he was working on an alternative history of the West, which emphasized synergy and humanistic values rather than the reckless historical egotism of kings and generals.)

The end of this blissful era was announced by a dream. Michael was at work on an amazing book, following an environmental research project. There was a frightening depletion of the honeybee population, involving something called colony collapse disorder. No one seemed able to pinpoint the cause. Michael set out to document the problem, researching areas in Europe and America. Finally he felt he had determined the cause: something called neonicotinoids, an insecticide added routinely to garden pesticides in extremely small amounts, was disorganizing the bees' nervous systems, so they could not find their colony—hence the collapse! Under a publishing deadline, Michael worked 24/7 for eight months, at which point the book was submitted for publication.

But then Barbara had a horrific dream. Michael was on the floor in a pool of blood, and there was a hole in his heart. After she woke up she told him the dream; he thought it was just anxiety. Three days later, he felt unwell, but Barbara was vigilant. Because of the advance warning the dream had given, she diagnosed the symptoms as stroke and rushed him to the nearest emergency room in Kingston, New York. But when the cardiologist saw him and the scan, she realized it was an aortic dissection—a rupture of the aorta leading from heart to brain. They medivac lifted him to Albany immediately. Emergency surgery took eight hours. Barbara was told Michael had a 50 percent chance of survival, but if he survived, he had a 50 percent chance of having a stroke. Both happened! Michael survived, but the stroke destroyed most of his brain's left hemisphere. He spent months in intensive care, then in rehabilitation at the Northeast Center for Special Care (a head injury facility near Kingston, New York).

After Michael left the Northeast Center he got an apartment in Woodstock Commons, and we enjoyed many good times together. Barbara took wonderful care of him, bringing him to weekly then semimonthly neurofeedback treatments at our facility, Stone Mountain Center, in nearby New Paltz. During that time, Michael kept mentioning "book . . . book." I told him he already had his beautiful *A Spring without Bees* in print. He shook his head. Then Barbara brought in, in a paper bag, the manuscript that he had been working on for thirty years.

Together, we finished it! I (Stephen) wrote the introduction (which also tells Michael's story), and Inner Traditions published the amazing book, truly an offering to transform the world, under the title *Global Awakening: New Science and the 21st-Century Enlightenment.*

More than a year later, at my fiftieth wedding anniversary party, Michael sat joyfully in the middle of more than a hundred people. Here he autographed and sold his book. When the last one was gone (out of a carton) he sat wreathed in smiles, as if his job was done. Beaming, he later gave Barbara, the woman he loved (who had not been able to attend the event), all the money he'd collected. Michael Schacker passed away a week and a half later, on October 30 (the same day that Joseph Campbell had died years earlier), on Dia de los Muertos, when the veil between the world is at its thinnest. (The couple had had six and a half years together after Michael's stroke!)

A few months passed, and Barbara had the following dreams, in fairly quick succession. She thought they were so consistent with who Michael was (or apparently *is!*).

Michael was there, looking fine, healthy, young. He had a tall man with him. He told me, "This is a good man, he will love you." I talked to this man for a little while, while Michael went into other room. When I opened the door and went in there, Michael was looking out the window with a big smile on face.

Michael appeared to me, and apologized that he obsessed about his own work toward the end of his life. He smiled at me and said, "Now it's your turn!"

Barbara told me as I was writing this chapter, "If he had made it until December, we would have been married forty years—and I wouldn't have missed any of those years for all the world!"

This may seem strange to those of us who think of the romance between a man and a woman as lasting, well, *forever.* It brought to mind a story my friend Elmer Green had told me a few years earlier. Elmer's wife, Alyce, had been about twelve years older than he was. When she was in her seventies, she had developed Alzheimer's. Formerly a brilliant scientist and Elmer's partner in his groundbreaking work on consciousness at the Menninger Foundation, Alyce was, like many Alzheimer's victims, "in and out," and finally died of the disease. Elmer, ninety-six as of this year (2016), lived on—with a brilliant and uncompromised mind.

As the turn of the millennium approached, Alyce appeared to Elmer in a dream. "Elmer," she said, "you aren't doing too well living alone. You need a companion."

"Alyce," he replied, "You were the love of my life. I can't imagine being with anyone else; you're my one and only!"

"Don't be silly, Elmer," she responded, emphatically. *It doesn't work that way over here!*"

Elmer Green has always taken dreams seriously—and ones with Alyce *very* seriously. (See the three-volume *Ozawkie Book of the Dead* on his conversations with her—during her Alzheimer's and beyond her death.) After awakening, he wondered just what to do—a widower in his eighties, living in rural Kansas. He had no use for social media.

Then he remembered Gladys.

She had been his high school sweetheart. They had been in love sixty years earlier but life has funny ways of setting people on divergent pathways. Somehow he found her phone number and called her up.

"Gladys?" he asked tentatively.

"Elmer?"—Amazed, she nonetheless had recognized his voice.

He told her about what had happened, and his dream of Alyce. Gladys replied, "It's kind of funny, but my husband died a few years ago, and I've been kind of lonely. . . ."

When Robin and I were invited in 2001 to keynote at the legendary Council Grove Conference in Kansas, Elmer and Gladys were holding hands like newlyweds—which they, in fact, were. What could we say? (It was unbelievably cute!)

When I talked to Elmer in 2015 (I phone him every couple of months), I pointedly asked him about the outcome of the story above, fourteen years after his remarriage. "Was it worth it?" I asked. "Starting a new relationship in your eighties?"

"I asked Gladys how she would like to spend her last decade," he replied. 'I'd kind of like to see the world,' she told me. Well, Stephen, we had a blast—every major country in Europe, the Middle East, India, Asia . . . we went everywhere. I wouldn't have missed any of it!"

I smiled at my friend's eternal joie de vivre.

"You know," Elmer said kind of shyly, unsure, perhaps, if my spiritual beliefs went as far as his own, "There is no death!"

To begin working with your dreams is to enter a great mystery, the mystery of soul and destiny, the mystery of daring to know something, while, in truth, we float on a great sea of unknowing. As W. H. Auden put it, "We are lived by powers we pretend to understand."[11] Or as the Khalahari Bushman affirmed, "There's a dream dreaming us."

James Hillman wrote that when we are in the dream "the dream has us," but when we awaken in the morning, the ego takes over and we say, "Last night *I* had a dream!" But when the dream was happening, *who had who?* We are in the hands of our dreams, and in our experience, they are loving, mysterious hands. They hold us and seem to know more about us than we know about ourselves, and, as we have tried to reveal in these pages, they always seem to have our best interests at heart.

The Dream Portal Method

This method is used by Stephen and Robin Larsen in their dream groups. It can be printed out as a single-page reference for your dreaming colleagues and friends.

All warm-blooded creatures, including birds, are known to dream. REM sleep was identified about sixty years ago. It is a rarity to remember a complete dream. More commonly we have a fragment of a dream (still valuable!); 99.9 percent of dreaming occurs without our ever becoming aware of it at all. Because dreams rise from the depths of the psyche, they arise through the layers of who we really are. The suggestions and points below are to help you understand yourself and others (family, friends, and dream colleagues) through dreamwork.

- Never dismiss a dream as being "just a dream." Be willing to believe that it can carry the imprint of the whole (yours or another's) psyche.
- Dreams may come in two varieties: big and small. Even small dreams can be very, very useful, while the big ones eerily beg your attention and awareness.
- Dreams come from another side of ourselves through a portal; they require special attention and awareness, even techniques, to remember them regularly—otherwise they all too easily slip back into the source realm from which they emerged.

- You may want to keep a journal or a tape recorder near you at night for the purpose of recording the dreams—or you can tell them to a sleeping partner or a friend as soon as you awaken. Infrequently, you may recall a dream later in the day.
- Since time immemorial, people have worked on dreams in groups. The main requirement is that the group be seriously playful about the work and respectful of the dream and the dreamer's psyche and process.
- No one aside from the dreamer—even Dr. Freud or some Sherlock Holmes of dreams—can establish an authoritative analysis of what the dream means. Dreams carry multiple meanings and can be explored from many angles and approaches, yielding useful results.
- Dreams, being made of metamorphic, psychic stuff, lend themselves readily to poetry, art, inspiration, and new inventions. Be willing to let the impulse for some creative project arise as a result of the dream.
- To enrich your ability to work with dreams, read mythology of many kinds from many cultures.
- Be ready for your process of working on your dreams to evolve, unfold, and mature, as do you yourself in working on them.
- Dreams may have an objective as well as a subjective level. Don't ignore premonitions, clairvoyance, or telepathy.
- In your dream you can fall great distances, die, or dream of death without dying.
- Use association, amplifications, or active imagination to work with dreams.

Sweet dreams!

Notes

INTRODUCTION.
BIG DREAMS, LITTLE DREAMS

1. Joseph Campbell and Bill Moyers, "The Hero's Adventure."

CHAPTER 1. ANCIENT DREAMING

1. Herzog, *Cave of Forgotten Dreams* (documentary film).
2. Lawlor, *Voices of the First Day*.
3. Campbell, *Way of the Animal Powers*.
4. Gimbutas, *Goddesses and Gods of Old Europe*.
5. Eliade, *Shamanism*.
6. Campbell, *Hero with a Thousand Faces* and *Masks of God*.
7. Hoffman, "Dumuzi's Dream."
8. Bierbrier, *The Tomb-builders of the Pharaohs*.
9. McKechnie and Guillame, *Ptolemy II Philadelphus and His World*.
10. Kingsley, *In the Dark Places of Wisdom*.
11. Kerényi, *Askelpios*.
12. Kingsley, *In the Dark Places of Wisdom*.
13. Ibid., 110.
14. Ibid., 112.
15. Kingsley, *Story Waiting to Pierce You*.
16. Hesiod, *Theogony*, 116–24.
17. Homer, *Odyssey*, book 19, 560–69.
18. Yeats, *Vision*.
19. National Institute of Health, "Brain Basics: Understanding Sleep."
20. For more about Patanjali, see Wikipedia, s.v. "yoga sutras of Patanjali," last modified

January 23, 2017, https://en.wikipedia.org/wiki/Yoga_Sutras_of_Patanjali.

21. Harp and Smiley, *Three Minute Meditator.*

22. Synesius, *On Dreams,* 7.

23. Ibid.

24. Ibid., 11.

25. Ibid., 12.

26. Synesius, "On Dreams," in Johnson, *The Platonist,* 224.

27. Synesius, *On Dreams,* 15.

28. Ibid.

29. Synesius, "On Dreams," in Johnson, *The Platonist,* 228.

30. Hillman, "Peaks and Vales," 59.

31. Synesius, *On Dreams,* 18.

32. Ibid., 19.

33. Ibid., 20.

34. Synesius, "On Dreams," in Johnson, *The Platonist,* 282.

35. Synesius, *On Dreams,* 25.

36. Ibid., 26.

37. Ibid.

38. Ibid., 34.

39. Campbell, *The Mythic Image,* 7.

40. Synesius, *On Dreams,* 34.

CHAPTER 2. THE DREAMING BRAIN

1. Verny and Kelly, *Secret Life of the Unborn Child.*

2. Larsen, *Neurofeedback Solution.*

3. Grof, *Realms of the Human Unconscious.*

4. Division of Sleep Medicine at Harvard Medical School, "Natural Patterns of Sleep."

5. Freud, *Interpretation of Dreams.*

6. See LaBerge, *Lucid Dreaming.*

7. Hurd, "Allen Hobson and the Neuroscience of Dreams."

8. Hobson, Hong, and Friston, "Virtual Reality and Consciousness Inference in Dreaming," containing a quote by Revonsuo, *Inner Presence,* 55.

9. Hurd, "Allan Hobson and the Neuroscience of Dreams."

10. Ibid.

11. Green, Ullman, and Tauber, "Dreaming and Modern Dream Theory."

12. Larsen, *Neurofeedback Solution.*

13. See Volkow, "Marijuana's Lasting Effects on the Brain."

14. Larsen, *Neurofeedback Solution.*

CHAPTER 3. REMEMBERING OUR DREAMS

1. Reed, *Getting Help from Your Dreams,* 15.
2. Synesius, *On Dreams,* 8, 10, 20.
3. Stephen Larsen's discussion of Dr. Ira Progoff's work is mainly drawn from personal experience in journaling seminars with Dr. Progoff.
4. Hillman, *The Dream and the Underworld,* 126.
5. Levertov, *Denise Levertov: Poems 1972–1982.*
6. Leviton, "The Barefoot Philosopher of the Imagination," 2.
7. Ibid., 7, quoting Bachelard.
8. For an overview of Calvin Hall's work by his collaborator, see Van de Castle, *Our Dreaming Mind.*

CHAPTER 4. WHAT MAKES FOR A BIG DREAM?

1. Solomonova, Frantova, and Nielsen, "Felt Presence: The Uncanny Encounters."

CHAPTER 5. STANDING NAKED BEFORE THE DREAM

1. Bair, *Jung: A Biography.*
2. Maidenbaum, *Jung and the Shadow of Anti-Semitism.*
3. Tranströmer, "Romanesque Arches," in *Half-finished Heaven.*
4. Larsen and Larsen, *Fire in the Mind.*
5. Ibid., 18–19.
6. Campbell, *Inner Reaches,* 110.

CHAPTER 6. ARCHAEOLOGIST OF MORNING

1. Mary Oliver, *House of Light,* 57.
2. Wikiquotes, s.v. "Novalis," last modified November 28, 2016, https://en.wikiquote.org/wiki/Novalis.
3. Quoted in Stevens, *Private Myths,* 338.

CHAPTER 7. PRECOGNITION, TELEPATHY, AND SYNCHRONICITY IN DREAMS

1. Brown, "The Life and Martyrdom of Polycarp."
2. Ibid.
3. St. Augustine, *Confessions,* book 3.

4. Aquinas, *Great Books*, vi.

5. Moss, *Secret History of Dreaming*, 146.

6. Ibid.

7. Ibid.

8. Ibid., 149.

9. Ibid., 168.

10. Kagan, *Lucrecia's Dreams*.

11. Moss, *Secret History of Dreaming*, 171.

12. Bradford, *Harriet Tubman: The Moses of Her People*, 75–76.

13. Ibid.

14. Moss, *Secret History of Dreaming*, 179.

15. Shafton, *Dream Singers*.

16. Ibid.

17. Tolaas and Ullman, "Extrasensory Communication and Dreams."

18. Ibid.

19. Ibid.

20. Ibid.

21. Ibid.

22. Ullman, "Dream Telepathy—Experimental and Clinical Findings."

23. Wikipedia, s.v. "list of multiple discoveries," last modified January 12, 2017, https://en.wikipedia.org/wiki/List_of_multiple_discoveries.

24. Shafton, "African Americans and Predictive Dreams," 1.

25. Chinkwita, *Usefulness of Dreams*.

26. Teish, *Jambalaya*.

27. Chinkwita, *Usefulness of Dreams*.

28. Moss, *Secret History of Dreaming*, 184–85.

29. Shafton, "African Americans and Predictive Dreams," 4.

30. Cayce, *Dreams and Visions*, xvii.

31. Cayce, *The Edgar Case Collection*, 82.

CHAPTER 8. DREAM INCUBATION

1. Oliver, *New and Selected Poems*.

2. Ibid.

3. Garfield, *Creative Dreaming*, 9–11.

4. Garfield, *Dream Book*, 56.

5. Sigerist, *A History of Medicine*, vol. 2, 64.

6. Ibid., 65–67.

7. Jung, *Civilization in Transition*, 304.

8. Hillman, *The Dream and the Underworld*.

9. Progoff, *At a Journal Workshop*, 64.

10. Woodman and Mellick, *Coming Home to Myself*, 178.

11. Machado, "Is My Soul Asleep?" in Bly, *The Soul Is Here for Its Own Joy*, 24.

12. Ullman and Zimmerman, *Working with Dreams*, 209.

13. Ullman, "An Approach to Closeness."

14. Berdyaev, in Rogers, *On Becoming a Person*, 26.

15. Watkins, *Waking Dreams*, 24–25.

16. Personal conversation Tom had with John Weir Perry after a talk Perry gave at the University of Vermont in the 1980s.

17. Thoreau, *Walden*.

18. Nance, *The Gentle Tasaday*.

19. Heidigger, *An Introduction to Metaphysics*, 206.

20. von Franz, *On Dreams and Death*, vii.

CHAPTER 9. THE
CAULDRON OF INEXHAUSTIBLE GIFTS

1. Bruner, *On Knowing*.

2. Sacks, *Migraine*, 53.

3. Kiefer, "Biographical Sketches of Memorable Christians."

4. Bosma, *The Electronic Cry*, 24, citing Viñao's liner notes.

5. Kiefer, "Biographical Sketches of Memorable Christians."

6. Hildegard quoted in Fox, *Original Blessing*.

7. Eliot, "Dante."

8. "Famous Dreams: Dante Alighieri," www.dreaminterpretation-dictionary .com/famous-dreams-4.html (accessed May 16, 2017).

9. Lambdin and Lambdin, *A Companion to Old and Middle English Literature*, 191.

10. Sarhan, "Dream Vision in Chaucer's Poetry."

11. Gorman, "Ed Gorman Calling: We Talk to Richard Matheson."

12. *Wikipedia*, s.v. "Frankenstein," last modified January 4, 2017, https:// en.wikipedia.org/wiki/Frankenstein.

13. Shelley, *Frankenstein*, preface.

14. Maguire, *Night and Day*, 177.

15. Wikipedia, s.v. "Yesterday (Beatles song)," last modified January 8, 2017, https://en.wikipedia.org/wiki/Yesterday_(Beatles_song).

16. Miles, *Paul McCartney*, 201–5.

17. Ibid.

18. Ibid.

19. Roberts, *Serendipity*, 83–91.

20. Ibid., 77.

21. Ibid.

22. "Benzene and Other Aromatic Compounds."

23. Benfey, *Journal of Chemical Education,* vol 35 (1958), page 21—cited in Roberts, *Serendipity,* 77.

24. Seltzer, "Influence of Kekulé Dream," 22; and Wotiz and Rudofsky, letter to the editor, 3.

25. Todman, "Inspiration from Dreams in Neuroscience Research." For more on this topic, see McIsaac, "5 Scientific Discoveries Made in Dreams."

26. Todman, "Inspiration from Dreams in Neuroscience Research," 3.

27. McIsaac, "5 Scientific Discoveries Made in Dreams."

28. Einstein, *Autobiographical Notes,* 8–9.

29. Calaprice, *The Expanded Quotable Einstein,* 287.

30. George Sylvester Viereck, "What Life Means to Einstein," interview with Albert Einstein, *Saturday Evening Post,* October 26, 1929, was the first source of this often-quoted phrase, according to http://quoteinvestigator.com/2013/01/01 /einstein-imagination (accessed January 25, 2017).

31. Einstein, *Autobiographical Notes,* 8–9.

32. Root-Bernstein and Root-Bernstein, "Einstein on Creative Thinking."

33. Ibid.

CHAPTER 10. DREAMING WHILE AWAKE, WAKING IN THE DREAM

1. Peniston and Kulkosky, *Peniston/Kulkosky Brain Wave Neurofeedback Therapy.*

2. Watkins, *Waking Dreams;* and Singer, *Inner World of Daydreaming.*

3. Watkins, *Waking Dreams,* 60–67.

4. Berne and Savary, *Dream Symbol Work.*

5. Ibid.

6. Larsen and Larsen, *Mythic Imagination;* and Larsen and Larsen, *Parabola.*

7. Watkins, *Waking Dreams.*

8. Berne and Savary, *Dream Symbol Work.*

9. Gallegos, *Personal Totem Pole.*

10. Goleman, *Emotional Intelligence.*

11. Moss, *Dreamways of the Iroquois.*

12. The full text of the *Jesuit Relations* documents can be found at http://moses .creighton.edu/kripke/jesuitrelations (accessed January 25, 2017).

13. Watkins, *Waking Dreams,* 145–46.

14. Van de Castle, *Our Dreaming Mind,* 340.

15. Blake, *The Complete Poems,* 337.

CHAPTER 11.
DREAMS AND THE POETIC IMAGINATION

1. Hillman, *Re-Visioning Psychology.*
2. Cox, *Seduction of the Spirit,* 13.
3. Joan of Arc quote, www.azquotes.com/quote/921157 (accessed January 25, 2017).
4. Hillman, *Dreams and the Underworld,* 200.
5. Levertov, "Interweavings," 139.
6. Hillman, *Dream and the Underworld,* 126.
7. Wikipedia, s.v. "pantoum," last modified January 15, 2017, https://en.wikipedia .org/wiki/Pantoum.
8. Hirsch, *Poet's Glossary,* 441.
9. Freud, *The Interpretation of Dreams.*
10. Hillman, *Re-Visioning Psychology,* x.
11. Ibid.

EPILOGUE.
WHAT DREAMS MAY COME . . .

1. Hillman, *Insearch,* 57–60.
2. Ibid., 57.
3. Whitmont and Perera, *Dreams, a Portal to the Source,* 2.
4. Marcuse, *Eros and Civilization.*
5. von Franz, *On Dreams and Death,* especially chapter 3.
6. Ibid., viii–ix.
7. Hoffman, "A New Vision for Dreams of the Dying."
8. Ibid.
9. Ibid.
10. Solomonova, Frantova, and Nielsen, "Felt Presence: The Uncanny Encounters."
11. Auden, *Another Time.*

Bibliography

Aquinas, Thomas. *Great Books of the Western World*. Vol. 19. Chicago: Encyclopaedia Britannica, 1952.

Aserinsky, Eugene, and Wallace Mendelson. "In Memory of Eugene Aserinsky (1921–1998)." *Journal of the History of Neurosciences* 7, no. 3 (December 1998): 250–51. Published online 2010. www.tandfonline.com/doi/abs /10.1076/jhin.7.3.250.1859 (accessed January 17, 2017).

Auden, W. H. *Another Time.* new ed. London: Faber and Faber, 2007. First published 1940.

Avens, Roberts. *Imagination Is Reality*. Ann Arbor, Mich.: Spring Publications, 1980.

———. *Imaginal Body: Para-Jungian Reflections on Soul, Imagination, and Death.* Lanham, Md.: University Press of America, 1982.

Bachelard, Gaston. *The Poetics of Reverie: Childhood, Language, and the Cosmos.* Boston: Beacon Press, 1971.

———. *The Psychoanalysis of Fire*. Boston: Beacon Press, 1987.

———. *The Poetics of Space: The Classic Look at How We Experience Places.* Boston: Beacon Press, 1994.

Bair, Deirdre. *Jung: A Biography*. New York: Back Bay Books/Little Brown and Company, 2003.

Baldwin, Christina. *Life's Companion*. New York: Bantam Books, 1990.

Barasch, Marc Ian. *Healing Dreams: Exploring the Dreams That Can Transfigure Your Life.* New York: Riverhead Books, 2000.

"Benzene and Other Aromatic Compounds." www2.chemistry.msu.edu/faculty /reusch/virttxtjml/react3.htm (accessed March 8, 2017).

Berne, Patricia H., and Louis M. Savary. *Dream Symbol Work: Unlocking the Energy from Dreams and Spiritual Experiences.* New York/Mahwah, N.J.: Paulist Press, 1991.

Bierbrier, Morris. *The Tomb-builders of the Pharaohs.* London: British Museum Publications, 1982.

Blake, William. *The Complete Poems.* 3rd ed. Edited by W. H. Stevenson. New York: Routledge, 2007.

Bly, Robert. *News of the Universe.* San Francisco, Calif.: Sierra Club Books, 1980.

———. *The Soul Is Here for Its Own Joy.* Hopewell, N.Y.: The Ecco Press, 1995.

Bly, Robert, James Hillman, and Michael Meade, eds. *The Rag and Bone Shop of the Heart.* New York: HarperCollins Publishers, 1992.

Bosma, H. M. *The Electronic Cry: Voice and Gender in Electroacoustic Music.* University of Amsterdam, 2013. Available at https://pure.uva.nl/ws/files /2112129/130704_08.pdf (accessed March 7, 2017).

Bosnak, Robert. *A Little Course in Dreams.* Boston: Shambhala, 1988.

Bradford, Sarah H. *Harriet Tubman: The Moses of Her People.* New York: George R. Lockwood and Son, 1886. Available online at Project Gutenberg: www .gutenberg.org/files/9999/9999-h/9999-h.htm (accessed January 17, 2017).

Brown, David L. "The Life and Martyrdom of Polycarp." Logos Resource Pages, http://logosresourcepages.org/History/polycarp.htm (accessed March 24, 2017).

Bruner, Jerome. *On Knowing: Essays for the Left Hand.* new ed. Cambridge, Mass.: Belknap Press, 1979.

Bryant, Dorothy. *The Kin of Ata Are Waiting for You.* New York: Moon Books/ Random House, 1971.

Calaprice, Alice, ed. *The Expanded Quotable Einstein.* Princeton, N.J.: Princeton University Press, 2000.

Campbell, Joseph. *The Hero with a Thousand Faces: The Collected Works of Joseph Campbell.* New York: Pantheon Books, 1949.

———. *The Masks of God.* 4 vols. New York: Viking Press, 1959–68.

———. *The Mythic Image.* Bollingen Series C. Princeton, N.J.: Princeton University Press, 1974.

———. *The Inner Reaches of Outer Space: Metaphor as Myth and Religion.* New York: Harper and Row, 1986.

———. *The Way of Animal Powers.* Vol. 1 of *The Historical Atlas of World Mythology.* New York: HarperCollins, 1988.

Campbell, Joseph, and Bill Moyers. "The Hero's Adventure." *Joseph Campbell and the Power of Myth,* PBS episode 1, aired June 21, 1988.

Campbell, Joseph, with Bill Moyers. *The Power of Myth.* New York: Anchor, 1991.

Cavalli, Thom F., and Robert A. Johnson. *Alchemical Psychology: Old Recipes for Living in a New World.* New York: Jeremy P. Tarcher/Putnam, 2002.

Cayce, Edgar. *Dreams and Visions.* Virginia Beach, Va.: A.R.E. Press, 2008.

———. *The Edgar Case Collection*. n.p.: Wings Books, 1988.

Chinkwita, Mary. *Usefulness of Dreams*. Newark, Vt.: Janus Press, 1993.

Cirlot, Juan Eduardo. *A Dictionary of Symbols*. New York: Philosophical Library, 1962.

Cox, Harvey. *The Seduction of the Spirit*. New York: Simon and Schuster, 1973.

Craig, Paula. *Build Your Own Dream House*. Virginia Beach, Va.: A.R.E. Press, 1974.

De Becker, Raymond. *The Understanding of Dreams*. New York: Bell Publishing Company, 1968.

Delaney, Gayle. *Living Your Dreams*. New York: Harper and Row, 1988.

Division of Sleep Medicine at Harvard Medical School. "Natural Patterns of Sleep." Last reviewed December 18, 2007. http://healthysleep.med.harvard.edu /healthy/science/what/sleep-patterns-rem-nrem (accessed June 2, 2017).

Domhoff, G. William. *The Mystique of Dreams*. Berkeley and Los Angeles: University of California Press, 1985.

Einstein, Albert. *Autobiographical Notes*. Edited and translated by Paul A. Schilpp. Chicago: Open Court Publishers, 1999. First published in 1946.

Eliade, Mircea. *Shamanism: Archaic Techniques of Ecstasy*. Princeton: Princeton University Press, 1964.

Eliot, T. S. "Dante." In *Selected Essays*, 199–237. New York: Harcourt, Brace and Company, 1950.

Epel, Naomi. *Writers Dreaming*. New York: Carol Southern Books, 1993.

Faraday, Ann. *Dream Power*. New York: Berkeley Books, 1972.

———. *The Dream Game*. New York: Harper and Row, 1974.

Feinstein, David, and Stanley Krippner. *The Mythic Path*. New York: Jeremy P. Tarcher, 1997.

Fontana, David. *The Secret Language of Symbols*. San Francisco, Calif.: Chronicle Books, 1993.

Fox, John. *Poetic Medicine: The Healing Art of Poem-Making*. New York: Jeremy P. Tarcher/Putnam, 1997.

Fox, Matthew. *Original Blessing*. New York: Tarcher, 1983.

Freud, Sigmund. *The Interpretation of Dreams*. Translated and Edited by James Strachey. New York: Basic Books, 1955. First published in 1899.

Fromm, Erich. *The Forgotten Language*. New York: Grove Press, 1951.

Gallegos, Eligio Stephen. *Personal Totem Pole: Animal Imagery the Chakras and Psychotherapy*. 2nd ed. Embudo, New Mex.: Moon Bear Press, 1990.

Garfield, Patricia. *Creative Dreaming: The Mysterious World of Dreams Revealed*. New York: Ballantine Books, 1974.

———. *Creative Dreaming: Plan and Control Your Dreams to Develop Creativity, Overcome Fears, Solve Problems, and Create a Better Self*. Updated ed. New York: Touchstone, 1995.

———. *The Dream Book*. Toronto: Tundra Books, 2002.

Garrison, Andrea R. *The Presence of Angels: Reflections on Mattie Pearl and Emanuel Swedenborg.* West Chester, Penn.: The Swedenborg Foundation, 2013.

———. *The Crossing Over of Mattie Pearl.* Create Space, 2008. Kindle edition published 2012.

Gimbutas, Marija. *The Goddesses and Gods of Old Europe: Myths and Cult Images.* Chicago: University of Chicago Press, 2007.

Goleman, Daniel. *Emotional Intelligence: Why It Can Matter More Than IQ.* Tenth anniv. ed. New York: Bantam, 2005.

Gorman, Edward J. "Ed Gorman Calling: We Talk to Richard Matheson." *Mystery File: Crime Fiction Research Journal.* Revised version published online in 2006, www.mysteryfile.com/Matheson/Interview.html.

Green, Maurice R., Montague Ullman, and Edward Tauber. "Dreaming and Modern Dream Theory." In *Modern Psychoanalysis,* edited by Judd Marmor, 146–86. New York: Basic Books, 1986.

Grof, Stanislav. *Realms of Human Unconscious: Observations from LSD Research.* reprint ed. London: Souvenir Press, 1996.

Guin, Ursula Kroeber. *The Word for World Is Forest.* New York: Ace Books, 1972.

Gurney, E. and F. W. H. Podmore Myers. *Phantasms of the Living.* London: Trubner Co., 1886.

Harp, David, and Nina Smiley. *The Three Minute Meditator.* N.p.: Mind's I Press, 2008.

Heidegger, Martin. *An Introduction to Metaphysics.* New Haven, Conn.: Yale University Press, 1959.

Herzog, Werner. *Cave of Forgotten Dreams.* Written and directed by Werner Herzog. Los Angeles, Calif.: Creative Differences Productions, 2010.

Hesiod. *Theogony.* Available at www.sacred-texts.com/cla/hesiod/theogony.htm (accessed May 12, 2017).

Hillman, James. *Insearch.* Irving, Tex.: Spring Publications, 1967.

———. *Re-Visioning Psychology.* New York: Harper and Row, 1975.

———. *The Dream and the Underworld.* New York: Harper and Row, 1979.

———. "Peaks and Vales." In *Puer Papers,* edited by Cynthia Giles. Irving, Tex.: Spring Publications, 1979.

———. *A Blue Fire.* New York: Harper and Row, 1989.

———. *The Soul's Code: In Search of Character and Calling.* New York: Random House, 1996.

Hillman, James, and Wilhelm Heinrich Roscher. *Pan and the Nightmare: Two Essays.* Dallas, Tex.: Spring Publications, 1972.

Hillman, James, and Michael Ventura. *We've Had a Hundred Years of Psychotherapy— And the World's Getting Worse.* San Francisco: HarperCollins, 1992.

Hirsch, Edward. *A Poet's Glossary.* New York: Houghton Mifflin Harcourt, 2014.

Hobson, J. A. *The Dreaming Brain*. New York: Basic Books, 1988.

Hobson, J. A., Charles C.-H. Hong, and Karl J. Friston. "Virtual Reality and Consciousness Inference in Dreaming." *Frontiers of Psychology* (October 9, 2014). http://dx.doi.org/10.3389/fpsyg.2014.01133 (accessed January 17, 2017).

Hobson, J. A., and R. W. McCarley. "The Brain as a Dream-State Generator: An Activation-Synthesis Hypothesis of the Dream Process." *American Journal of Psychiatry* 134 (1977): 1335–48.

Hoffman C. "Dumuzi's Dream: Dream Analysis in Ancient Mesopotamia." *Dreaming* 14, no. 4: 240–51.

Hoffman, Jan. "A New Vision for Dreams of the Dying." *New York Times,* February 2, 2016.

Homer. *The Odyssey*. Translated by Samuel Butler. Available at http://classics .mit.edu/Homer/odyssey.html (accessed May 12, 2017).

Hope, Jane. *The Secret Language of the Soul*. San Francisco: Chronicle Books, 1997.

Hurd, Ryan. "Allan Hobson and the Neuroscience of Dreams." Dream Studies Portal. www.dreamstudies.org/2010/01/07/neuroscience-of-dreams (accessed January 17, 2017).

Ione. *This a Dream! A Handbook for Deep Dreamers*. Kingston, N.Y.: Ministry of Maat Press, 2000.

Jaynes, Julian. *The Origins of Consciousness in the Breakdown of the Bicameral Mind*. Boston: Houghton Mifflin Company, 1990.

John, E. Roy. "Principles of Neurometrics." *American Journal of EEG Technology* 30 (1990): 251–66.

Johnson, Robert A. *She: Understanding the Feminine Psychology*. New York/San Francisco: Harper and Row, 1976.

———. *We: Understanding the Psychology of Romantic Love*. San Francisco: Harper SanFrancisco, 1983.

———. *Inner Work: Using Dreams and Active Imagination for Personal Growth*. New York: Harper and Row, 2009.

Jones, Gwyn, and Thomas Jones, eds. *The Mabinogion*. Everyman's Library. New York: Dutton, n.d.

Joyce, James. *Finnegans Wake*. New York: The Viking Press, 1947.

———. *Ulysses*. New York: Vintage, 1961.

———. *A Portrait of the Artist as a Young Man*. New York: Viking Press, 1964.

Jung, Carl Gustav. *Psychology and Religion*. New Haven, Conn.: Yale University Press, 1938.

———. *The Development of Personality: Papers on Child Psychology, Education, and Related Subjects*. Vol. 17 in *The Collected Works of C. G. Jung,* translated by R. F. C. Hull and Gerhard Adler. Princeton, N.J.: Princeton University Press, 1954.

————. "Marriage as a Psychological Relationship." In *The Development of Personality: Papers on Child Psychology, Education, and Related Subjects.* Vol. 17 of *The Collected Works of C. G. Jung.* New York: Pantheon Books, 1954.

————. *Modern Man in Search of a Soul.* Translated by W. S. Dell and Cary F. Baynes. New York: Harcourt, Brace, and World, 1955.

————. *The Archetypes and the Collective Unconscious.* Vol. 9, part 1 of *The Collected Works of C. G. Jung.* New York: Pantheon/Bollingen, 1959.

————. "The Psychology of Dementia Praecox." In Psychogenesis of Mental Disease. Vol. 3 of *The Collected Works of C. G. Jung,* translated by R. F. C. Hull, 8. Princeton, N.J.: Princeton University Press, 1960.

————. *Memories, Dreams, Reflections.* Edited by Aniela Jaffee. Translated by Richard Winston and Clara Winston. New York: Pantheon Books, 1961.

————. *Symbols of Transformation: An Analysis of the Prelude to a Case of Schizophrenia.* Vol. 5 of *The Collected Works of C. G. Jung,* translated by R. F. C. Hull, 5. Princeton, N.J.: Princeton University Press, 1967.

————. *Psychology and Alchemy.* Vol. 12 of *The Collected Works of C. G. Jung.* Princeton, N.J.: Princeton University Press, 1968.

————. "On the Nature of the Psyche," in *Structure and Dynamics of the Psyche.* Vol. 8 of *The Collected Works of C. G. Jung,* edited by G. Adler, Herbert Read, Michael Fordham, translated by R. F. C. Hull. Princeton, N.J.: Princeton University Press, 1969.

————. *Practice of Psychotherapy.* Vol. 16 of *The Collected Works of C. G. Jung,* translated by R. F. C. Hull and Gerhard Adler. Princeton, N.J.: Princeton University Press, 1969.

————. "The Stages of Life." In *The Structure and Dynamics of the Psyche: Including "Synchronicity: An Acausal Connecting Principle."* Vol. 8 of *The Collected Works of C. G. Jung,* translated by R. F. C. Hull. Princeton, N.J.: Princeton University Press, 1969.

————. *Analytical Psychology: Its Theory and Practice.* Foreword by E. A. Bennet. New York: Vintage, 1970.

————. *Psychological Types.* Revised edition by R. F. C. Hull. Vol. 6 of *The Collected Works of C. G. Jung,* translated by H. G. Baynes. Princeton, N.J.: Princeton University Press, 1971.

————. *Two Essays on Analytical Psychology.* Vol. 7 of *The Collected Works of C. G. Jung,* translated by R. F. C. Hull and Gerhard Adler. Princeton, N.J.: Princeton University Press, 1972.

————. "Answer to Job." In *Psychology and Religion: West and East.* Vol. 11 of *The Collected Works of C. G. Jung,* translated by R. F. C. Hull. Princeton, N.J.: Princeton University Press, 1973.

————. *Experimental Researches.* Vol. 2 of *The Collected Works of C. G. Jung,* edited by Gerhard Adler, translated by R. F. C. Hull. Princeton, N.J.: Princeton University Press, 1973.

———. *Psychological Reflections: A New Anthology of His Writings, 1905–1961*. Princeton, N.J.: Princeton University Press, 1973.

———. *Civilization in Transition*. Vol. 10 of *The Collected Works of C. G. Jung*, translated by R. F. C. Hull. Princeton, N.J.: Princeton University Press, 1970.

———. *Mysterium Coniunctionis: An Inquiry into the Separation and Synthesis of Psychic Opposites in Alchemy*. Vol. 14 of *The Collected Works of C. G. Jung*, translated by R. F. C. Hull and Gerhard Adler. Princeton, N.J.: Princeton University Press, 1977.

———. *Psychology and the East (from Volumes 10, 11, 13, and 18 of Collected Works)*. Translated by R. F. C. Hull. Princeton, N.J.: Princeton University Press, 1978.

———. *Aion: Researches into the Phenomenology of the Self*. Vol. 9, part 2 of *The Collected Works of C. G. Jung*. Translated by R. F. C. Hull and Gerhard Adler. Princeton, N.J.: Princeton University Press, 1979.

———. *The Psychology of Transference*. N.p.: Ark Paperbacks, 1983.

———. *Essays on Contemporary Events: The Psychology of Nazism*. Translated by R. F. C. Hull and Gerhard Adler. Material from volumes 10 and 16 of *The Collected Works of C. G. Jung*. Princeton, N. J.: Princeton University Press, 1989.

———. *The Psychoanalytic Years*. Translated by R. F. C. Hull, and edited by Leopold Stein and Diana Riviere. Material from volumes 2, 4, 17 of *The Collected Works of C. G. Jung*. Princeton, N.J.: Princeton University Press, 2016.

Jung, Carl Gustav, and Aniela Jaffé, eds. *C. G. Jung: Word and Image*. Princeton, N.J.: Princeton University Press, 1979.

Jung, Carl Gustav, and Carl Kerényi. *Essays on a Science of Mythology: The Myth of the Divine Child and the Mysteries of Eleusis*. Material from volume 9 of *The Collected Works of C. G. Jung*. Princeton, N.J.: Princeton University Press, 1969.

Jung, Emma. *Animus and Anima*. New York: Spring Publications, 1969.

Kagan, Richard L. *Lucrecia's Dreams: Politics and Policies in Sixteenth-Century Spain*. Berkeley: University of California Press, 1995.

Kaku, Michio. *The Future of the Mind: The Scientific Quest to Understand, Enhance, and Empower the Mind*. New York: Doubleday, 2014.

Keen, Sam, and Anne Valley-Fox. *Your Mythic Journey*. New York: Jeremy P. Tarcher, 1989.

Kelsey, Morton T. *God, Dreams, and Revelations*. Minneapolis, Minn.: Augsburg Publishing House, 1974.

Kerényi, Karl. *Dionysos: Archetypal Image of Indestructible Life*. The Princeton/Bollingen Series in World Mythology: Bollingen Series 65, translated by Ralph Manheim. Princeton, N.J.: Princeton University Press, 1996.

——. *Asklepios: Archetypal Image of the Physician's Existence*. Archetypal Images in Greek Religion. Bollingen Series 65, translated by Ralph Manheim, 3. Princeton, N.J.: Princeton University Press, 1959.

Kiefer, James E. "Biographical Sketches of Memorable Christians of the Past: Hildegard of Bingen, Visionary." http://justus.anglican.org/resources /bio/247.html (accessed January 25, 2017).

Kingsley, Peter. *In the Dark Places of Wisdom*. Inverness, Calif.: The Golden Sufi Center, 1999.

——. *A Story Waiting to Pierce You: Mongolia, Tibet, and the Destiny of the Western World*. Point Reyes, Calif.: The Golden Sufi Center, 2010.

LaBerge, Stephen. *Lucid Dreaming: A Concise Guide to Awakening in Your Dreams and Your Life*. Louisville, Colo.: Sounds True, 2009. First published 1986.

Lambdin, Laura Cooner, and Thomas Lambdin. *A Companion to Old and Middle English Literature*. United States: Greenwood Publishing Group, 2002.

Larsen, Robin, ed. *Emanuel Swedenborg: A Continuing Vision*. New York: The Swedenborg Foundation, 1988.

Larsen, Stephen. "The Healing Mask." *Parabola* (Summer 1980).

——. "The Soul and the Abyss of Nature." In *Emanuel Swedenborg: A Continuing Vision*, edited by Robin Larsen. New York: The Swedenborg Foundation, 1988.

——. *The Mythic Imagination: Your Quest for Meaning Through Personal Mythology*. New York: Bantam Books, 1990.

——. "Mending the Mind of Childhood." *Chronogram* 1997. First in a series of three articles.

——. "Mid-Life Metamorphosis." *Chronogram* 1997. Second in a series of three articles.

——. "Re-Magicking the World." *Chronogram* 1997. Third in a series of three articles.

——. "The Other Side of Life." *Chronogram* 1998.

——. *The Shaman's Doorway*. Rochester, Vt.: Inner Traditions, 1998.

——. "The Tao of Neuroscience: Len Ochs' Magic Lights and the Realization of Cortical Flexibility." Winter Brain Conference (Futurehealth.org). Palm Springs, Calif.: 1998.

——. "The Use of Flexyx Treatment Modality with Patients with Multiple Brain and Spinal Cord Injuries." Winter Brain Conference (Futurehealth.org). February 2001.

——. *The Healing Power of Neurofeedback: The Revolutionary LENS Technique for Restoring Optimal Brain Function*. Foreword by Thom Hartmann. Rochester, Vt.: Healing Arts Press, 2006.

——. *The Fundamentalist Mind*. Wheaton, Ill.: Quest Books, 2007.

——. *The Neurofeedback Solution: How to Treat Autism, ADHD, Anxiety, Brain*

Injury, Stroke, PTSD, and More. Rochester, Vt.: Healing Arts Press, 2012.

Larsen, Stephen, and Robin Larsen. *A Fire in the Mind: The Life of Joseph Campbell.* New York: Doubleday, 1991.

———. "The LENS with Animals: Preliminary Observations." PowerPoint presentation with accompanying video. International Society for Neuronal Regulation, National Conference. Fort Lauderdale, Fla., 2004.

Lawlor, Robert. *Voices of the First Day.* Rochester, Vt.: Inner Traditions, 1991.

Levertov, Denise. *Relearning the Alphabet.* New York: New Directions Books, 1970.

———. "Interweavings: Reflections on the Role of Dream in the Making of Poems." *Dreamworks: An Interdisciplinary Quarterly* 1, vol. 2 (Summer 1980): 133–41.

———. *Denise Levertov: Poems 1972–1982.* New York: New Directions Books, 2001.

Leviton, Richard. *The Barefoot Philosopher of the Imagination—Gaston Bachelard's Reverie of the Elements.* PDF. 1994. Available at www.blueroomconsortium.com/pdfs/article_the-barefoot-philosopher.pdf (accessed January 17, 2017).

Maguire, Jack. *Night and Day.* New York: Simon and Schuster, 1989.

Maidenbaum, Aryeh, ed. *Jung and the Shadow of Anti-Semitism: Collected Essays.* Berwick, Maine: Nicholas-Hays, 2002.

Marcuse, Herbert. *Eros and Civilization: A Philosophical Inquiry into Freud.* New York: Vintage Books, 1961.

Martin, Kathleen, ed. *The Book of Symbols.* Cologne, Germany: Taschen, 2010.

May, Rollo. *The Courage to Create.* New York: W. W. Norton and Company, 1975.

McGrath, Thomas. *Selected Poems 1938–1988.* Port Townsend, Wash.: Copper Canyon Press, 1988.

McIsaac, Tara. "5 Scientific Discoveries Made in Dreams," *Epoch Times,* June 4, 2015. www.theepochtimes.com/n3/1380669-5-scientific-discoveries-made-in-dreams, last updated July 29, 2015 (accessed January 17, 2017).

McKechnie, Paul, and Phillip Guillame, eds. *Ptolemy II, Philadelphus and his World.* Leiden and Boston: Brill, 2008.

Miles, Barry. *Paul McCartney: Many Years from Now.* New York: Henry Holt and Company, 1997.

Moss, Robert. *Dreamgates: An Explorer's Guide to the Worlds of Soul, Imagination, and Life Beyond Death.* New York: Three Rivers Press, 1998.

———. *The Dreamer's Book of the Dead: A Soul Traveler's Guide to Death, Dying, and the Other Side.* Rochester, Vt.: Destiny Books, 2005.

———. *Dreamways of the Iroquois: Honoring the Secret Wishes of the Soul.* Rochester, Vt.: Destiny Books, 2005.

———. *The Secret History of Dreaming: A Thorough Historical Account of Dreaming from Many Cultures.* Novato, Calif.: New World Library, 2009.

Myss, Caroline. *Sacred Contracts.* New York: Harmony Books, 2001.

Nance, John. *The Gentle Tasaday: A Stone Age People in the Philippine Rain Forest.* San Diego, Calif.: Harcourt Brace Jovanovich, 1975.

National Institute of Health, "Brain Basics: Understanding Sleep." www.ninds .nih.gov/Disorders/Patient-Caregiver-Education/Understanding-Sleep (accessed March 8, 2017).

Oliver, Mary. *House of Light.* Boston: Beacon Press, 1992.

———. *New and Selected Poems.* Boston: Beacon Press, 1992.

Piaget, Jean. *Play, Dreams, and Imitation in Childhood.* New York: The Norton Library, 1962.

Peniston, E. G., and P. J. Kulkosky. *The Peniston/Kulkosky Brain Wave Neurofeedback Therapy for Alcoholism and Posttraumatic Stress Disorders: Medical Psychotherapist Manual.* Certificate of Copyright Office. The Library of Congress, 1989, 1995, 1–25.

Popper, K. R., and J. C. Eccles. *The Self and Its Brain.* Berlin/New York: Springer International, 1977.

Progoff, Ira. *At a Journal Workshop.* New York: Dialogue House Library, 1975.

Reed, Henry. *Getting Help from Your Dreams.* New York: Ballantine Books, 1985.

Reed, Henry, ed. *Sundance I.,* no. 1 (1985). Virginia Beach, Va.: Atlantic University.

———, ed. *Sundance I.,* no. 2. (1985) Virginia Beach, Va.: Atlantic University.

Revonsuo, Antti. *Inner Presence: Consciousness as a Biological Phenomenon.* Cambridge, Mass.: MIT Press, 2006.

Robbins, Jim. *A Symphony in the Brain: The Evolution of the New Brain Wave Biofeedback.* New York: Grove Press, 2008.

Roberts, Royston M. *Serendipity: Accidental Discoveries in Science.* Foreword by Derek H. R. Barton. Wiley Science Editions. Hoboken, N.J.: John Wiley and Sons, 1989.

Rogers, Carl. *On Becoming a Person: A Therapist's View of Psychotherapy.* New York: Houghton Mifflin, 1961.

Root-Bernstein, Michele, and Robert Root-Bernstein. "Einstein on Creative Thinking: Music and the Intuitive Art of Scientific Imagination." *Psychology Today* (blog), March 31, 2010. www.psychologytoday.com/blog /imagine/201003/einstein-creative-thinking-music-and-the-intuitive-art -scientific-imagination (accessed January 25, 2017).

Rūmī, Jalāl ad-Dīn Muhammad. *Open Secret.* Translated by John Moyne and Coleman Barks. Putney, Vt.: Threshold Books, 1984.

Sacks, Oliver. *Migraine.* Revised expanded edition. New York: Vintage, 1999.

Sanford, John. *Dreams: God's Forgotten Language.* San Francisco: Harper and Row, 1989.

Sarhan, Qassim Salman. "Dream Vision in Chaucer's Poetry." College of Education, University of Al-Qadissiya. www.iasj.net/iasj?func=fulltext &aId=93357 (accessed January 25, 2017).

Segaller, Stephen, and Merrill Berger. *The Wisdom of the Dream*. Boston: Shambhala Publications, 1989.

Seltzer, Richard. "Influence of Kekulé Dream on Benzene Structure Disputed." *Chemical and Engineering News* 63, no. 44 (November 4, 1985): 22–23.

Shafton, Anthony. *Dream-Singers: The African American Way with Dreams; Ancestor Visitations, Numbers, Predictions, Visions, Signs, Déjà Vu, and More.* New York: John Wiley and Sons, 2002.

———. "African Americans and Predictive Dreams." *Dream Time* [magazine of the International Association for the Study of Dreams], 2003. www .asdreams.org/magazine/articles/african_prediction_dreams.htm (accessed May 15, 2017).

Shelley, Mary. *Frankenstein; or, the Modern Prometheus*. London: Henry Colburn & Richard Bentley, 1831.

Siegel, Alan, and Kelly Bulkeley. *Dreamcatching*. New York: Three Rivers Press, 1998.

Sigerist, Henry Ernst. *A History of Medicine*, vol. 2. *Early Greek, Hindu, and Persian Medicine*. New York: Oxford University Press, 1961.

Singer, Jerome L. *The Inner World of Daydreaming*. New York: Harper and Row, 1975.

Solomonova, Elizabeth, Elena Frantova, and Tore Nielsen. "Felt Presence: The Uncanny Encounters with the Numinous Other. *AI and Society* 26 (2011): 171–78. doi:10.1007/s00146-010-0299-x.

St. Augustine. *Confessions*. Oxford: Oxford University Press, 1991.

Stevens, Anthony. *Private Myths: Dreams and Dreaming*. Cambridge, Mass.: Harvard University Press, 1995.

Synesius [St. Synesios, Bishop of Cyrene]. *On Dreams*. Translated by Isaac Myer. Philadelphia: Published by the translator, 1888.

Synesius, "On Dreams," translated by Isaac Myer. In Thomas Moore Johnson, *The Platonist, An Exponent of Philosophic Truth*. Vol 4, issues 1–6. Osceola, MO.: 1888.

Taylor, Jeremy. *Dreamwork: Techniques for Discovering the Creative Power in Dreams*. New York/Ramsey, N.J.: Paulist Press, 1983.

———. *Where People Fly and Water Runs Uphill*. New York: Warner Books, 1992.

———. *The Living Labyrinth: Exploring Universal Themes in Myths, Dreams, and the Symbolism of Waking Life*. New York/Mahwah, N.J.: Paulist Press, 1998.

Teish, Luisah. *Jambalaya: The Natural Women's Book of Personal Charms and Practical Rituals*. reprint ed. New York: HarperOne, 1988.

Tick, Edward. *The Practice of Dream Healing: Bringing Ancient Greek Mysteries into Modern Medicine.* Foreword by Stephen Larsen. Wheaton, Ill.: Quest Books, 2001.

Todman, D. "Inspiration from Dreams in Neuroscience Research." *The Internet Journal of Neurology* 9, no. 1 (2007). http://ispub.com/IJN/9/1/10059 (accessed January 25, 2017).

Tolaas, Jon, and Montague Ullman. "Extrasensory Communication and Dreams." In *Handbook of Dreams—Research, Theories, and Applications.* Edited by Benjamin B. Wolman. Consulting Editors Montague Ullman and Wilse B. Webb. New York: Van Nostrand Reinhold Company, 1979. Available at http://siivola.org/monte/papers_grouped/copyrighted /Parapsychology_&_Psi/Extrasensory_Communication_and_Dreams.htm (accessed January 26, 2017).

Tranströmer, Tomas. *The Half-finished Heaven: The Best Poems of Tomas Tranströmer.* Translated by Robert Bly. Minneapolis, Minn.: Graywolf Press, 2001.

Ulanov, Ann Belford. *The Feminine in Jungian Psychology and in Christian Theology.* Evanston Ill.: Northwestern University Press, 1971.

Ullman, Montague. "An Approach to Closeness: Dream Sharing in a Small Setting." In *Closeness in Personal and Professional Relationships,* edited by Harry A. Wilmer. Boston: Shambhala, 1992.

———. "Dream Telepathy—Experimental and Clinical Findings." In *Lands of Darkness: Psychoanalysis and the Paranormal,* edited by Nick Totton. London: Karnac Books, 2003.

———. "The Significance of Dreams in a Dream Deprived Society." http:// siivola.org/monte/papers_grouped/uncopyrighted/Dreams/significance _of_dreams_in_a_dream_deprived_society.htm (accessed January 17, 2017).

Ullman, Montague, and Claire Limmer, eds. *The Variety of Dream Experience.* New York: Continuum, 1987.

Ullman, Montague, and Nan Zimmerman. *Working with Dreams.* New York: Delacorte Press, 1979.

Van de Castle, Robert. *Our Dreaming Mind.* New York: Ballantine, 1994.

Verny, Thomas, and John Kelly. *The Secret Life of the Unborn Child.* New York: Summit Books, 1981.

Volkow, Nora. "Marijuana's Lasting Effects on the Brain." Messages from the Director, March 2013. www.drugabuse.gov/about-nida/directors-page /messages-director/2012/09/marijuanas-lasting-effects-brain (accessed January 26, 2017).

von Franz, Marie-Louise. *C. G. Jung: His Myth in Our Time.* Translated by William H. Kennedy. New York: G. P. Putnam's Sons, 1975.

———. *On Dreams and Death: A Jungian Interpretation.* Boston: Shambhala Publications, 1987.

———. *Shadow and Evil in Fairytales,* revised edition. Boston: Shambhala Publications, 1995.

———. *Dreams: A Study of the Dreams of Jung, Descartes, Socrates, and Other Historical Figures.* Boston: Shambhala Publications, 1998.

Wakefield, Dan. *Creating from the Spirit.* New York: Ballantine Books, 1996.

Watkins, Mary. *Waking Dreams.* New York: Harper Colophon Books, 1976.

———. *Invisible Guests: The Development of Imaginal Dialogues.* Burlingame, Calif.: The Analytic Press, 1986.

Whitmont, Edward C., and Sylvia Brinton Perera. *Dreams, a Portal to the Source.* New York: Routledge, 1989.

Wiseman, Ann Sayre. *Nightmare Help.* Berkeley, Calif.: Ten Speed Press, 1989.

Woodman, Marion, and Jill Mellick. *Coming Home to Myself: Reflections for Nurturing a Woman's Body and Soul.* York Beach, Maine: Conari Press, 2000.

Woolger, Jennifer Barker, and Roger J. Woolger. *The Goddess Within: A Guide to the Eternal Myths That Shape Women's Lives.* New York: Fawcett Columbine, 1989.

Wotiz, John H., and Susanna Rudofsky. Letter to the editor. *Chemical and Engineering News* 64, no. 3 (January 20, 1986): 3–4.

Yeats, William Butler. *A Vision: An Explanation of Life Founded upon the Writings of Giraldus and upon Certain Doctrines Attributed to Kusta Ben Luka.* N.p: Kessinger Publishing Co., 2003. First published in 1925.

Index

activation/synthesis theory of dreaming, 52–53, 54

African Americans
Garrison's grandfather, 192–93
Mutwa, 187–89
psychic abilities of, 166–68, 187–93
Tubman, 166–68, 187, 190

AIM model of consciousness, 54

air element, 80

alarm clocks, 76

Alexander, Eban, 299, 300

alpha-theta training, 254–55

ancient dreaming
in the Bible, 87, 158–61
in cave imagery, 7–8
dream incubation, 11–16, 202–4
Egyptian dream lore, 10
in Mesopotamia, 9–10
oracular and prophetic, 158–61
Serapis cult and, 10–11
shamanic, 7–9
from time immemorial, 6
true vs. false dreams, 17–18
valued in preliterate societies, 6–7

animals, dreaming by, 39

Apollo, 13–14, 15

Aquinas, Thomas, 162

architecture of dreams, 80–81

Asclepius, 12, 13, plate 2

attic in dreams, 80

Auden, W. H., 295, 306

Augustine, St., 162

AUM, stages of, 26–28

Australian initiation rite, 116

ayahuasca ceremonies, 62

babies, dreaming by, 39–40

Bachelard, Gaston, 79, 274

basement in dreams, 80

Basic Perinatal Matrices (BPM), 41

Berger, Hans, 48–49, 186

Berne, Patricia, 258

Bible, big dreams in, 87, 158–61

big dreams, 86–108
in ancient Greece, 14
in the Bible, 87, 158–61
as blessings, 107–8
finding spirituality within, 94–107
"Hold Three Coins," 278–82
of indigenous peoples, 86–87
lessons in character, 90–94
Synesius on, 87
Uncle Remus dreams, 90–94

visiting dead relatives, 89–90
visiting God, 87–89
birth, impacts of, 41
Blake, Catherine, 20
Blake, William, 20, 44, 234, 235, 236,
    plate 10
blessings, big dreams as, 107–8
Bly, Robert, 128, 130, 143
body shop dreams, 179–80
books, recommended, 200, 292
brain
    hippocampus, 257
    neurotransmitters, 47–48
    singing and, 61
    Synesius's view of, 33
brain waves
    ADHD and, 58–59
    alpha-theta training, 254–55
    in dream imagery, 60
    EEG for recording, 48–49
    frequencies of, 50
    interpenetration of, 253, 256–57
    states of consciousness and, 50, 253
    symphony metaphor for, 60–61, 62
brakes failing dream, 151–56, 275
"Breeze at Dawn, The" (poem), 86, 138
Bruner, Jerome, 223
Byron, Lord, 237

Campbell, Joseph
    on ancient caves, 7
    at Council Grove East conference,
        129–32
    early interest in Native Americans,
        132–34
    football injury of, 134–35
    Gimbutas's work and, 8
    Hero with a Thousand Faces, The, 8,
        24, 45, 113
    as Larsen's mentor, 129–32, 136

on Vishnu's dream, 36
    waking dreams of, 134–35
Caslant, Eugene, 257
cauldron of inexhaustible gifts. See also
    visionary dreamers of Europe
    Einstein's dream, 246–47
    expression required by, 228
    gifts from, 237, 239
    music and dream, 239–41
    other names for, 222–23
    principles for approaching, 223
    problem solving example, 248–49
    science and dreams, 241–47
    small gifts from, 249–50
cave imagery, 7–8
Cayce, Edgar, 56, 193–95
character, dream lessons in, 90–94
Chaucer, Geoffrey, 231–32
children
    books helpful for nightmares of, 200
    dreaming by babies, 39
    mother-child relationship, 39
    nightmares in, 42, 199–202
    night terrors in, 42–43
    Senoi, 199–200
Christian precognitive dreams, 161–62
clairvoyance. See paranormal dreams
Clinton, Bill, 187–88
Coleridge, Samuel Taylor, 235–36
compassion, dream on importance of,
    101–3, 105–6
compensatory dreaming, 37, 68, 155–56,
    251
Conference on the Great Mother,
    142–43
consciousness. See also specific states
    AIM model of, 54
    brain waves and states of, 50, 253
    drugs for altering, 47
    hard problem of, 46–47

interpenetrating states of, 253,
256–57
state-dependent learning, 257
Constantine, 158
Cox, Harvey, 272
crisis of dreams, 82
cross-cultural interpretation, 57

Dalai Lama, 32–33
Daniel and Nebuchadnezzar, 159–60
Dante Alighieri, 229–30, 231
Darwin, Charles, 169
Day, Dorothy, 141
daydreaming, 251, 256–58
dead relatives, visiting, 89–90
death
    dreams when approaching, 298–99
    love stories transcending, 300–306
    near-death experiences, 199, 300
    Thanatos, 296–300
death instinct, 297–98
deep sleep, M in AUM as, 27–28
Dement, William, 51
demons, 33
Descartes, René, 169
Desoille, Robert, 257
development of dreams, 82
dramatic structure of dreams, 81–82
Dream, The (painting), plate 11
Dream-Guessing Game, 262–63
dream incubation, 196–221. See also
    dream retreats
    in ancient Greece, 11–16, 202–4
    children's nightmares and, 199–202
    connecting with wisdom via, 196–97
    dream retreats for, 204–21
    inversion of, 23–24
    lucid dreaming vs., 198
    by the Senoi, 198–200, 263
    temple dreamers, 197–98

dreaming, in general
    activation/synthesis theory of, 52–53,
        54
    EEG during, 60
    need for, 196, 297
    paradigms of, 55–58
    rapid eye movement with, 45–46
    things that interfere with, 75–76
    U in AUM as, 26–27, 28
    waking world and, 196
dream journal
    approaching the dream, 293–94
    authors' use of, 72–73
    books to inspire, 292
    dramatic structure of dreams,
        81–82
    dream architecture in, 80–81
    four elements in, 79–80
    as friend and companion, 77–78
    methods for, 71, 73–74
    Present Period Log, 69–70, 206–7
    present tense for, 71–72
    recording dreams, 70–71
    as sacred place, 78
    tips for keeping, 68–69
    Working with Key Words/Images in
        the Dream, 288–92
Dream Muse exercise, 211
Dream Portal Method, 76–77, 151,
    307–8
dream retreats, 204–21
    creating for yourself, 287–88
    day one of, 207–10
    dream incubation during, 211–13
    Dream Muse exercise, 211
    eve of, 205–7
    finishing touches of, 210
    haiku use during, 205–6, 208, 219
    If This Were My Dream exercise,
        211–12

marine sniper's dreams, 213–17
owl queen dream, 217–20
dreams within dreams, 36–37
dreamwork. *See also* dream retreats
dialogue of, 68–69
four-step process of, 74
as soul work, 292–93
steps for remembering dreams,
67–71
as true yoga, 23
using poetry for, 275–76
wrestling in, 21–22, 23
drugs
for altering consciousness, 47
ayahuasca, 62
effect on dreaming, 75–76
hallucinogenic, 23–24
long-term effects of marijuana,
64
teenage use of, 63–64
Dumuzi's dream, 10

earth element, 79
Eccles, John, 245–46
Egyptian Dream Book, 10, plate 1
Ehrenwald, Jan van, 178
Einstein, Albert, 246–47
electroencephalography (EEG), 48–49,
58, 60
elements in dreams, 79–80
Eliot, T. S., 230, 286, 295
emotional intelligence, 261
Evans, Ron, 262
Evil-Eye Fleagle, 121–22
exercises
Dream-Guessing Game, 262–63
Dream Muse, 211
Gates of Horn and Ivory, 37–38
If This Were My Dream, 211–12
Three Minute Meditator, 29

Working with Key Words/Images in
the Dream, 288–92
exposition of dreams, 81

"Faith of Mind" (poem), 97, 103–4
fear and power, 200
felt presence, 300
fire element, 80
Flagg, Clara Stewart, 199, 265
Frankenstein, 236–37, 238
Frantova, Elena, 300
Freud, Sigmund, 142, 155, 272, 284,
297
Freudian view, 34–35, 52–53, 171
Frobenius, Leo, 14

Gallegos, Stephen, 260
Garfield, Patricia, 199
Garrison, Andrea, 192–93
Gates of Horn and Ivory exercise, 37–38
Gehrig, Lou, 134–35
Gimbutas, Marija, 8, 11
God, 87–89, 273, 278
Greece, ancient, dream incubation in,
11–16, 202–4
Green, Elmer, Alyce and Gladys, 304–6
Gregor, Elmer, 134
Grof, Stanislav, 41

haiku use in dreamwork, 205–6, 208,
219, 284–85
hallucinogenic drugs, 23–24
Harrison, George, 240
Heidegger, M., 220–21
helping animal archetype, 111
helping dreams, 148–50, 151–56
Heraclitus, 151, 274
Hesiod's *Theogony,* 16–17
Hildegard of Bingen, 162, 222, 224–29,
plate 7

Hillman, James
  on befriending dreams, 295
  on control and dreams, 306
  on dream ambiguities, 274
  on dream imagery, 272, 273
  on listening to dreams, 293–94
  on the soul, 204
  as Verner's mentor, 141, 142
hippocampus, 257
Hobson, Alan, 46, 52–55, 171
Hoffman, Jan, 299
"Holding in Tenderness" (poem),
  283–84
"Hold Three Coins" dream, 278–82
"Hold Three Coins for the Old Wise
  Man" (poem), 281
Howe, Elias, 252
"Hsin Hsin Ming" (poem), 97, 103–4
Hurd, Ryan, 55
hypnagogia, 60
hypnopompia, 60

iatromantis tradition, 12, 14
If This Were My Dream exercise, 211–12
indigenous big dreams, 86–87
indwelling practice, 259, 260–61
interpreting dreams
  in the Bible, 159–60
  cross-cultural interpretation, 57
  personal nature of, 109
  by Synesius, 29–32
Iroquoian dream lore, 261–63
Israel, 22

Jacob and the angel, 21–22
James, William, 300
Jean, Guy, 210
Joan of Arc, 163–64, 273
Johnson, Robert, 74
Johnston, Jack, 198, 199

Joseph and the Pharaoh, 159
journal. *See* dream journal
Joyce, James, 127
Jung, Carl
  on an acorn's dream, 286
  authors' dreams of, 118, 144–47
  balance principle of, 143
  on dreams as compensatory, 37, 68,
    155–56
  on dreams at the end of life, 298
  on Eastern traditions, 16
  on ethical demands of dreams, 142
  Larsen's meeting with, 118–19
  on psyche as image, 272
  as Verner's mentor, 139, 143
  waking imagination and, 270
Jung Foundation, 113–14

Karloff, Boris, 238
Kekulé, Friedrich August, 222, 241–44
Kerttu, 283–84
Kiefer, James E., 226
King, Martin Luther, Jr., 142
Kingsley, Peter, 12–16
kitchen in dreams, 81
Kleitman, Nathaniel, 45, 51
Kübler-Ross, Elisabeth, 88

Larsen, Robin Searson
  art from dreams by, 73, plate 3
  cancer bout of, 94
  dating Stephen at NYU, 115
  dream parallels with Stephen, 83–84
  marriage to Stephen, 120
  poem for Kerttu's dream, 283–84
  Stephen's dream of, 123–24
Larsen, Stephen
  about, 1
  birth of, 110
  Campbell as mentor for, 129–32, 136

childhood nightmares of, 110–11
collaborative process of, 3–4
dating Robin at NYU, 115
dream of Jung, 118
dream of Robin and puppets, 123–24
dream parallels with Robin, 83–84
dream remembering experience,
    83–85
early dream journal of (1965), 114–15
initiation crisis of, 116–18
José (Fleagle) and, 121–23
at the Jung Foundation, 113–14
marriage to Robin, 120
mask workshops by, 125, plate 5
meeting with Jung, 118–19
on mentors, 136
studies in psychology by, 112–14
teachers of, 1–2
teenage mind exploration by, 111–12
therapy framework of, 126–28
Whitmont as mentor for, 114–18,
    119–20, 123, 124, 126, 136
on Whitmont's character, 109–10
letters, dreams as, 78
Leuner, Hanscarl, 257–58
Levertov, Denise, 79, 273–74
Leviton, Richard, 79
Lewinsky, Monica, 188
Limmer, Claire, 77
Lincoln, Abraham, 168
living room in dreams, 80–81
Loewi, Otto, 245
Lou Gehrig's disease, 135
love
    as beyond good and evil, 100–101
    stories transcending death, 300–306
lucid dreaming
    dream incubation vs., 198
    ethics of, 256
    interventions for adults, 265–67

managing the dream, 263–65
with recurring dreams, 267–70
Senoi teaching of, 199–200, 264–65
sewing machine invention in, 252
Lucrecia de Leon, 165–66
lysis of dreams, 82

Machado, Antonio, 210
"Magic Song for Those Who Wish to
    Live," 137
Marzano, Jim, 87–89
mask workshops, 125, plate 5
Matheson, Richard, 232–33, 234
McCarley, R. W., 52, 53, 54, 171
McCartney, Paul, 240–41
McGrath, Thomas, 221
meditation, 207, 208, 265–66
Memories, Dreams, Reflections, 139, 143
Mendeleev, Dmitri, 241–42
mercy, 106
Mesopotamia, 9–10
metaphors from dreams, 282–85
mind, movement of, 26, 29
miracles, dream, 150
Monster Dream Playshops, 201–2
Morpheus, 16, 18–20, 22, 23, 25
Mortier, Shams, 145, 147
Moss, Robert, 30, 162, 163, 164, 165,
    166, 261
mother-child relationship, 39
motivation, in dream recall, 68
Moyers, Bill, 135
music, 61, 62, 227, 239–41
Mutwa, Vusamazulu Credo, 187–89
Myss, Caroline, 288

near-death experiences (NDE), 199,
    300
Nebuchadnezzar and Daniel, 159–60
Nell, Renée, 147–48

neurofeedback
    for ADHD, 59
    alpha-theta training, 254–55
    cumulative benefits of, 49
    dreaming affected by, 62–63
    dream theory and, 59–60
    for nightmares, 63, 65–66
    Vietnam vet's experience with,
        178–79
neurotransmitters, 47–48
Nielsen, Tore, 299, 300
nightmares
    in adults, 43
    in ancient times, 44
    books helpful for children's, 200
    as dream incubation inversions,
        23–24
    helping children cope with, 42,
        199–202
    illness leading to, 44–45
    neurofeedback for, 63, 65–66
    positive attitude toward, 20
    prevalence of, 43
    shared, 263–64
night terrors, 42–43, 63
Nobel, Alfred, 241, 244
Novalis, 145, 151

Ochs, Len, 62–63
"Ode: Intimations of Immortality . . . ,"
    235
"Old Cathedral with the Warm Heart,
    The" (poem), 277–78
Oliver, Mary, 150, 197–98, 286
On Dreams, 29, 30–31, 35
Oneiroi
    chthonic origins of, 17
    dwelling place of, 16
    genealogy of, 20–21
    Thanatos, 296–300

owl queen dream, 217–20

pantoum writing, 276–78, 281
paradigms of dreaming
    neurofeedback and, 59–60
    neurology/content clash, 58
    scientific, 169–72
    varieties of, 55–57
paranormal dreams
    of body shop, 179–80
    of Cayce, 193–95
    experiments in clairvoyance, 175–76
    murdered people sheltered, 185–86
    precognitive, 161–68, 187–89
    of prerevolutionary home, 181–84
    shared waterslide dreams, 180–81
    transcending time and space, 186–87
    Ullman's telepathic dream, 177–78
partners in dreaming, 76–77
Patanjali, 25–26
Pema Chödrun, 280, 282
Penelope, 17, 34, 35
Persphone, 14
Phantasms of the Living, 172–74
place-taking, 259–61
poetic imagination, 272–94
    in dream journaling, 288–94
    of dreams, 273–74
    dreams honored by use of, 284
    expressing experiences, 286–87
    God speaking through, 273
    haiku use in dreamwork, 205–6, 208,
        219, 284–85
    in "Hold Three Coins" dream,
        278–82
    metaphors from dreams, 282–85
    pantoum writing, 276–78, 281
    reality of, 272–73
    soul as the source of, 272
    using, in dreamwork, 275–76

Pollak, Felix, 274–75
Polycarp of Smyrna, 161
precognitive dreaming
    Christian era, 161–62
    by Lincoln, 168
    by Mutwa, 187–89
    by women dreamers, 163–68
prerevolutionary home, 181–84
Present Period Log, 69–70, 206–7
problem solving with a dream, 248–49
Progoff, Ira, 69, 77, 78, 206
psychic abilities. See also paranormal
        dreams
    of African Americans, 166–68,
        189–93
    of Cayce, 193–95
    telepathy, 173–81, 186

Quill, Timothy E., 299

Ramana Maharshi, 97
rapid eye movement (REM)
    discovery of, 51
    during dreams, 45–46
    REM vs. non-REM dreams, 59
    as simulacra of waking state, 58
recurring dreams, 267–70
Reed, Henry, 67, 204, 287
remembering dreams
    as an art, 67
    dream journal for, 68–69, 70–74,
        77–78
    Larsen's experience in, 83–85
    meditation for, 207, 208
    Present Period Log for, 69–70
    recording dreams, 70–71
    repression preventing, 59
    slow-wave sleep preventing, 59
    steps for, 67–71
    telling them to partners, 76–77

things that interfere with, 75–76
    tips and tricks for, 74–75
Remus, dreams of Uncle, 90–94
Rhine, J. B., 174, 175
Robbins, Jim, 60, 61
Roberts, Royston, 243
Rossetti, Dante Gabriel, 230–31, plate 9
Rumi, 86, 138

Sacks, Oliver, 225
Savary, Louis, 258
Schacker, Michael and Barbara, 301–4
Schneemann, Carolee, 181–85
Schopenhauer, Arthur, 135
scientific paradigm, 169–72
scientist's dreams
    Eccles's, 245–46
    Einstein's, 246–47
    Kekulé's, 241–44
    Loewi's, 245
    Mendeleev's, 241
seeding the unconscious, 69, 84, 198,
        223, 289
Sengcan, Jianzhi, 97, 103–4
Senoi dream lore, 198–200, 263,
        264–65, 268
Serapis cult, 10–11
sewing machine invention, 252
Shabalala, Joseph, 240
Shafton, Anthony, 168, 187, 190–91,
        192
Shakespeare, William, 106, 230,
        232–33, 296
shamanic dreamwork, 7–9, 16
Shelley, Mary, 236–37
Sibyllene oracles, 31, 32
Singer, Jerome, 256
sleep, stages of, 51
Society for Psychical Research, 171–72
Solomonova, Elizaveta, 300

soul
    dreamwork as soul work, 292–93
    Heraclitus on, 151
    Novalis on the seat of, 145, 151
    as poetic imagination's source,
        272
spirituality
    finding in a big dream, 94–107
    science and, 169–72
state-dependent learning, 257
Stewart, Kilton, 198–99, 261
"strained," meaning of, 106
Swedenborg, Emanuel, 234
Synesius of Cyrene
    on big dreams, 87
    dreaming and the brain for, 33
    dream interpretation by, 29–32
    on dreams and writing, 35–36
    on dreams as gifts, 35
    on dreams as oracle, 69
    on dreams within dreams, 36–37
    Freud's view opposed by, 34–35

Taoism, 104
Tartini, Guiseppi, 239, plate 8
Telemachus, 22
telepathy, 173–81, 186. *See also*
    paranormal dreams
temple dreamers, 197–98
terrorist dreams, 33
Thanatos, 296–300
Theophilus, Pope, 37
Three Minute Meditator exercise, 29
Thule Inuit song, 137
Thurber, James, 251
Thurston, Mark, 207
Todman, D., 246
Tolaas, Jon, 173
Transtrommer, Tomas, 128
Tripp, Linda, 188

true vs. false dreams, 17–18, 37–38
Tubman, Harriet, 166–68, 187, 190
turiya state, 15, 28

Ullman, Montague, 77, 173, 176–78,
    211
universe, as a friendly place, 135
unpacking dream symbols, 258–60

"Vacillation" (poem), 108
Van de Castle, Robert, 267
Verner, Sangeeta, 89–90
Verner, Tom
    about, 1
    big dream of, 90–94
    birth of, 137
    collaborative process of, 3–4
    commentary by, 128–29
    Conference on the Great Mother
        attended by, 142–43
    Day as mentor for, 141
    dream journal of, 72, plate 4
    dream of Jung, 144–47
    dream of Nell's brother's death,
        148–50
    dreams' importance for, 142
    at Duquesne University, 140
    early morning walks by, 137–38
    fingerprinting by, 93
    Hillman as mentor for, 141, 142
    journal keeping by, 138–39
    Jung as mentor for, 139, 143
    monastic youth of, 138–39
    mother as first teacher of, 142
    poetry loved by, 140–41
    teachers of, 1–2
    work with dream of brakes failing,
        151–56
    work with Nell, 147–50
Verny, Thomas, 40

Viñao, Alejandro, 227
visionary dreamers of Europe
    Blake, 235, plate 10
    Chaucer, 231–32
    Coleridge, 235–36
    Dante Alighieri, 229–30, 231
    Hildegard of Bingen, 162, 222,
        224–29, plate 7
    Rossetti, 230–31, plate 9
    Shakespeare, 232–33
    Shelley, 236–37
    Swedenborg, 234
    Wordsworth, 235
von Franz, Marie Louise, 221, 298

waking dreams. *See* daydreaming
waking state
    A in AUM as, 26, 28
    dreamlike reveries in, 58
    EEG during, 60
    effect of dreams on, 46
water element, 79–80
waterslide dreams, 180–81
Watkins, Mary, 256, 257, 259, 267
What Dreams May Come, 232–33, 234
Whitman, Walt, 128

Whitmont, Edward C.
    context emphasized by, 57
    imposing character of, 109–10
    as Larsen's mentor, 114–18, 119–20,
        123, 124, 126, 136
    on the uses of dreams, 296
Williams, Strephon Kaplan, 265
women dreamers
    Hildegard of Bingen, 162, 222,
        224–29, plate 7
    Joan of Arc, 163–64
    Lucrecia de Leon, 165–66
    Tubman, 166–68, 187, 190
Woodman, Marion, 208–9
Wordsworth, William, 235
Working with Key Words/Images in the
    Dream, 288–92
wrestling in dreams, 21–22, 23
"Writing in the Dark" (poem), 79

Yeats, W. B., 17, 108
"Yesterday" (song), 240–41
Yiskah, 18–20, 23, 33
yoga, 23, 26–28

Zimmerman, Nan, 77, 211